DRAW FAERIES

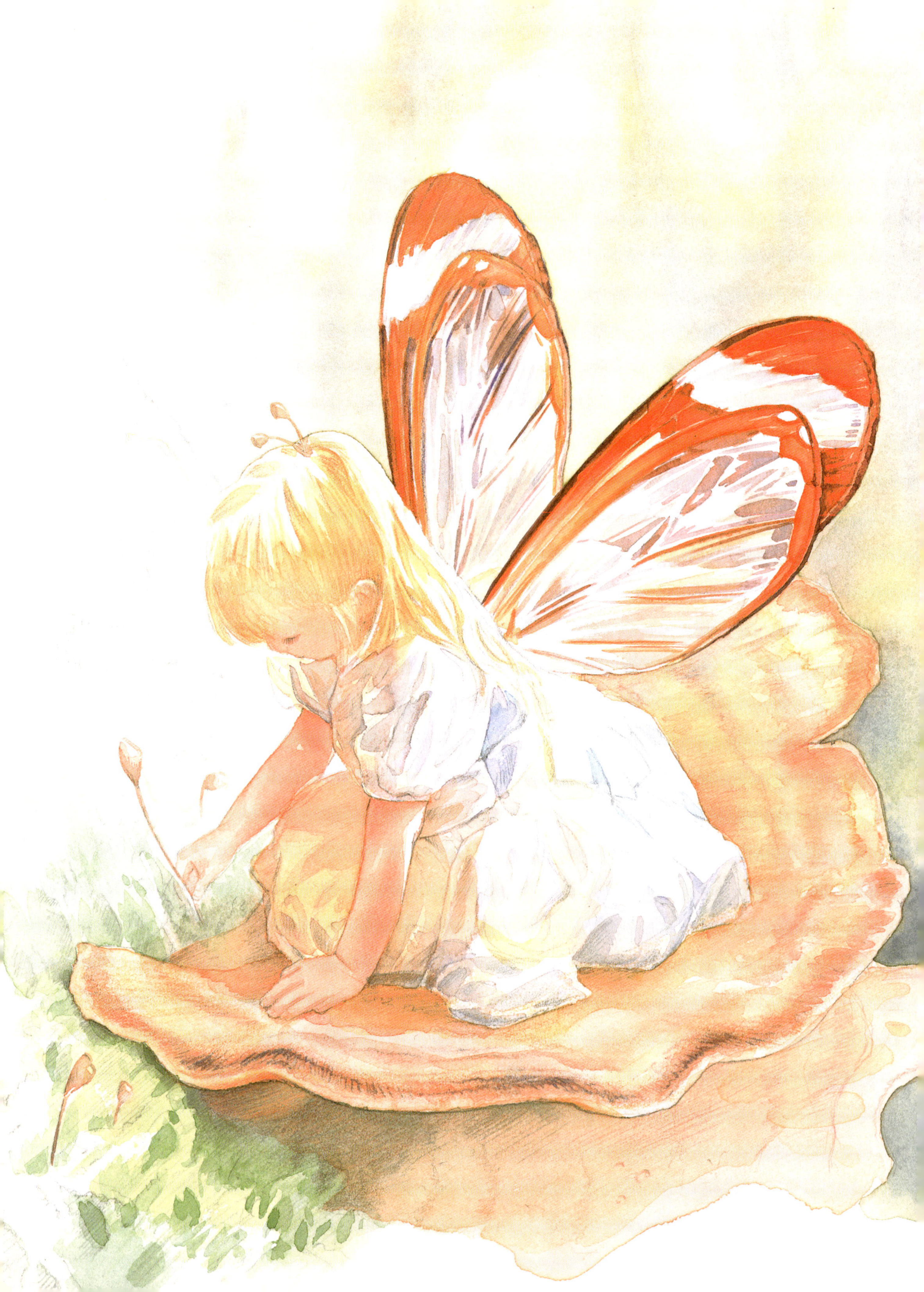

DRAW
FAERIES

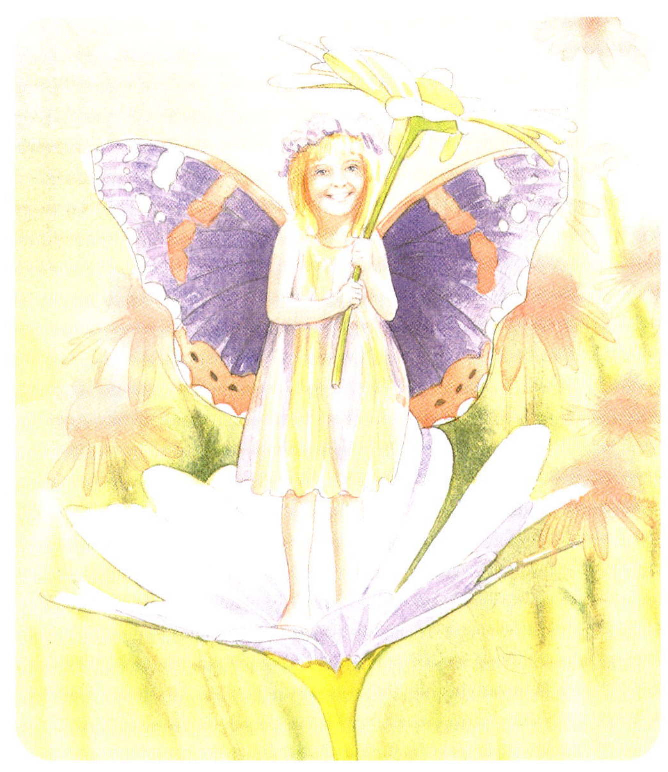

Melanie Phillips

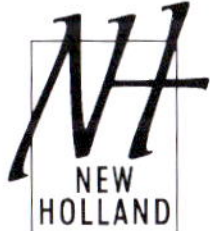

Reprinted in 2009
First published in 2009 by
New Holland Publishers (UK) Ltd
London • Cape Town • Sydney • Auckland

Garfield House, 86–88 Edgware Road
London W2 2EA
www.newhollandpublishers.com

80 McKenzie Street, Cape Town 8001
South Africa

Unit 1, 66 Gibbes Street, Chatswood,
NSW 2067, Australia

218 Lake Road, Northcote, Auckland
New Zealand

Text and illustrations copyright © 2009
New Holland Publishers (UK) Ltd
Copyright © 2009 New Holland Publishers (UK) Ltd

Melanie Phillips has asserted her moral right to be identified as
the author of this work.

All rights reserved. No part of this publication may be reproduced, stored in a retrieval system, or transmitted in any form or by any means, electronic, mechanical, photocopying, recording or otherwise, without the prior written permission of the publishers and copyright holders.

ISBN: 978 1 84773 327 6

Editor: Amy Corstorphine
Designer: Neal Cobourne
Production: Laurence Poos
Editorial direction: Rosemary Wilkinson

Reproduction by Pica Digital Pte Ltd, Singapore
Printed and bound in Malaysia by Times Offset
(M) Sdn Bhd

3 5 7 9 10 8 6 4 2

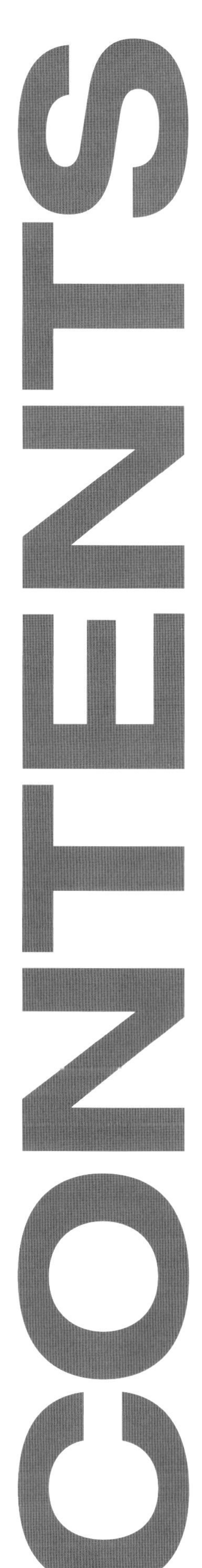

Introduction

How do you draw a faerie if you can't see one? Faeries can seem a pretty challenging subject to draw but they aren't really. They can be closely based on the human figure, both young and mature, their wings can be taken from many wonderful creatures, such as butterflies, moths, dragonflies – even oddly-shaped leaves and flowers. Add to all this some fairytale surroundings adapted from the natural world and you have the start of a wonderful faerie drawing or painting. This book aims to start you on a magical journey of experimentation, imagination and inspiration, so that you will be confident in designing your very own faeries.

Finding inspiration

Before you start your journey, it's a good idea to keep a folder or file of clippings and photographic references that inspire you. It could be filled with pictures of models in fashion magazines or catalogues, you could collect photos of woodlands and plants, or you may be able to take photographs in your garden or local park. Look for unusual trees and roots, plants and flowers and anything interesting that you may find. Use your imagination: if you were a faerie, where would you like to live?

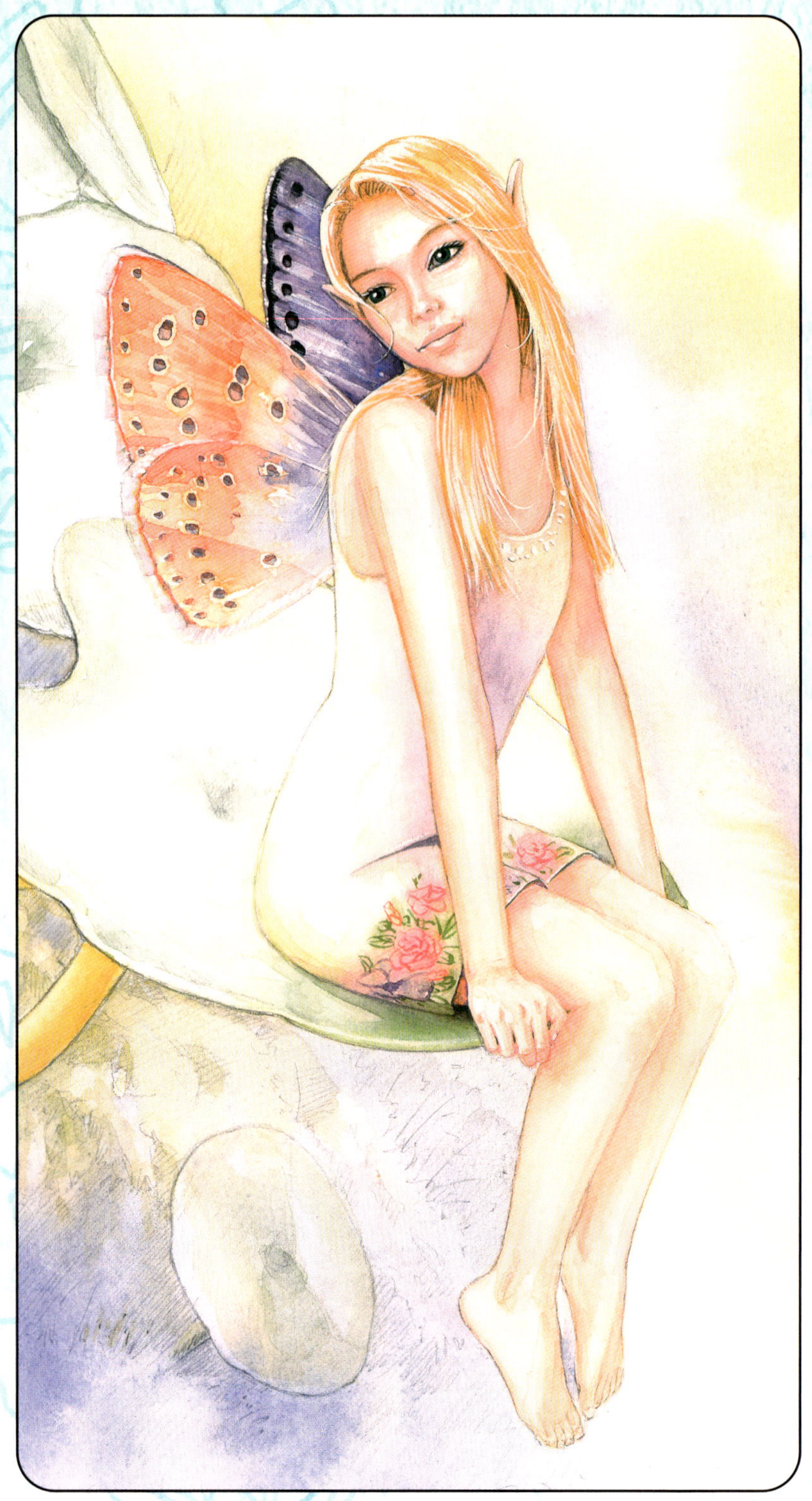

Sketching

Try to draw and sketch as much as possible. The secret to creating a great faerie drawing is practice! Observe the world around you and draw what you see. Collect objects in nature, for instance leaves, twigs, bark, shells, stones, flowers and grasses, and sketch them from different angles and in different compositions.

Famous faeries and faerie artworks

There are many famous faeries that we learn about in our childhood: the tooth faerie, the faerie godmother and Tinkerbell, from *Peter Pan*, are just a few. There are also many famous faerie artists, who have produced a variety of wonderful paintings of faeries. Cicely Mary Barker dedicated her life to painting flower faeries and created a faerie for almost every garden flower. Brian Froud is another greatly admired artist who takes his work one step further. He adds another dimension to his faeries by delving deep into the fantasy world and often combines good and bad faeries in the same painting.

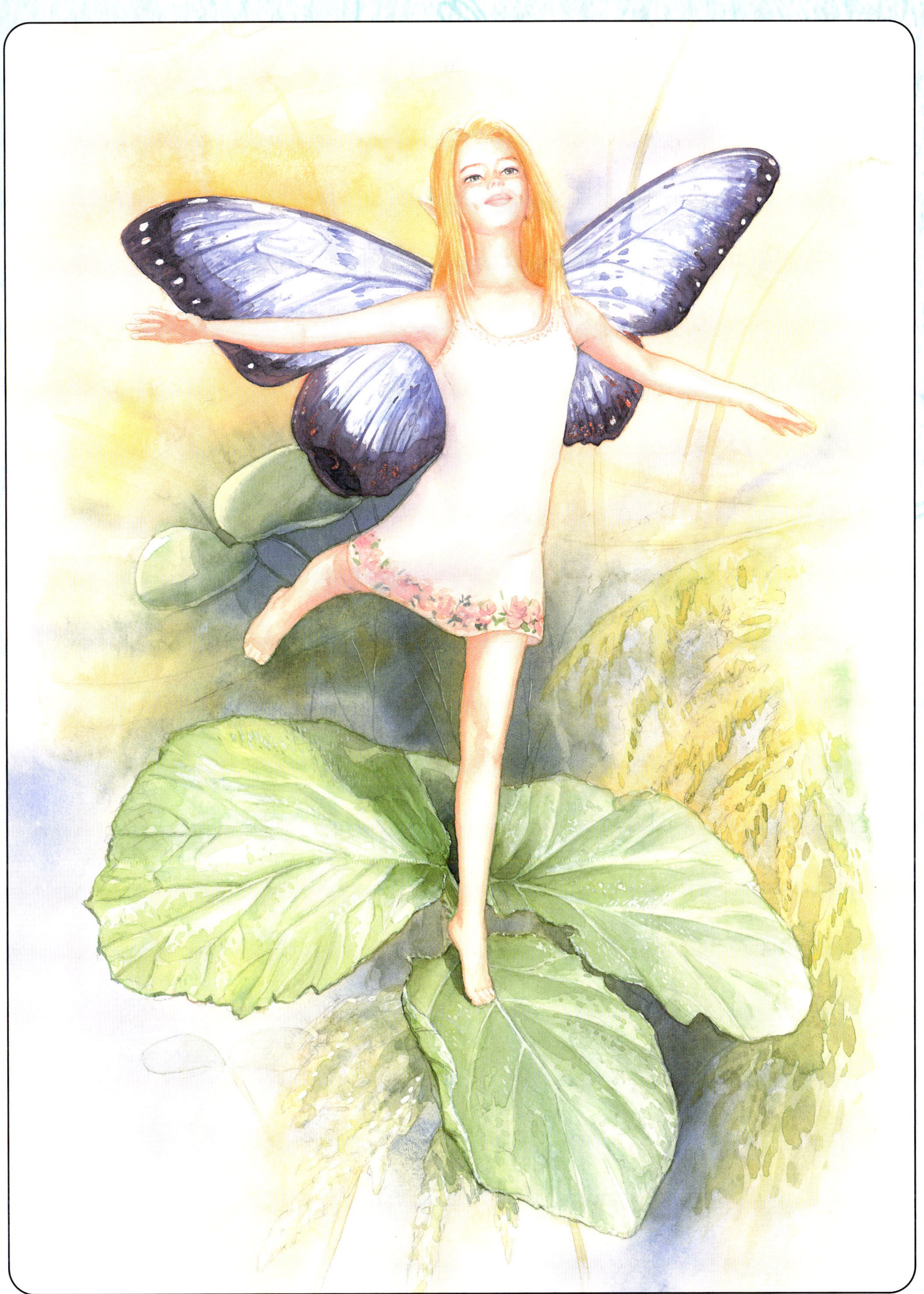

TYPES OF FAERIES

There are many different types of faeries in the magical world. Listed below are just a few with a short explanation for each.

Flower faeries

These live in and look after the flowers in your garden. They wear clothes made from petals or leaves and skip, dance and play in the blossom all day long.

Dryads or woodland faeries

Dryads are faeries who live far away from prying eyes; they live in the woodland trees and are said to belong to one tree, and one tree only. They protect and nurture their tree and, once it dies or is felled, the dryad will die along with it.

Nymphs

Nymphs are small delicate creatures. There are many variations of nymphs and they look after the various natural places of the earth, from the fresh streams to the mountain peaks.

Naiads or water faeries

Water faeries look after streams, seas and oceans and can appear in many forms. If you are lucky you may see a beautiful silky-haired faerie; if you upset them though, they could appear to you in a ghastly form.

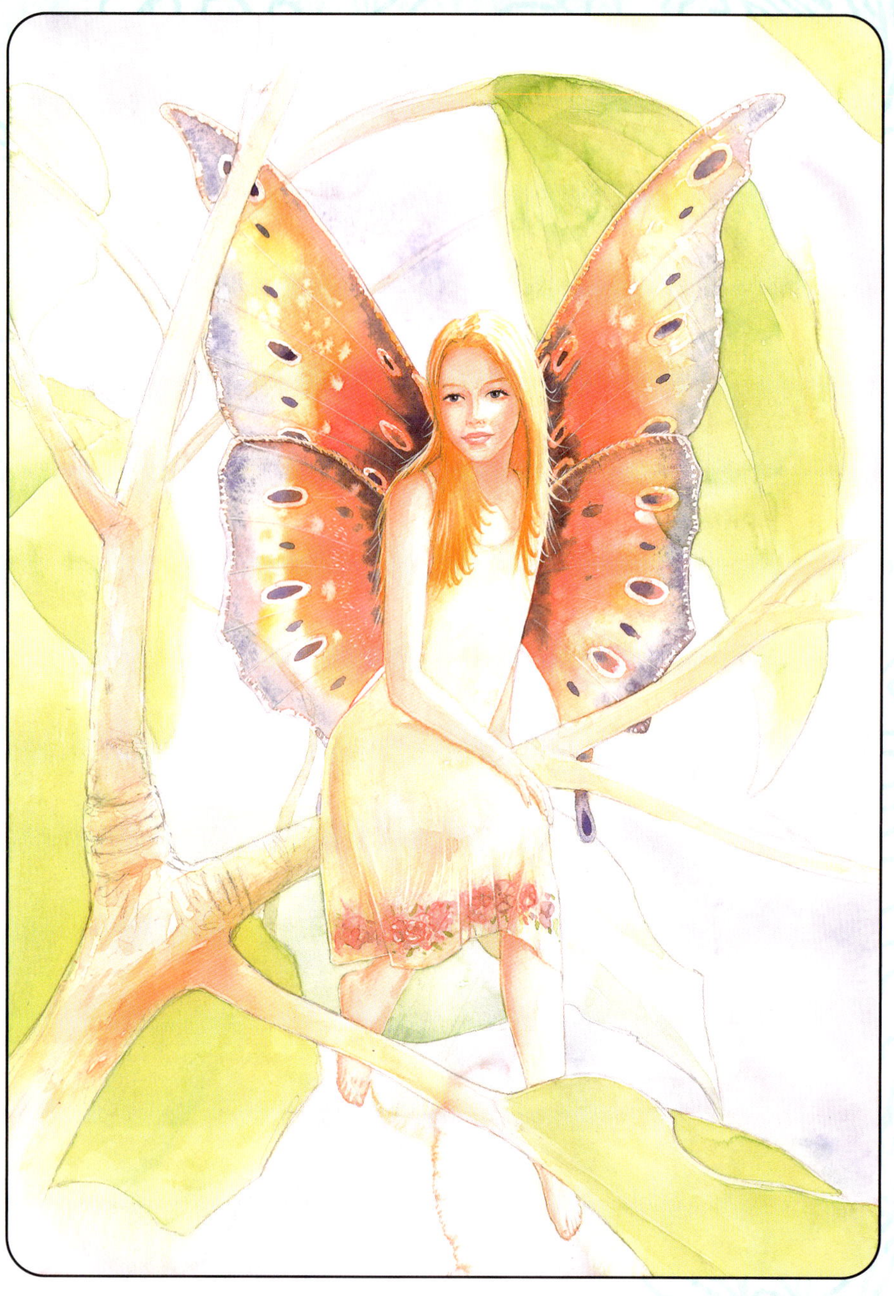

Ethereal faeries

Ethereal faeries are the most divine of all magical faeries. They move like ballerinas, graceful and serene, and are closer to the spirit world than the other faeries.

Sylphs

Sylphs live in the air, free as a bird, riding the thermals. They can often resemble a bird in their characteristics and are delicate and graceful, dancing and gliding as they move.

Sprites

Sprites are generally known for helping the autumn change to winter and they are often depicted playing in the autumn leaves or in a snowy and icy environment.

Devas

Devas are known to inhabit the plane between the magical world and the human world. They are Nature's spirits and it's said that every plant has its own deva.

Dark faeries

Dark faeries are some of the most popular faeries to illustrate, as they can be beautiful and mystical yet they do have a wicked side. They can take on many shapes and forms and don't have to be female.

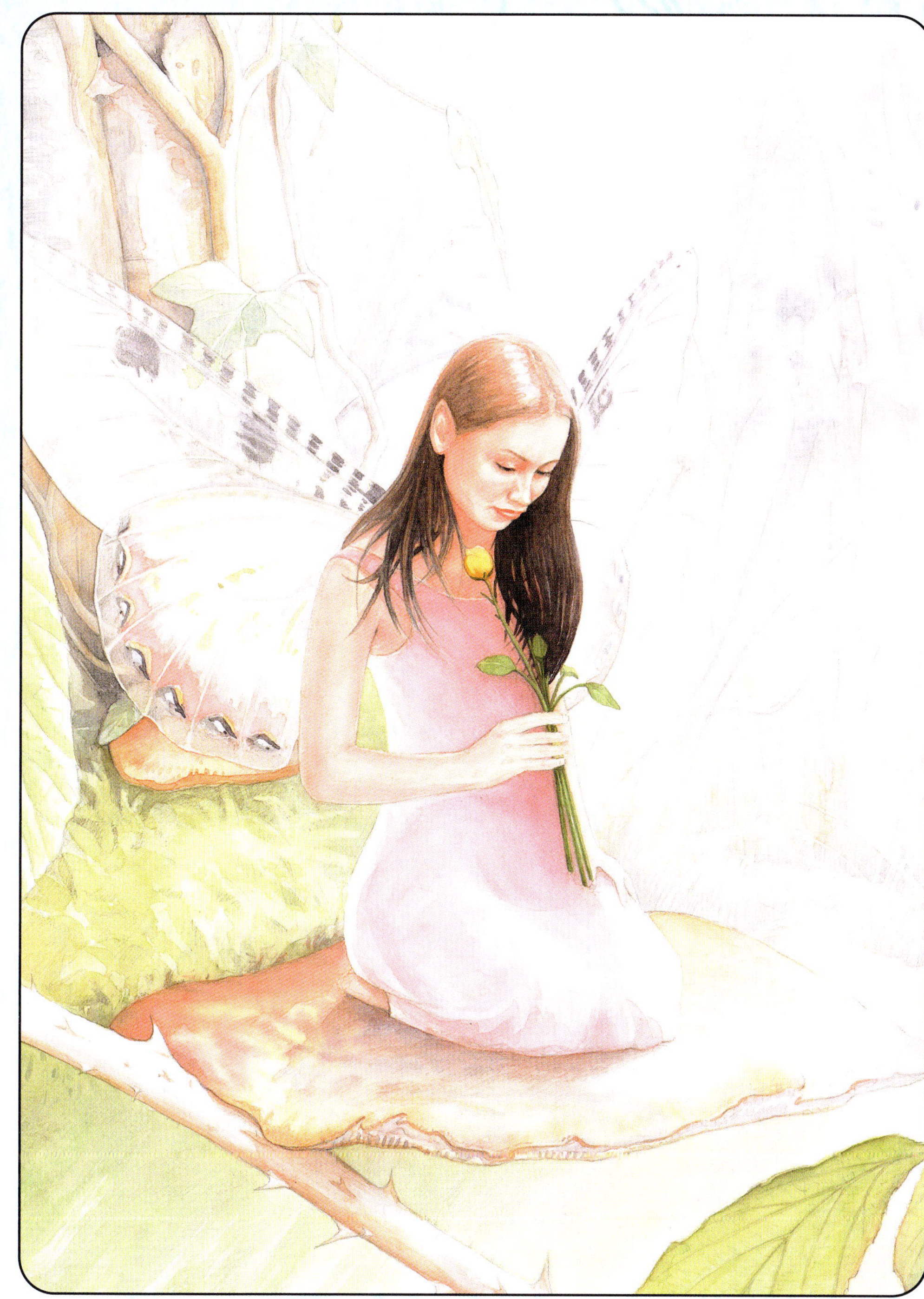

spread rapidly all over Europe. They live in mossy clefts in rocks and among the roots of ancient trees, although they never stay very long in the same place.

Banshees

Banshees are known for their lamenting wails, which they make while visiting a household to warn them that someone in the family is about to die. They are Celtic in origin.

Pixies

Pixies, or piskies, are little people who are believed to live on the moors of Cornwall. One of their favourite pastimes is stealing horses and ponies, riding them wildly in the night and returning them in the morning. They can also be very helpful, though, often assisting humans with their work.

Elves

Elves live in woodlands and are known for their immortality and magical powers. They are said to be the size of humans, or even taller, and are very beautiful with long pale hair.

Sirens

Sirens are associated with the sea and can be illustrated as nymphs or mermaids. In Greek mythology they are depicted as creatures with the head of a female and the body of a bird. They live on islands and, with the irresistible charm of their song, lure mariners to their destruction on the rocks.

Goblins

Goblins are a more grotesque variety of a gnome. They are known to be playful, but at other times they can be evil. Goblins are said to have originated in France and

Gnomes

Gnomes are dwarf-like creatures that dwell in the earth (their name literally means 'earth dweller'). They are extremely small in size and it is said that they don't like the sun, whose rays turn them to stone.

Leprechauns

Leprechauns are very small sprites who make shoes for elves and are often described as merry little creatures dressed in old-fashioned green-coloured clothes, with a red cap, leather apron and buckled shoes.

MATERIALS AND EQUIPMENT

There is a huge range of materials and equipment you can use to create different types of faerie artwork. You don't have to buy every single piece of art equipment from your local art shop if you want to draw or paint faeries, or even purchase the very best or the most expensive. With a few basic art materials you can produce some wonderful results. The following pages provide details of some of the materials you could use; read through them and choose a range that you feel you could work with. Really try to envisage how you would like your faerie artwork to look, and choose your tools accordingly.

Drawing equipment

Many artists use professional drawing tables or easels to work on. These are excellent and can be purchased at any art shop but aren't always necessary. As long as you have a sturdy table and a comfortable chair, you should be able to work with ease. If you want to create an angle to work on, you could lean on a folder or use a drawing board with a book underneath. You can even make your own drawing board from a piece of either hardboard or MDF cut to size. Lay the board on your table and place a book underneath at the far edge so that the board is raised up slightly. This will help with your posture while drawing or painting.

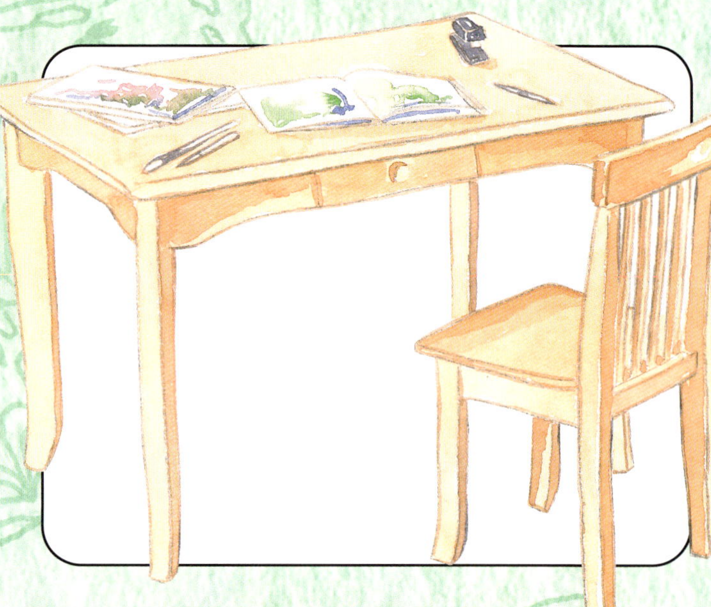

Papers and boards

When you are just starting out, particularly when drawing preliminary sketches, you can simply use inexpensive copy paper to draw on and use greaseproof paper for tracing. If you wish to branch out a little though, there is a wide range of papers available in your local art shop, which can be bought either in pads or in single sheets. Sketch pads are perfect for dry media and both pads and single sheets are available in different weights and qualities.

Cartridge paper is usually the cheapest and there are often many brands to choose from.

Watercolour paper is very popular to work on and is produced in a wide range of textured surfaces, both in pads and single sheets. Watercolour paper can be used with a variety of media including pen and ink, coloured and graphite pencils, acrylics – and, of course, watercolour paints.

Specialist pastel papers are also available in sheets and pads with a great selection of wonderful textures and colours to choose from.

Canvas can be used for oil and acrylic paints. Art shops sell canvas in different formats, the most popular being 'stretched canvas', i.e. canvas stretched over a wooden frame. It is also available in canvas panels, i.e. canvas stretched and glued onto lightweight board. However, by far the most cost-effective way of practising on the texture of canvas is to buy canvas paper. This is also available in pads and single sheets.

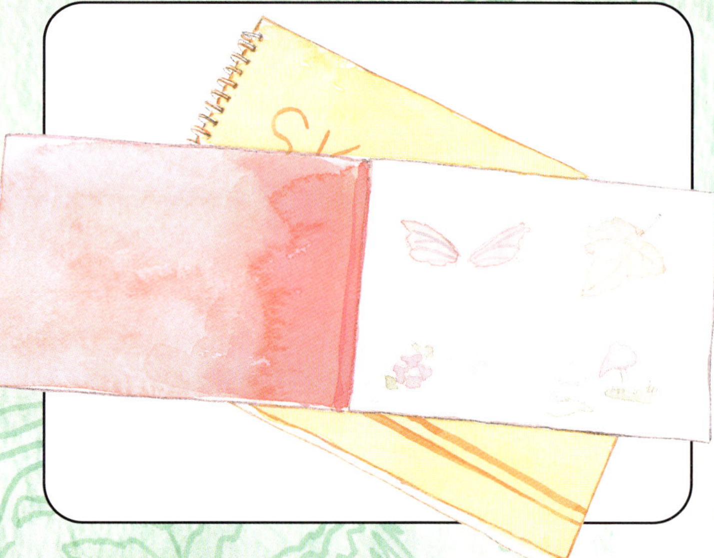

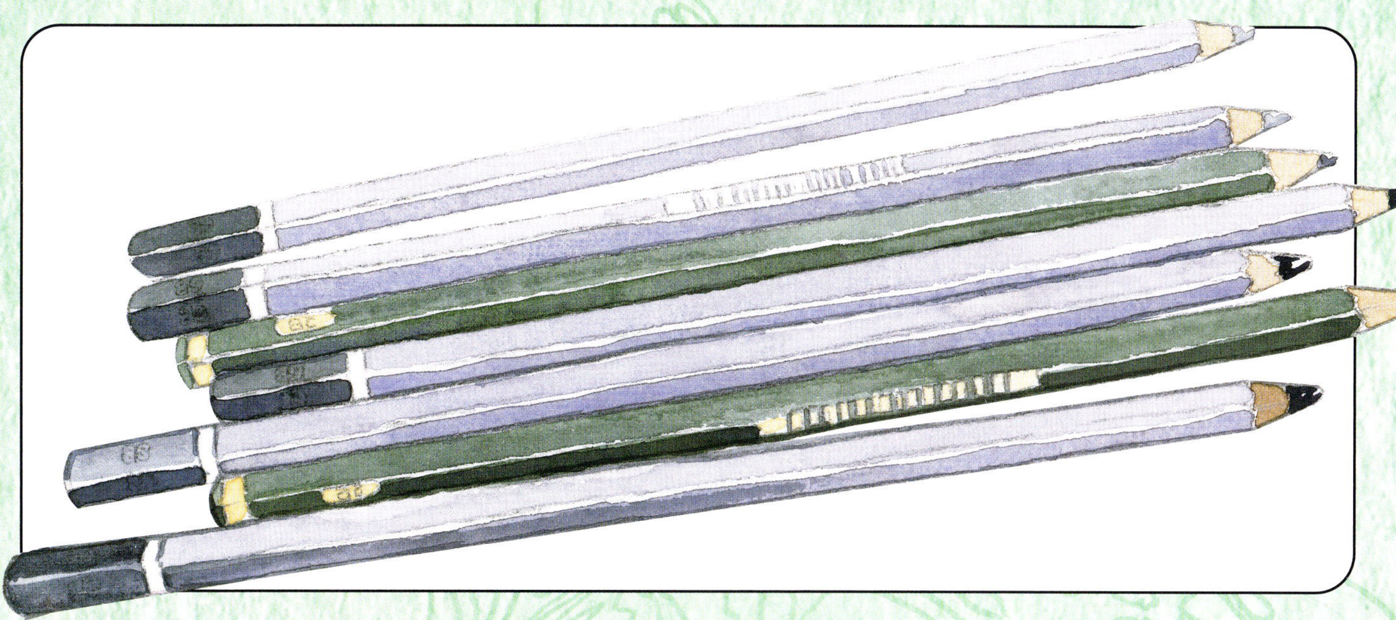

Graphite pencils

All artists need a good range of graphite pencils. You will naturally reach for a pencil to sketch ideas, to outline your drawings before adding colour or to create full graphite pencil drawings. Owning a variety of pencil grades is essential for any artist. They can be purchased in all art shops and range from 9H (which is very hard), to 9B (which is very soft). The softer the pencil, the thicker and darker the line it produces, so experiment with all the different grades This way you will know which one is best to use and when.

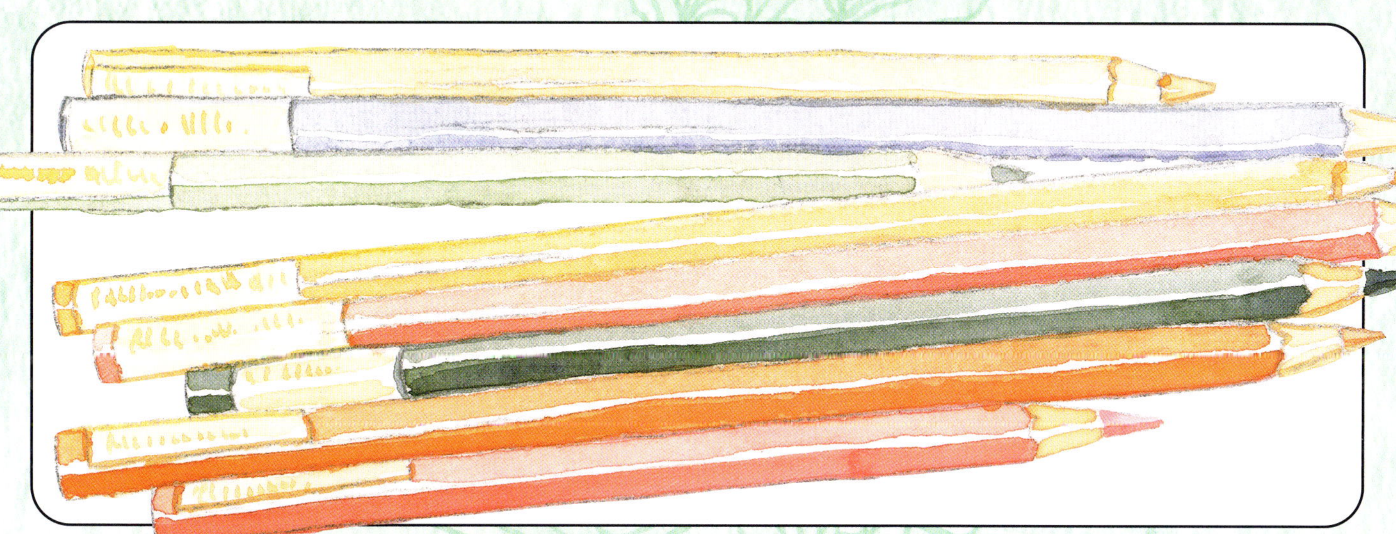

Coloured pencils

If you have never used paint before, coloured pencils are one of the easiest colour media to work with. Most people will be familiar with using coloured pencils from school, but artists' coloured pencils are much more enjoyable to work with, as the quality is far better. Coloured pencils can't be pre-mixed on a pallet, so a wide range of colours have been made to give the artist enough choice. Large sets can be expensive though, so I would recommend just purchasing a small set of between 10 and 20 to start with, then buy any further colours individually when needed. Alternatively, as there are many different types and brands of pencil, it may be an idea to purchase a few of each brand to see which you like working with best. Some are soft and waxy and some are hard wax. You can also purchase water-soluble pencils which can be used both wet and dry. Some brands are finer and chalkier which help in creating softer effects, and finally there are very hard pencils which are perfect for creating very fine detail. Whichever you choose to work with, for the best results always be sure to keep them sharp.

Pen and ink

Pen and ink can either be used as a standalone medium or in conjunction with watercolour. There are several different varieties of pen and ink you can use.

The oldest method is ink bottles and dip pens. You can buy sets of nibs that are different shapes for creating various qualities of line. There is also a wide range of coloured inks available to use with them – some are even glittery! You can purchase both waterproof and water-soluble inks, with the waterproof ones mainly used for outlining areas.

Fountain pens that hold cartridges can be useful as they are easy to control and you can use different coloured inks in the cartridges.

Many illustrators use rotring pens and these are very handy for drawing the features of faeries' faces as they have a very fine point.

There are also many everyday pens found in stationery shops that can be used in creating faerie artwork, such as fine-tipped writing pens, felt tips, markers, brush pens, and even ballpoint pens can work well.

Pastel sticks and pastel pencils

Pastels come in two forms; pastel sticks and pastel pencils. Pastel sticks are chunks of pastels that are made into short sticks or bullet shapes and are useful for covering large areas on your paper. There are many different brands of pastel sticks and their consistency can vary from very soft to very hard.

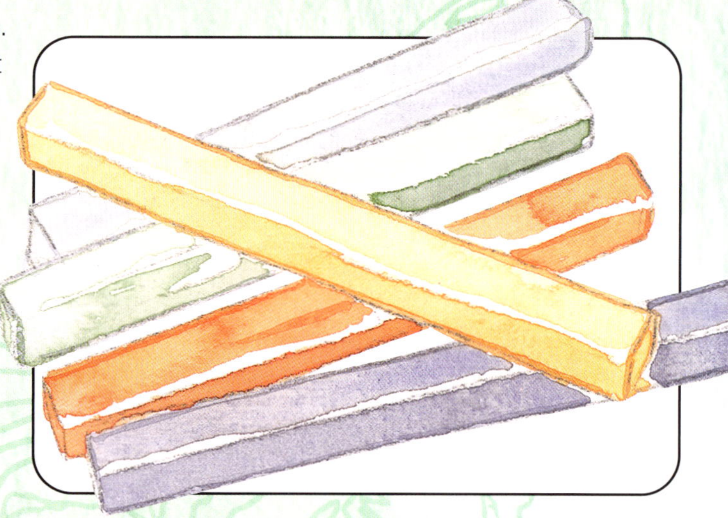

You can also purchase pastel pencils which look exactly like coloured pencils. They are wonderful for adding detail on top of your base coat if you have used pastel sticks for the under layers and backgrounds of your faerie drawings. You can also use them for sketching line drawings as you can produce very fine flowing lines with them, which creates movement within your work.

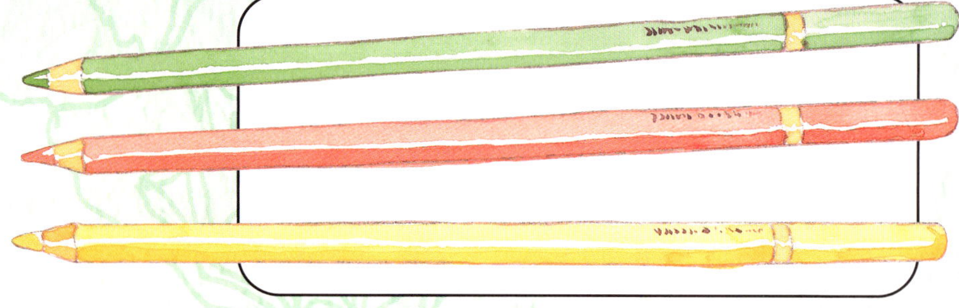

Watercolours

Watercolours are extremely versatile: you can start off sketching with a pencil in your notepad and if you want to add just a hint of colour, you can use a little watercolour to liven up your work in just a few washes. Watercolour tubes are very small and you need only a small amount of paint on your pallet, as you then mix it with plenty of water. They are also available in pens, which are compact and easily transportable, so you can take them with you when you are sketching in the field.

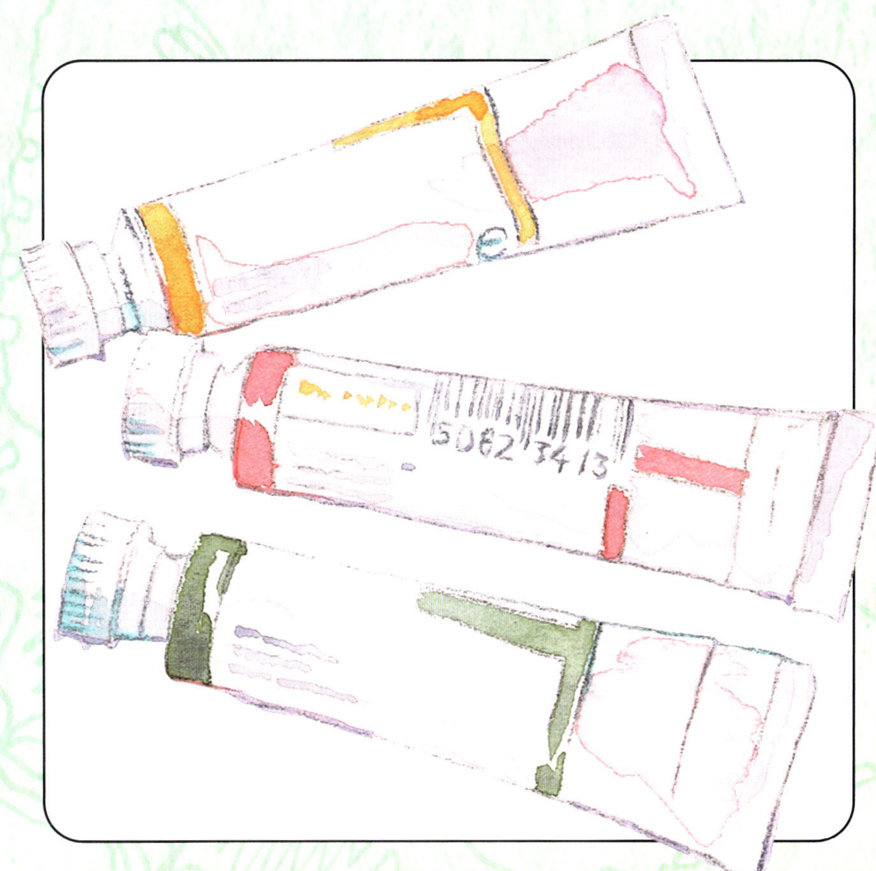

Acrylics

Acrylic paints are water-based, which means they can be diluted with water. They are easy to work with, easy to clean and they dry very quickly. They are also very versatile and you can paint on almost any surface with them.

Acrylics are sold in tubes, pots or bottles, so that you can squeeze a small amount onto your pallet and mix your desired colours. Acrylics can be purchased individually or in sets and, as for most materials, you have a variety of brands to choose from. The 'student' range of colours is the least expensive as these colours contain fewer pigments but they are perfect for any beginner.

Acrylics dry very rapidly which can make blending colours on paper and canvas more difficult, so a 'retarding medium' can be added which stops the water from evaporating so quickly. You add a small amount to your mix of paint but be careful not to use too much or the paints will become sticky.

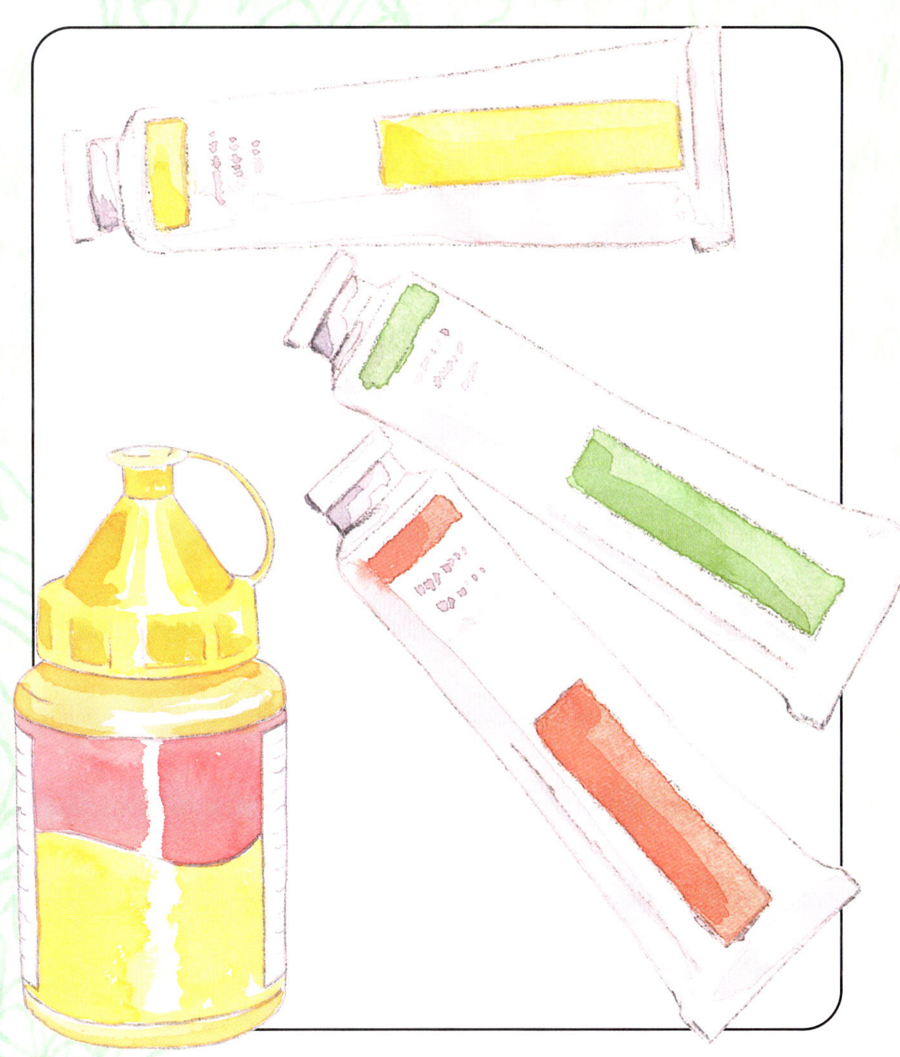

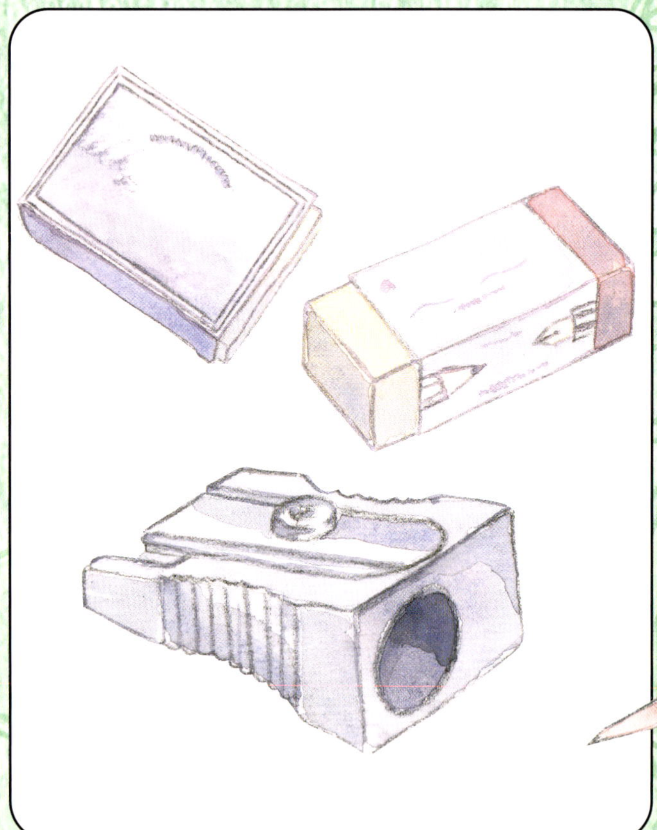

Accessories

Erasers and putty erasers are essential for making corrections. Putty erasers are especially useful as you can mould the eraser into a fine point for removing graphite accurately. I would suggest dabbing at the area rather than dragging the eraser across, to avoid scuffing the paper.

Pencil sharpeners and craft knifes are a must when working with graphite pencils, coloured pencils and pastel pencils. Try to maintain a sharp point on your pencil at all times as this really helps to keep your work precise and defined.

There are many different paintbrushes, depending on which medium you are working with. Brushes for all media come in various shapes, sizes and with different sized handles. Sable brushes are used for watercolour painting but tend to be quite expensive. The synthetic and sable blend brushes are much more economical. Synthetic brushes are used with oils and acrylic, as these are much more hardwearing.

The two main brush shapes are flat and round. Flat brushes are excellent for covering large areas, while round ones are perfect for detailed work.

Computers

A computer can be a useful tool for artists. Not only can we connect to the internet to look for reference photos and ideas for our paintings and drawings, but we can also use photo editing programs to create our artwork. There are a few photo editing programs that are free to download and these will enable you to draw with a range of pencils, paint with a large number of colours, create pre-defined shapes and even import your own photos, so that you can design the compositions of your faerie paintings. You can even produce your final paintings on the computer. If you have access to a scanner you can also scan in your artwork, then continue working on it at the computer for added effects.

If you enjoy working with the computer, there are many more advanced photo editing programs available for purchase. If you are interested in creating your faerie artwork using a computer, you may like to try a 'tablet and pen'. It can be very difficult to draw with a computer mouse, but with this method you can use the pen to draw on the surface of the tablet and your image will appear on the screen.

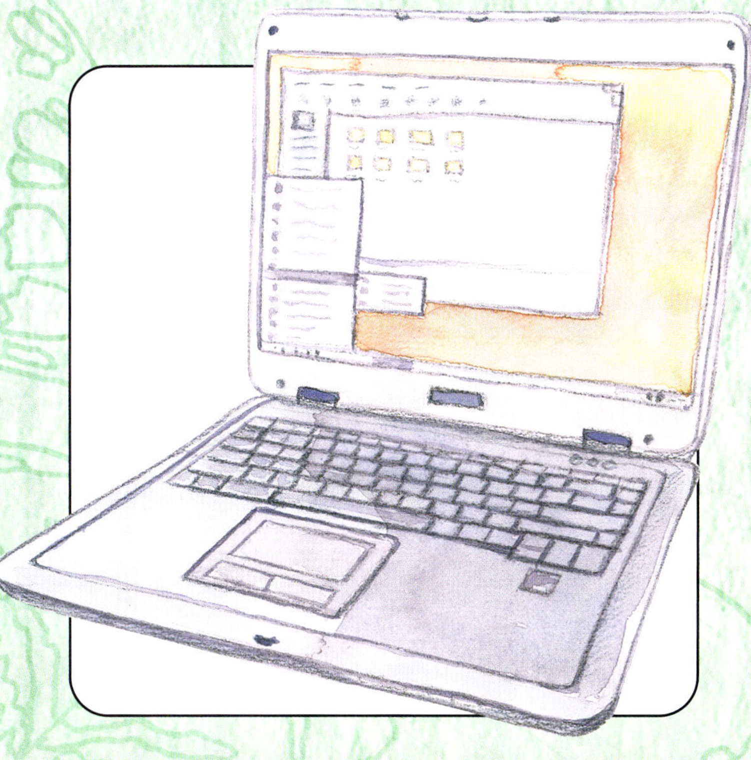

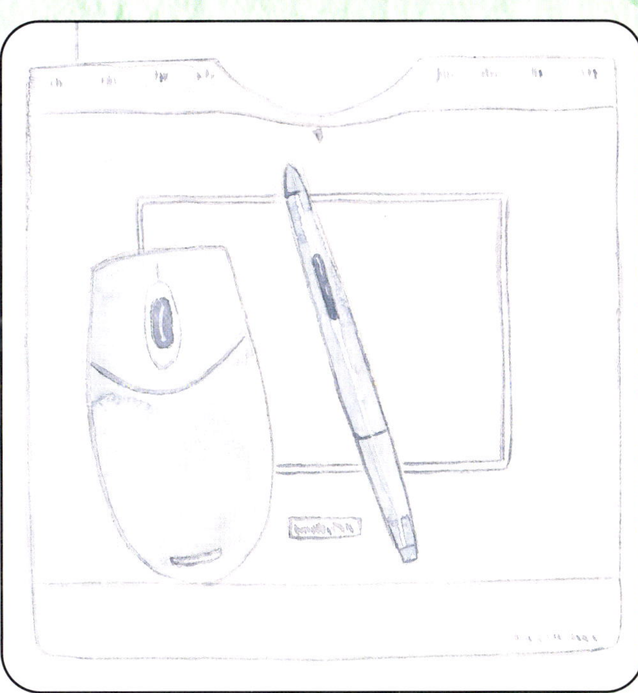

Digital cameras

If you have a digital camera, try to take it with you wherever you go so that you can collect photos for reference. Try to visit gardens and woods so that you can take photos of foliage, flowers, moss, toadstools and leaves. Landscape scenes and long distance shots of trees are excellent reference material for backdrops and if your camera has a close-up macro facility, try to take some shots of dew drops and tiny flowers. Keep all of these photos safely on your computer in an organized fashion, so that you can look though them easily when you are designing your faerie artwork.

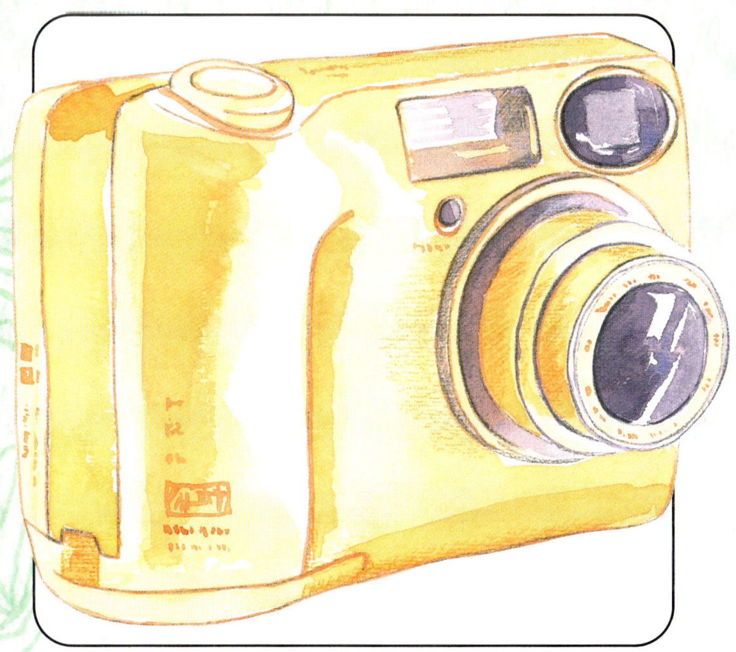

Experimenting with your materials

It is important to familiarise yourself with your art materials before you start to create your faerie artwork, especially if you are new to any of them. If you are using paints, see how thickly or thinly you can paint with them and which brushes produce thin lines and thick lines. Test out which colours mix together to make other colours and which colours don't mix at all! If you are using pencils and coloured pencils, see if you can layer the colours and tones over the top of each other. Try to draw using thin fine lines, or shade deep dark areas to create depth. Finally, experiment on a variety of papers and boards to see which materials work best on which surfaces. The following section will help you in your experimentations with all the media covered in this book.

GRAPHITE PENCIL

Graphite pencil is the easiest medium to work with. It is the most natural medium as we are used to holding a pencil from a very early age. It is usually the first medium an artist will choose to work with when creating preliminary drawings and sketches.

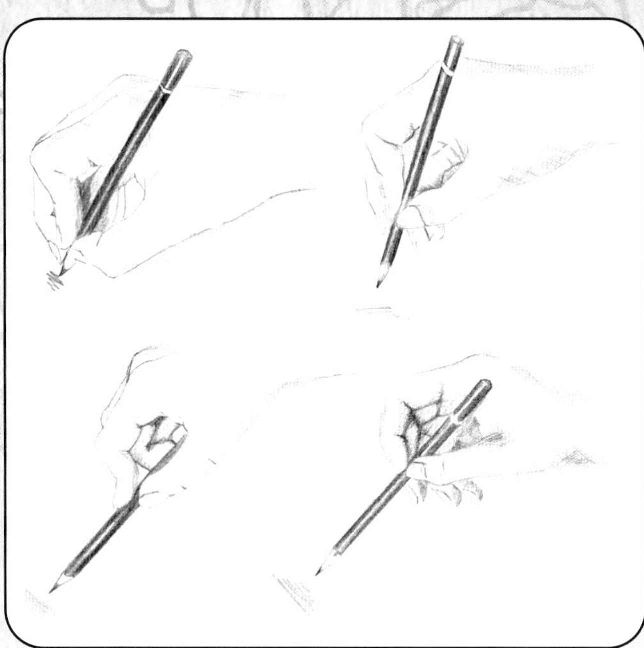

◄ Holding the pencil

It is important to hold your pencil correctly for shading and drawing and there are different positions for different lines. The first illustration shows the pencil being held in the normal writing position to draw fine controlled lines on the paper. The second position is holding the pencil a little further up away from the lead. This will enable you to be freer with your lines. The third example shows the pencil held half way up. This takes a while to get used to, but allows you to create a lot of movement in your sketching. It is helpful to have a larger piece of paper for this and if you can, try to create some long flowing lines. The final example shows that you can hold the pencil even towards the end. Lean your wrist gently on the paper and try creating flowing lines directly from the wrist and elbow, moving your whole arm in the process. Creating these flowing movements are very important in faerie drawings.

▲ Experimenting with lines

A good exercise is to test out all of your pencils and see which ones give soft thick lines and which give hard thin narrow lines. Experiment to create lines and patterns with the pencils, so that when you are drawing a picture and you need to create a certain line or set of lines in your work, you will know exactly which pencil will be best for the job. Remember to keep your pencils sharp by using your pencil sharpener or craft knife as this will give you finer and more exact lines.

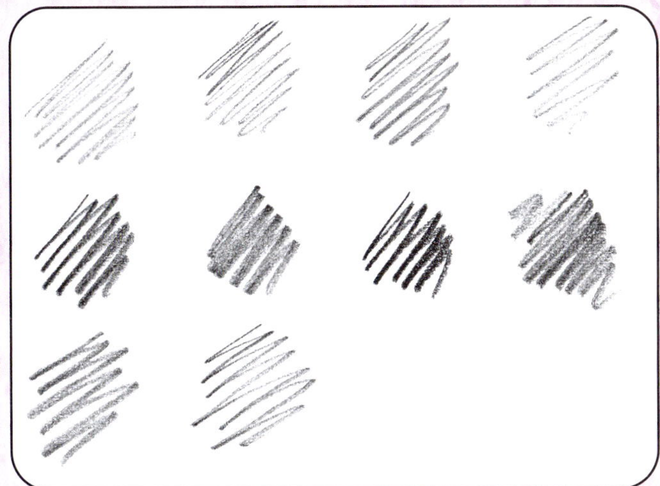

◀ Pencil grades

Pencils are manufactured in different grades, each classified by a number and a letter depending on how soft or hard they are. You need to work with a range of pencils and I would recommend choosing a variety of grades, ranging from 9H (the hardest) to 9B (the softest). I suggest a medium-grade pencil for sketching out your ideas, preferably a 2B. Draw preliminary lines lightly so you can easily erase them if you make a mistake. A 6B is good for building up the tones from your initial shading with the 2B; it allows you to add depth, and you can easily dab off areas with a putty eraser. Finally, a 9B is recommended for those deep, dark areas of shadow.

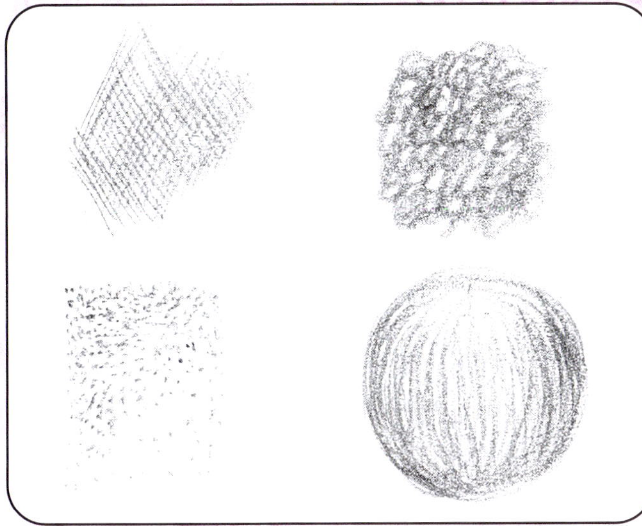

▲ Creating texture

It is easy to create texture, depth and three-dimensional forms with graphite pencil, as these examples show.

Cross hatching enables you to quickly create shading which has movement and texture. The lines are closer together for darker areas and spread further apart for lighter areas.

The scumbling example illustrates an almost fluffy texture and you create this by working the pencil around and around in tiny circles. The closer together the circles are, the darker the area will look.

Stippling is a lovely technique to use and, if you have the patience, whole drawings can be created in this technique. With a sharp pencil, preferably a 2B or a 4B, create simple dots on your page to make up the subject. The closer together the dots, the darker the area will seem.

Finally, contour lines are really handy if you have a solid object to illustrate; shading along its contour lines will give it form and three-dimensionality. Try these techniques yourself.

▲ Tonal strip

A good way to work out tonal values is to create a tonal strip. Start by drawing a rectangle split into six squares. Leave the first square on the left blank. This will be the lightest. Shade the next square with a 2B pencil as a flat tone. Try to create an all-over tone without any paper showing through your shading. Shade the third square also using a 2B pencil but this time layer the graphite with a second layer, creating a darker tone. Do the same with the fourth square, only this time use a softer grade of pencil and layer it three or four times. The last square will be the darkest and you will need to use your softest pencil. When you are layering, don't add pressure to darken the tone: just add layers to create an even build-up of tone. Once you have made your tonal strip you can use it to measure how dark or light objects are, by holding it against the object and matching the tone.

▲ Graduated strip

You can also make a graduated strip. This is similar to the tonal strip, but instead of shading flat squares try to graduate the tones from light to dark with a smooth transition. This can be hard to create and takes practice.

COLOURED PENCIL

If you have never used a colour medium before I would recommend starting with coloured pencils. The techniques involved are very similar to using graphite pencils. There are many brands available; some are softer to use than others and some are water-based.

Shading techniques

Coloured pencils are flexible and you can create textures in the same way as shown with graphite pencils on pages 16 and 17. You also have the advantage of layering various colours to create deeper tones.

▲ Basic shading

By using a single colour you can create horizontal shading for a flat base of any subject. Layering your pencil over and over, rather than adding pressure, will build up the tone gradually. To create a delicate effect from light to dark, and to preserve some luminosity, leave a little white paper underneath visible.

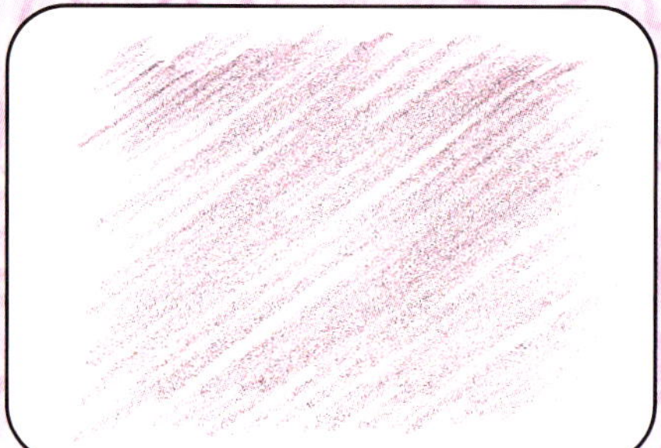

▲ Hatching

Hatching is one of the most common forms of shading. Rapid and regular lines that are evenly spaced convey texture and contours of the objects with ease. You can leave a little of the paper underneath showing through, as this adds to the technique. You can also vary the length of your line for variety.

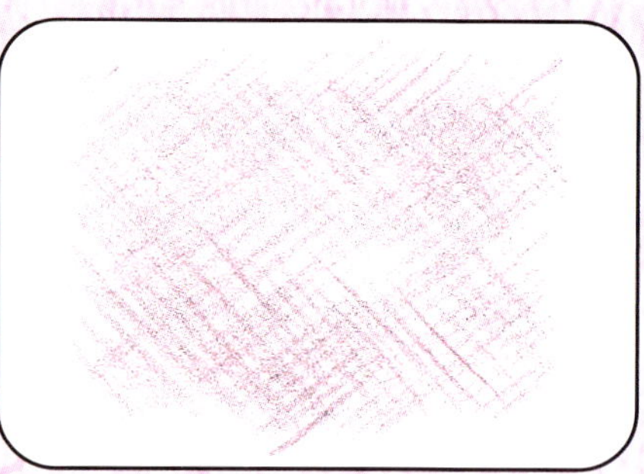

▲ Cross hatching

Cross hatching can add texture to an object and also depth of tone. Hatching overlaid at right angles can be created with different colours and even in multiple layers. The length of the lines can be varied depending on the contours and the subject.

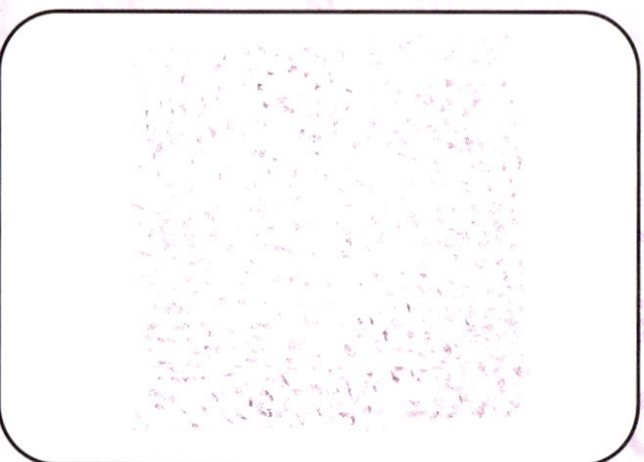

▲ Stippling

Stippling in coloured pencil is very easy but it is imperative that you keep your pencils sharp at all times. This technique can be used with one single colour or multiple colours and the dots can be spaced out for light areas and closer together for darker tonal areas.

▲ Gradient

To create a gradient, add more layers over just the upper area, rather than building up layers across the entire square.

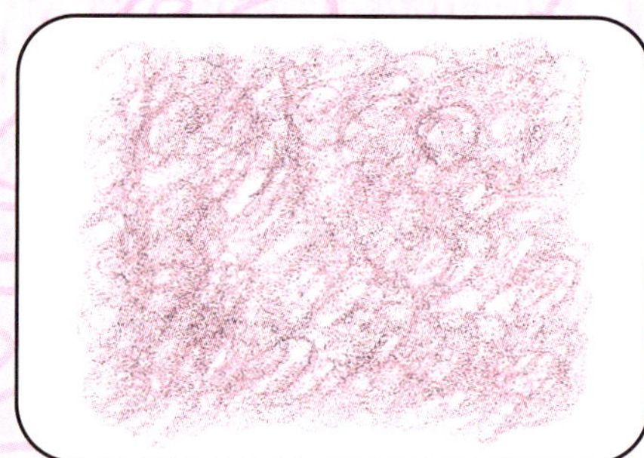

▲ Scumbling

This is a very useful technique that is really easy to create. Using your pencil in a circular motion, create tiny overlapping circles to create texture and tone. You can use one single colour for this technique or multiple colours. You can also vary the size of the circles.

▲ Layering

This technique is fundamental in coloured pencil drawing and shading. Start by adding a single layer within your square. Next add a second layer – what you are trying to achieve is a smooth flat tone, smoothing out your lines and removing any trace at all of white paper underneath.

▲ Horizontal shading

Horizontal shading is a style and technique of its own. Creating a drawing using only horizontal shading can give dynamic results. Shade using a sharp pencil, using multiple colours or just one single colour and create various lengths of short lines to convey the texture and contours of the object.

▶ Layering colours

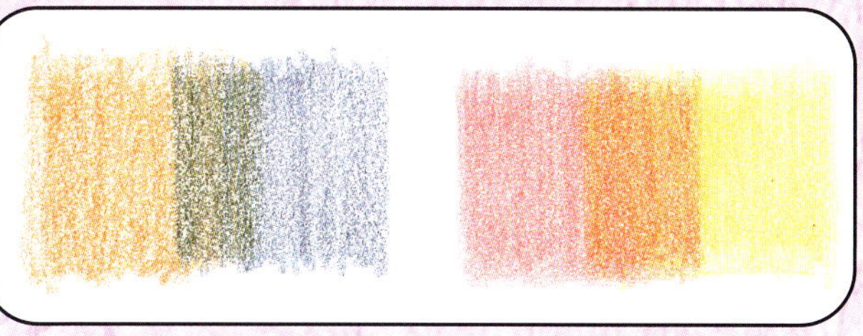

If you have a limited pallet of colours and you want to create a further specific colour, you can layer two colours to create a third. For instance, overlapping a block of yellow with a block of blue creates green. Similarly we can lay down a block of yellow overlapped with a block of red to create orange.

▶ Creating blacks

If you need to create a very dark area in your work, using black alone can make the area very flat and lifeless. Adding colours to the black can add some solidity and depth to it. Look at the black area you are copying or trying to create and work out if it's going to be a cold black or a warm black. If it's a cold black, add some dark blues into the mix, as shown on the right. If it's a warm black, add some warm reds and browns into the mix as shown in the middle. This will not only add depth but also liven up the area.

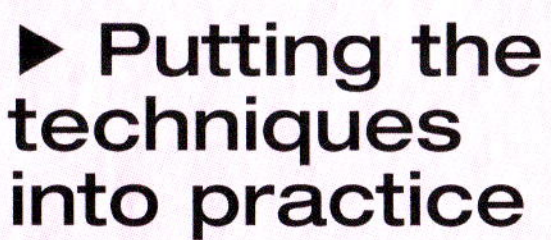

▶ Putting the techniques into practice

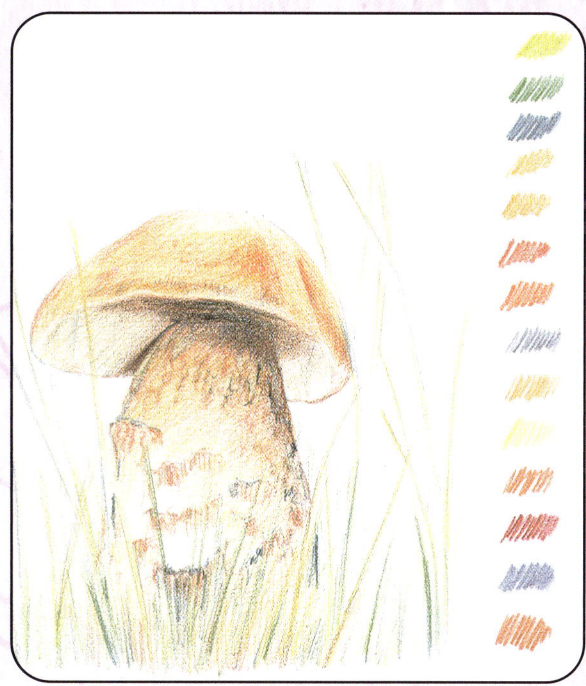

Once you have practised the techniques, try creating a drawing like this one of a toadstool. Here I have used simple shading and layering techniques to create depth and solidity. Try to use cooler colours for shadowed areas and warmer, lighter colours which allow the paper to show through where the light is hitting the subject. I have also included a colour swatch to show the range of colours I used. If you are shading grass, try to use only subtle greens and browns to give a more natural feel to the drawing.

WATERCOLOUR

Watercolour is a complex medium but I'm going to keep it as simple as possible to make it easy for a beginner. It is an exciting medium to work with, as it often seems to have a mind of its own! However, if you follow a few basic rules and keep your drawings and paintings simple, you will produce some wonderful results.

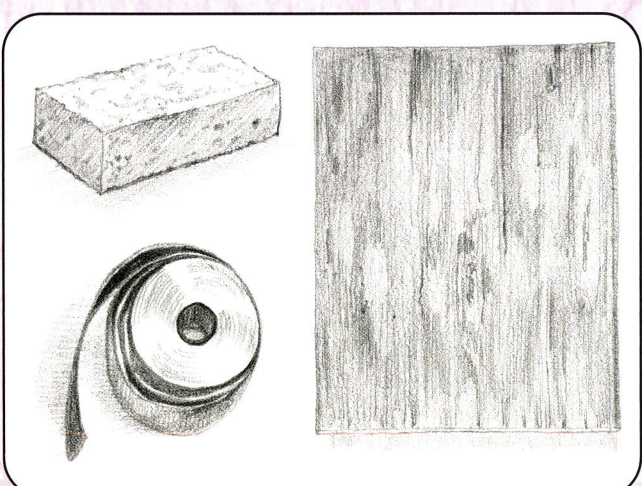

Stretching paper

Before you begin to paint, you will need to learn how to stretch your watercolour paper so that it doesn't crinkle when you paint on it. You will need a roll of gum tape, a clean sponge and a piece of plywood. Your ply board should be larger than the piece of paper you wish to stretch to allow room for the gum tape.

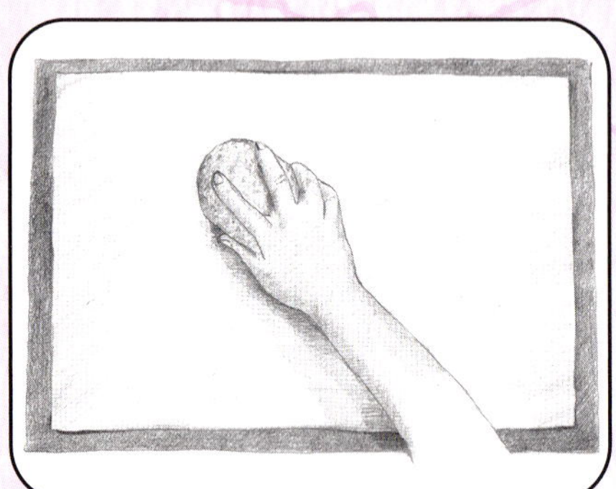

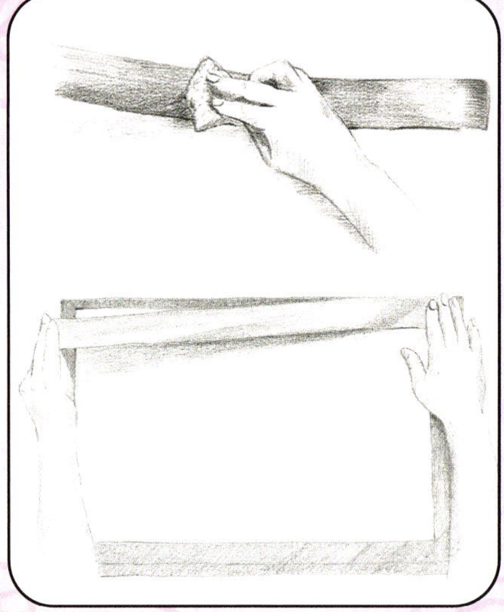

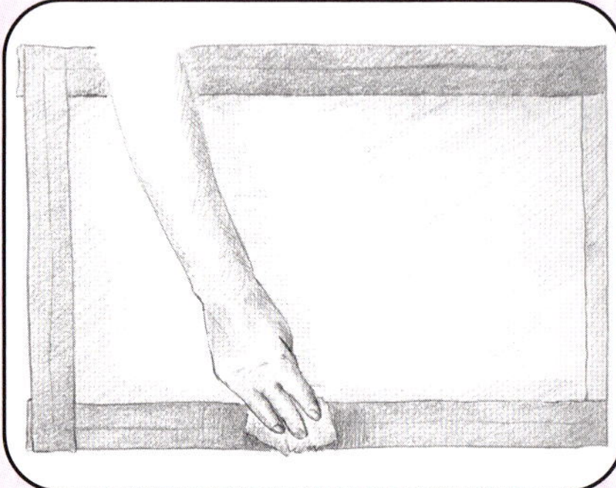

▲ Step 1

Measure the gum tape against each side of the paper and cut it into strips. The strips needs to be slightly longer than each side of the paper. Set them aside.

Soak your watercolour paper in water. You can lay it in a sink or in a bath if it is large. Leave it to soak for up to two minutes – but no longer, otherwise it could tear when you lift it out. Remove the paper from the water, allow it to drip for a few seconds, then lay it on the centre of board. Smooth it down, being careful not to leave too many bubbles or wrinkles. Use the clean sponge to smooth it out completely.

▲ Step 2

Use the damp sponge to wet the gum tape on both sides and lay it along one edge of the paper, overlapping onto the board, gum-side down. Repeat this process on the other three sides of the paper.

▲ Step 3

Very carefully remove any excess water from the edges of the gum tape with a piece of kitchen roll or a paper towel.

Leave your board somewhere flat to dry naturally, preferably overnight; the wrinkles and bubbles will disappear. The paper is now ready to be worked on. Once you have finished your painting, you can remove the paper using a craft knife, cutting around the edge of the paper just to the edge of the gum tape.

▶ Flat wash

This is the easiest of all washes in watercolour. Draw a square on your paper and mix your paint in a well on your pallet before you begin, adding plenty of water so that it is quite translucent. Watercolour dries quite quickly so you need to make sure you mix enough paint, otherwise you will end up with joining lines in the wash. Choose a large brush – it can be either flat or round, but flat is easier for this particular wash. Load your brush with the paint, start in the top corner and pull the brush in a straight line to the other side. Repeat this all the way to the bottom of the square, overlapping each line slightly, until you have covered the entire space with colour. If you need to load your brush with more paint, do so at the end of each line. Once you have filled the square, don't work back into it as you will ruin the effect. Now rinse out your brush well and try practising it again.

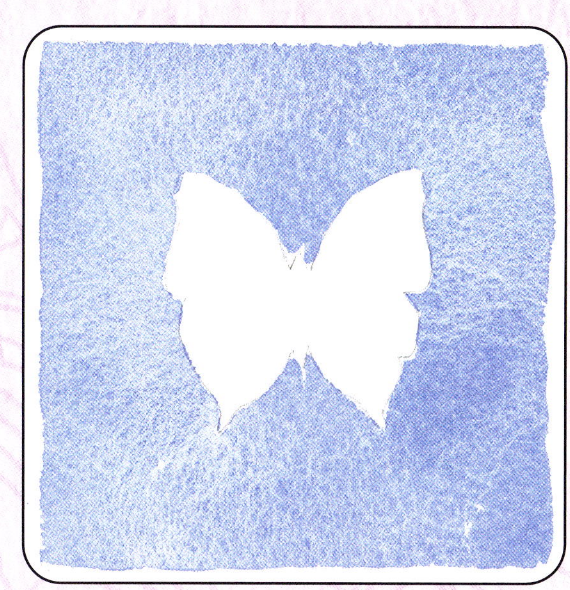

▶ Wet-in-wet wash

Draw a square on your paper and, using a sponge or a large brush, wet the square with clean water. It is very important to use clean water for this task. In general, when using watercolour it's a good idea to change your water regularly, otherwise your paintings can become dull. Once you have wet your square, mix up two colours in the wells of your pallet. Load your brush with the lighter colour and drop this into various areas of your square. Now rinse your brush, load it with the second colour and drop this into the spaces in your square. The paints will now spread and the two colours will diffuse across the paper. In this way you can create very soft background effects. The wet-in-wet technique is fun as you never know how it will turn out. As it isn't something you can plan easily, experiment with it using different colours and consistences.

▶ Graded wash

Draw a square on your page. Mix up a dark hue in one well of your pallet and a very light version in the second well by adding more water. We are going to start with the dark tones and work our way down to light. Load your brush with the darker hue, start at the top corner and work across to the other side. Rinse your brush, dry it with a paper towel and load it with the lighter mixture. Start your second line just slightly overlapping the top one and work your way to the other side. Next rinse your brush but this time, instead of drying it, leave plenty of water on the brush so when you load it with the lighter mixture of paint it will be even lighter. Create the third line in the square, still overlapping slightly so that the paint can disperse. You could then try experimenting using two different colours, for instance a blue and a crimson colour for a multicolour effect.

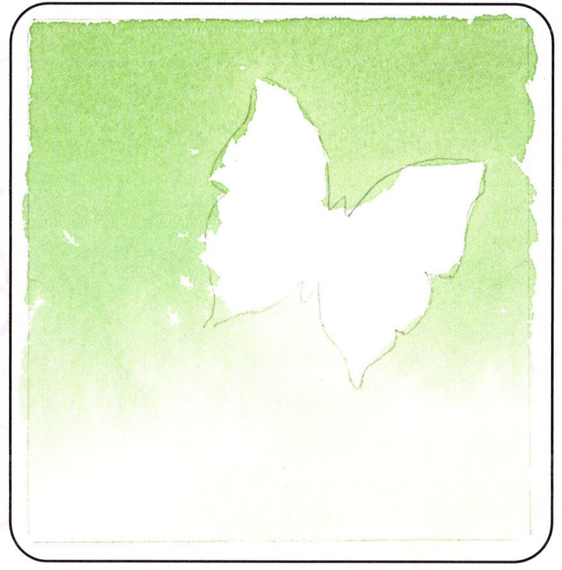

▶ Dry brush technique

You can use many different colours in the dry brush technique, as it is very versatile. Here a light green and a dark green illustrate how to start to create grass for your faerie paintings. To begin with I created a very light flat wash in the background and left this to dry. This is very important: if it is not left to dry, your dry brush technique will turn into a wet-in-wet technique. Once it is completely dry, mix up a darker green and load a little of it onto a clean, dry brush. Drag the brush from the base of the grass up to the tip, lightening the pressure as you go. If the brush is dry enough you should create a textured blade of grass; it also helps if you use textured paper. Experiment using wetter or drier paint to see the various results you can create. Also try using different consistencies of paint, to see the different effects you can create with thicker and thinner paints.

▶ Splatter technique

There are a few ways of creating this technique. I started by painting a flat wash to give a base; you could also wet the background and splatter into the wet paper for different results. Next, place some scrap paper on your table as this technique can be quite messy. Mix a few different colours in the wells of your pallet and collect a variety of brushes to experiment with. You can use different sized brushes or even a toothbrush to create the splatter effects. Load up a brush and gently flick it onto the paper. You can flick the bristles of the brush with your finger, but you will need to direct the brush closer to the paper for this technique. Use all the colours, remembering to rinse the brushes between each one. This also can't be fully planned and is exciting as you never know how it will look at the end. You can use this in your faerie paintings to create faerie dust and snow showers, and splatter effects in foliage will give detail.

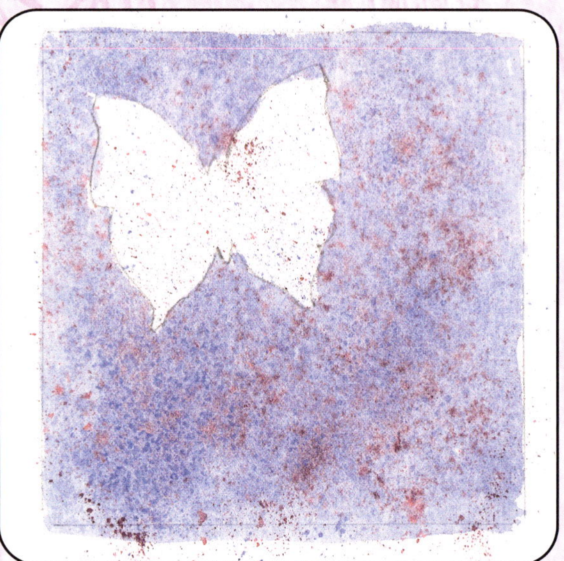

▶ Using salt

This is a fun technique to use and can turn a plain wash into something really special. Draw a square and fill your pallet with a couple of colours that you know will mix well together, for instance French Ultra Marine and Cobalt Blue. Using the wet-in-wet technique, drop the colours randomly in the square. Almost immediately, add grains of salt to the wet paper. As the wash dries the salt will absorb the pigment, gradually creating patterns and shapes in the paint. Different salts will create different patterns, so purchase a few different ones to experiment with. The larger the crystals, the larger the patterns and starry effects that you can create. Once the salt and the wet-in-wet wash are dry, brush the salt off with a clean dry hand or sponge. This is a very exciting technique and a must for everyone experimenting with watercolour.

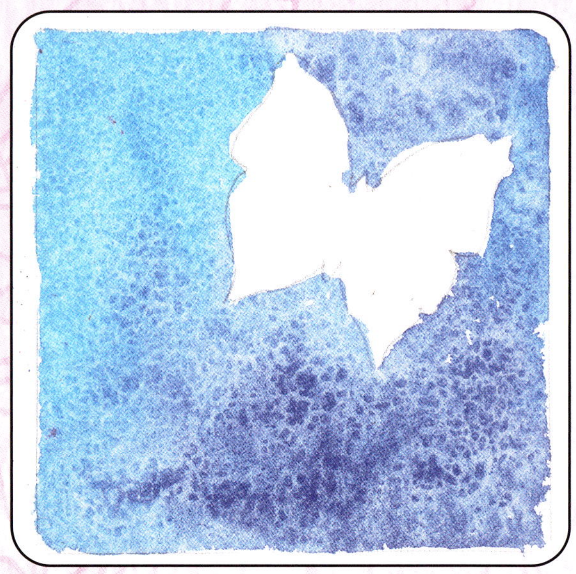

▶ Masking fluid

Masking fluid is a great way to retain the white of the paper in specific areas, enabling you to create smooth large washes around it. It's helpful if you want to paint large areas of background without having to paint carefully around the subject, which can be tricky and produce uneven washes. When you apply masking fluid, use a very old paintbrush and keep it solely for this use, as brushes can be ruined by it. Masking fluid is a latex and is difficult to remove from the bristles of the brush, so always rinse it thoroughly after application. If you have very small areas you wish to keep free of paint, use the end of the paintbrush or a cocktail stick. Apply the masking fluid and leave it to dry. Once dry, peel off the fluid, being careful not to rip the paper.

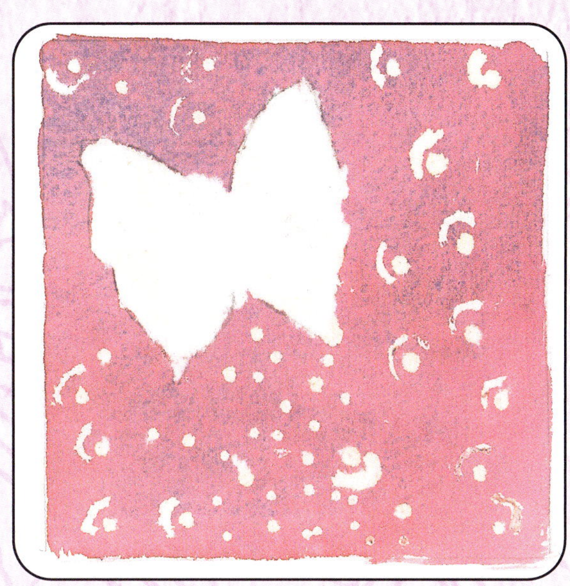

▶ Stippling

Stippling is a very easy technique to master and enables you to build up textures in precise areas. In this example I started with a simple flat wash using Yellow Ochre and left it to dry thoroughly. It is important that you use a stiff brush for stippling techniques; often watercolour brushes are soft and very flexible, so if possible it's better to use a brush made for acrylic or oil painting as they are more sturdy. Dip a dry, clean brush into a mixture of paint and, while holding the brush upright, dab the paint onto the paper. You will see that by dabbing across the paper you can stipple various colours and tones in patters where needed. I have used sap green and yellow ochre to represent a warm glade-like effect. Experiment using different-sized brushes and different colours and hues.

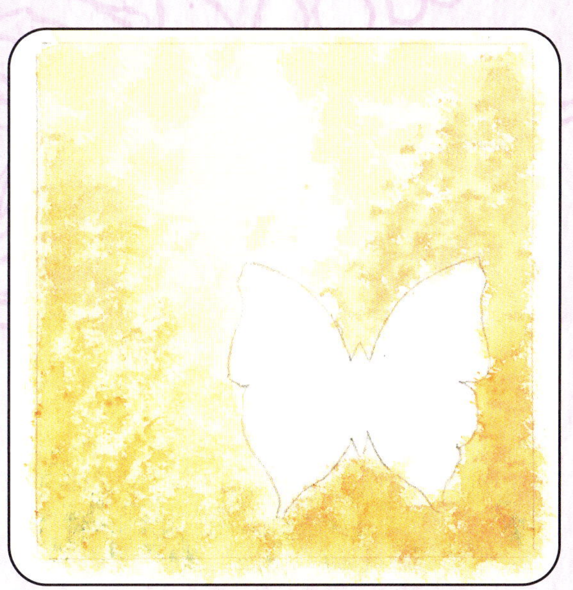

▶ Lifting off watercolour

You can use a variety of objects to lift off watercolour which will give you different patterns in the paint. I started by creating a light flat wash using blue and crimson. I left this to dry and then added a darker layer over the top. If you would like the paper to show through underneath, omit the first layer of colour. While the second layer was still wet, I lifted off some of the paint with a tissue to reveal the colour underneath. You could use all sorts of things to lift off the colour – a clean dry brush, a sponge, tissue paper, kitchen roll, cling film – the list is endless! Try to experiment to see what you can use and the different textures you can create. You can even scrape into the paint when it is dry to lift off the colour in lines, which is handy for grass and flower decoration.

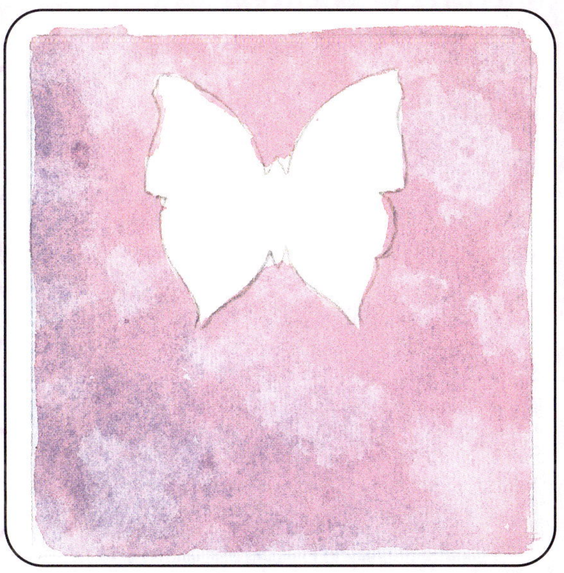

PEN AND INK

Pen and ink can be quite a tricky medium as once you have put pen to paper it can't be erased. This means you need to do some planning before you begin. If you draw out your picture with a graphite pencil first, this enables you to get the outline correct before you start adding any lines in pen. There are a variety of lines and washes that you can use, so experiment with them before you create a full picture. Many of them are similar to the techniques used with pencil.

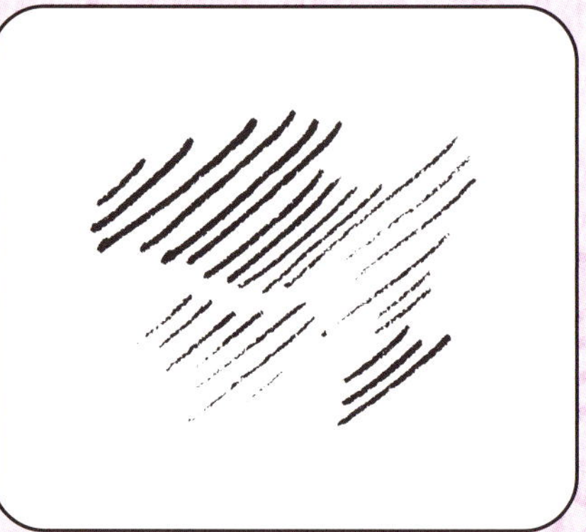

▲ Hatching

The most basic method of creating tones in pen and ink is simple lines. The closer together the lines are, the deeper the tones you can create. You can draw the lines at any angle, although vertically and diagonally are the most common.

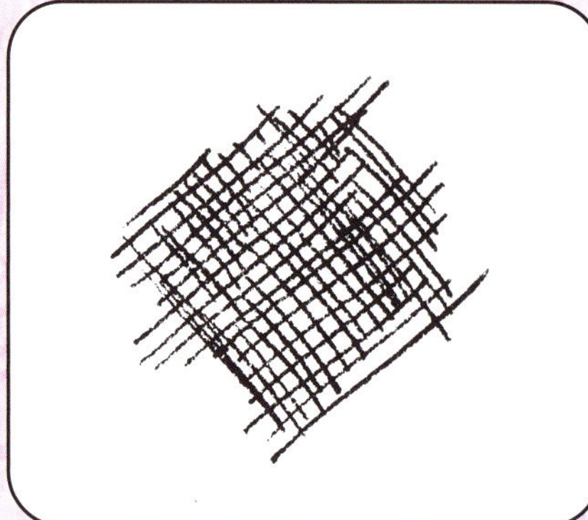

▲ Cross hatching

This is exactly the same with pen as with pencil. Using your pen, create a patch of lines in one direction and then draw more in the opposite direction on top. The closer together your lines are, the deeper and darker the tone will be.

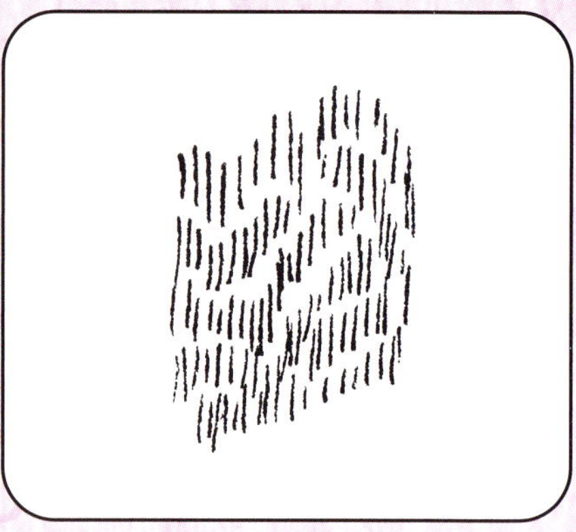

▲ Parallel lines

Using parallel lines can often describe an object or subject well. Create them freehand, try not to use a ruler and they will look more natural. Again, the closer together your lines are, the darker the tone will be.

▶ Direction of line

If you are illustrating a curved object it is important to draw lines within its contours. In these examples you can see lines have been drawn in a curve across a sphere, leaving a lighter area at the top where the light hits it. The first illustration shows the direction your pen should shade, the second shows single lines in one direction and the third shows more of a cross hatching effect across the sphere. This shading gives the sphere shape and three dimensional form.

You can do the same to a box shape or a triangle shape, or indeed any shape you choose, using simple lines to create a realistic 3D effect.

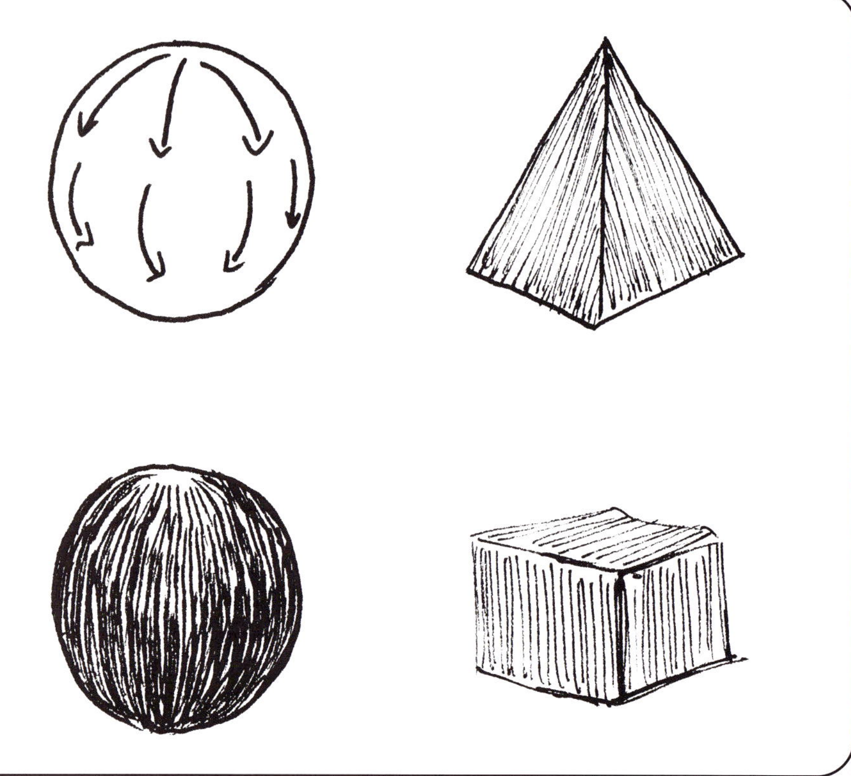

▶ Stipple

The two spheres illustrated here are created using only a few dots in the correct places. The first sphere has very few dots, yet you can still see the shape of the object. The second shade has many more dots and some are concentrated in the bottom left on the circle, helping to give the shape solidity and form.

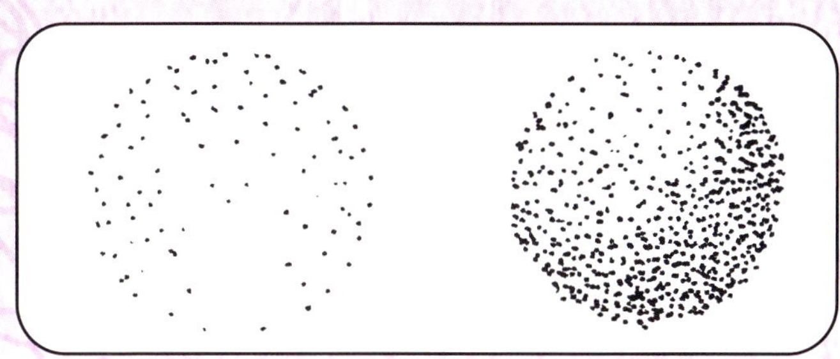

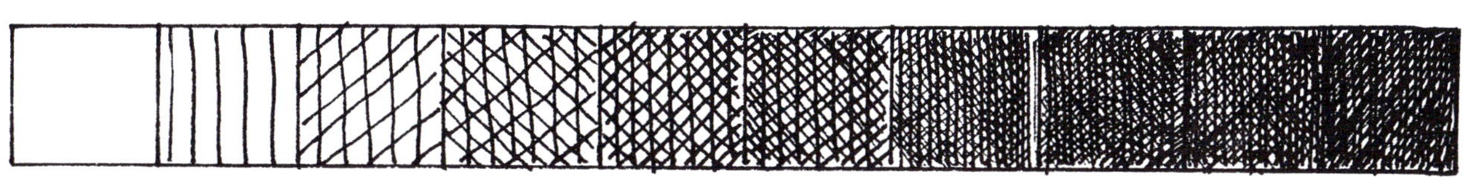

▲ Cross hatching value scale

The tonal strip shows how close together the lines have to be in order to create a deeper and darker tone. Draw a strip of 10 boxes. Start off by leaving the first one as the white of the paper. The second should have one layer of parallel lines. The third should have two layers of lines crossed. The fourth square then should have three layers of lines, and so on until you reach the end. Make sure that the last square is the darkest.

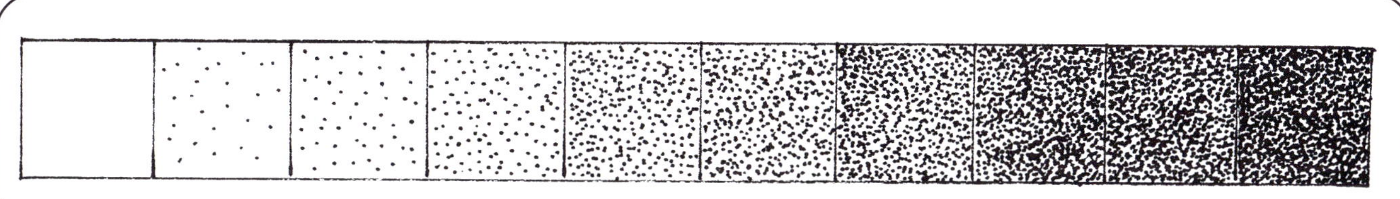

▲ Stipple value scale

This is created similarly to the cross hatch value scale, only this time using dots instead of lines. When you get to the last square it will still look like you have used dots, but most of them will be joined up, leaving a lovely stipple patterned effect. This technique is relatively time consuming but really worth the effort when complete.

▶ Putting the techniques into practice

Choose something simple to draw for your first attempt using pen and ink. Don't forget to draw the subject out in pencil first, get the outline exactly right and then start by creating a simple line drawing in pen. As you can see with this illustration of a toadstool, the pen can be very effective in a simple line form. This was completed using a felt tip pen.

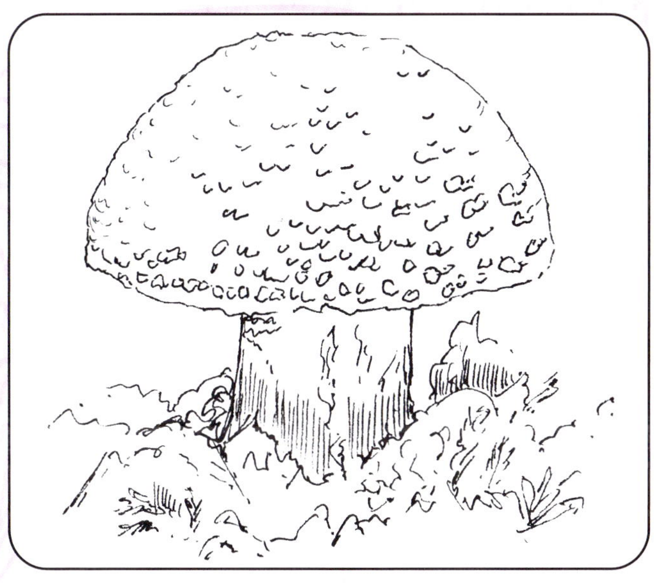

▶ This second illustration is the same picture but is shaded using a few techniques including cross hatching, hatching, and using different weights of line. This means that you press lighter for light lines and harder for darker lines – although don't press too hard, or you will release too much ink and the nib may get damaged.

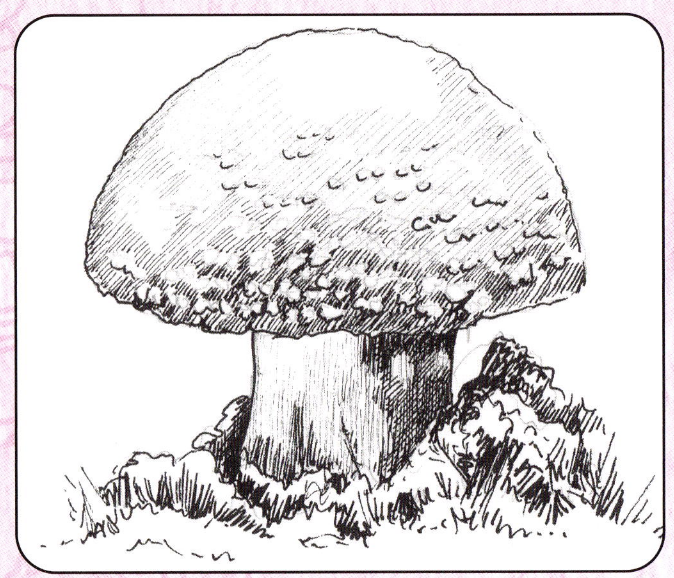

▶ The third illustration is pen and wash. Draw out your subject in pencil and create a line drawing over with pen. You can then use a brush and some sepia coloured ink to wash the tones over the subject where needed. Thus in this instance, the stem is darker as it's in shade, the top of the toadstool is much lighter and the grass and foliage around the base is painted randomly to create a textured effect.

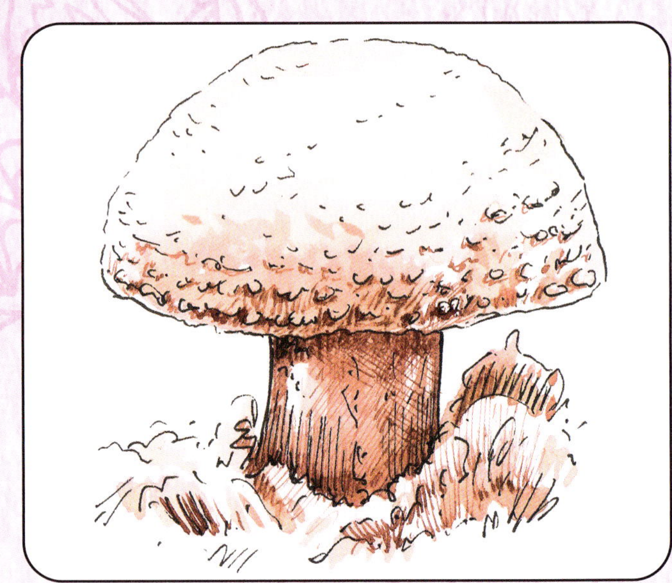

▶ The fourth illustration is created in the same way as the third but this time watercolour paint has been used to add some colour to the scene giving a little extra sparkle to the illustration. The two together give the illustration more detail, texture and colour.

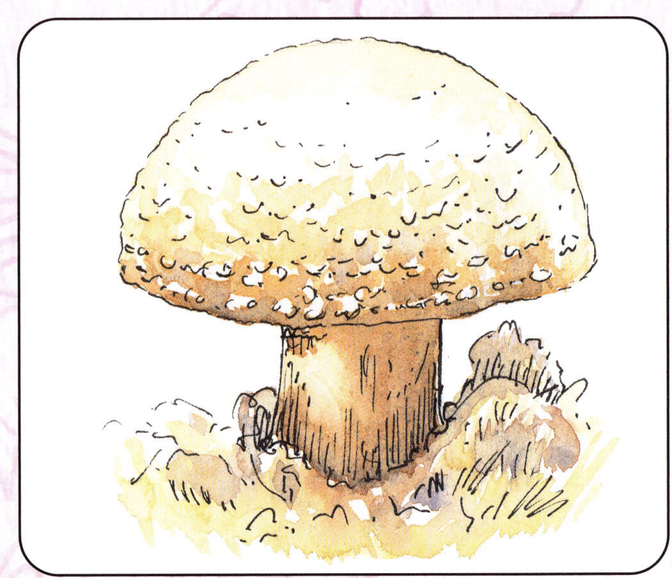

PASTELS

Pastels are lovely to work with and can produce very different results when used on different papers. Their softness is perfect for faerie drawings and illustrations, and because you can use different coloured papers, they can be really dynamic. Pastels can be messy: it's very easy to get the pastel over your fingers, so try to keep your work surfaces and paper clean so that you don't get finger prints on your drawings. It's good to have plenty of scrap paper handy so that you can lean your wrist on the paper instead of on your drawings.

▶ Making your mark with pastels

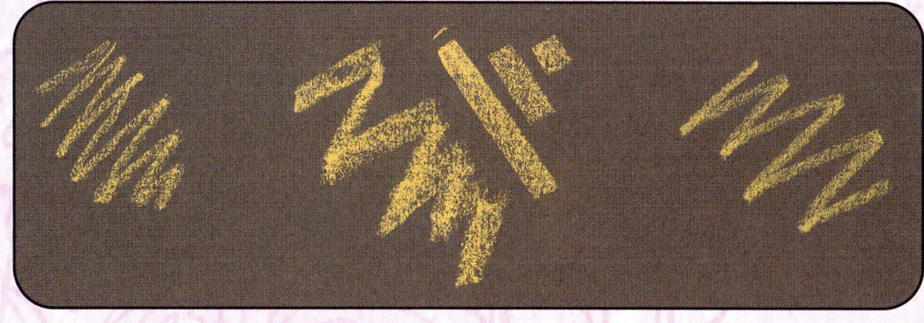

Experiment as much as you can with your pastels before you create your pastel faerie drawing. Discover how the pastel lies on different surfaces, and how you can create fine and thick marks with the various pastels available. These three illustrations show how thick or thin your lines can be. The first has been created using a sharp corner, or edge of a pastel stick. The second line is created by using the end of the pastel, and this allows you to draw thick and solid lines. The third illustration has been created by using a pastel pencil which is a little more controllable.

▶ Blending pastels

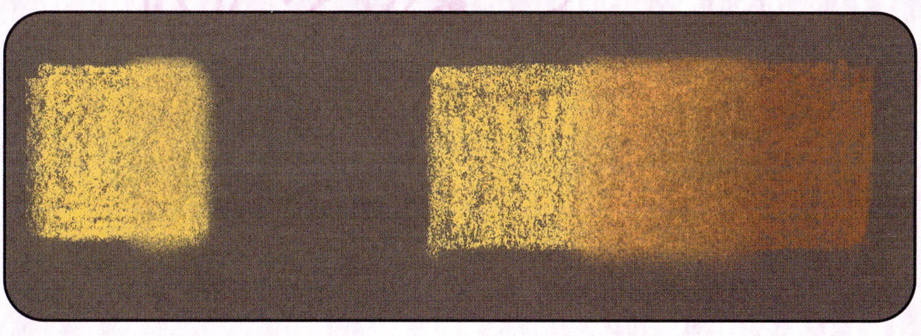

Pastels blend very easily using your finger to smooth them out. This isn't always necessary as it can remove the texture created by the pastel and the tooth of the paper; however, in certain areas of your work it may be needed, for a soft velvety background or sky, for example. You can see here that the left side of the yellow square is basic pastel drawn on pastel paper, while the right side is smoothed. We can also use blending to create other colours, as with coloured pencils. In the second illustration above the yellow box and the dark orange box are overlapped in the centre. When they are blended they create a lighter orange. You can do this with a variety of colours – experiment to see which work together and which don't.

▶ Hatching and cross hatching

Here you can see I have used cross hatching to cover an area, which provides texture as well as interest. The closer together you place your lines the deeper in tone the area will look. If you want a lighter area, add more distance between your lines. Alternatively, you can shade by just using a variety of lines in one direction, and if you vary the length of line it will add interest into the shading. With this technique, you can create shapes in the gaps between the lines.

Practising with pastels

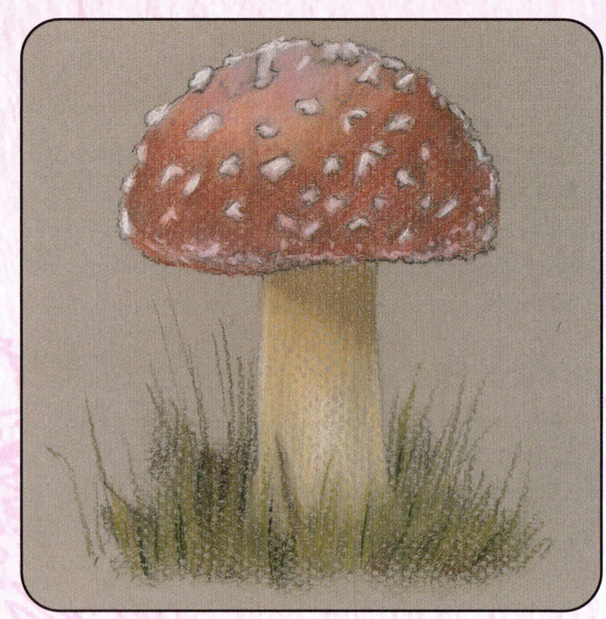

▶ Once you have familiarized yourself with pastels you can try out a very simple object to draw. This first Fly Agaric toadstool is drawn using a mixture of pastel pencils and pastel sticks on textured pastel paper. Draw your subject with a soft pencil and make sure you press as lightly as you can. This way you can erase any mistakes without damaging the paper. Once you are happy with the outline drawing, lay down your darkest tones first. In this example a dark red was used for the top of the toadstool, making sure gaps were left for the white areas. Dark ochre brown was then used for the stem and olive green for the grass. Once you have the basic tones, you can add your lighter tones. Finally, add detail on top with either the pastel sticks or the pastel pencils. The pencils are easier to control, so I would recommend these for fine lines such as the grass and the white on the top of the toadstool.

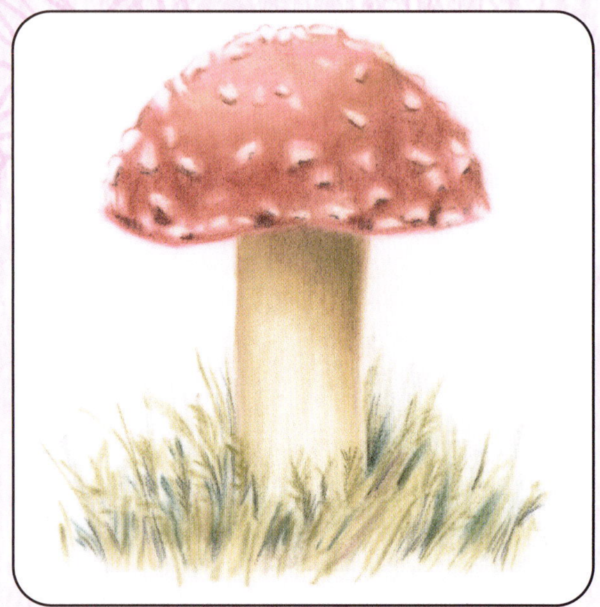

▶ The second illustration shows the difference when using a softer paper with the pastels. This is velour paper and can be purchased from specialist art shops online in pads or sheets. The velvet surface creates a very soft and smooth appearance and sometimes the final study appears to have more depth. I worked in exactly the same way as the first drawing, using both pastel sticks and pastel pencils, using the latter for all the final details.

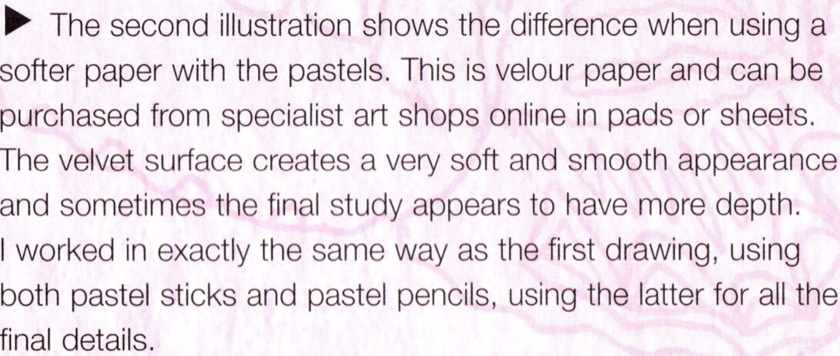

Make plenty of experiments with pastels, as they are a really dynamic medium and you can create drawings in colour and produce wonderful effective results in a short space of time.

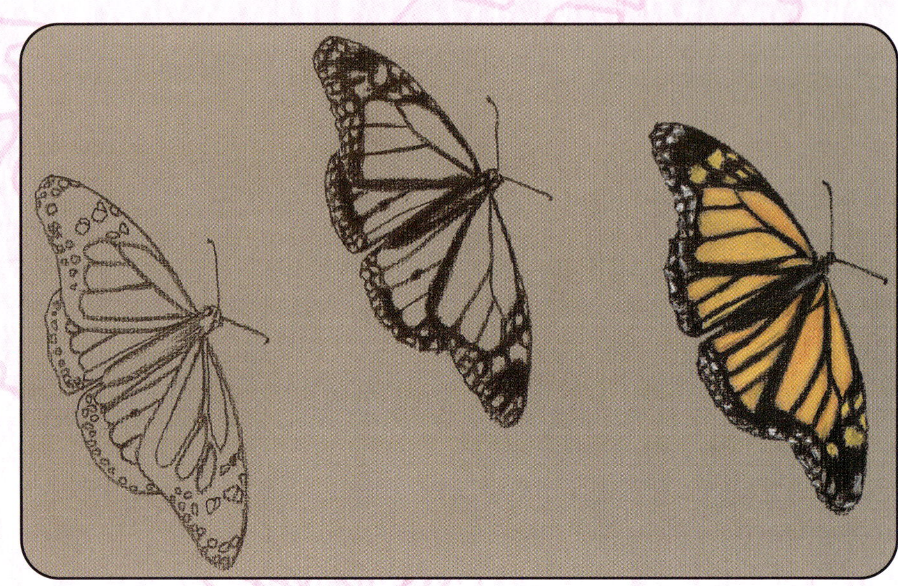

ACRYLIC

Acrylic is similar to watercolour in that you can use it for transparent washes but you can also mix acrylic thickly and and use it for solid colour. This enables you not only to work from light to dark, but also dark to light – so if you make any mistakes, you can just go over the top and fix them. It is thus a much more forgiving medium than, for example, ink, and a great one for beginners. It is also very versatile as you can paint on nearly any surface you can think of from wood to cardboard, paper or stones, and even dried foliage! Acrylic dries quickly, so stay-wet pallets are available to keep your colours wet on your pallet for longer. A good tip to make your own stay-wet pallet is to dampen some kitchen roll and place some greaseproof paper over the top. Lay out your colours on the greaseproof paper and the moisture from the kitchen towel will keep the colours from drying out too quickly.

▶ Thick and thin paint

The first square here is thick paint, mixed with very little water. The second square is half and half. The third is painted more like a watercolour: a lot of water was added to the mix. Don't use your best watercolour brushes for acrylic though, as they are too delicate. Brushes designed for acrylic are much more sturdy and robust and are very reasonably priced in any art shop.

▶ Building up your colours

In the swatch here you can see I have panted the entire strip a very dark blue and then created 5 squares of varying tones. For each square I mixed a little white in and consecutively worked my way up from dark to light.

▶ Glazes

You can create a similar effect using a watercolour style, whereby you glaze the colours over the top of each other. I started with a very light strip and then darkened each square consecutively.

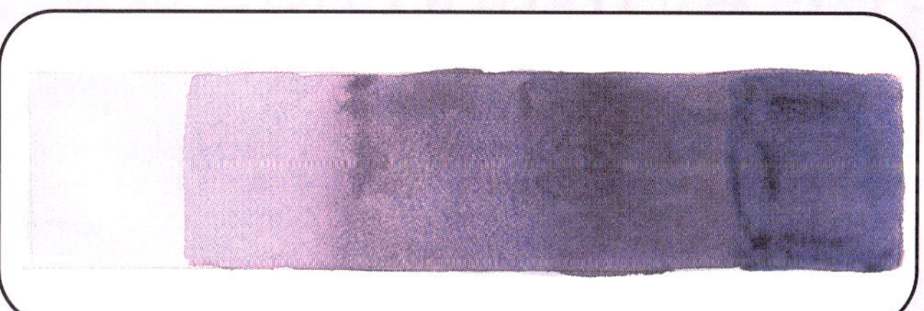

▶ Using masking fluid

Masking fluid can be used to prevent a background acrylic wash from colouring certain areas in exactly the same way as for watercolour paintings. Remember to use an old brush and always rinse with soap and water after use. The example here shows a daisy against a wet-in-wet acrylic wash. I painted masking fluid over the daisy and, when dry, I completed the wash behind. This allowed me to be free with the wash and not worry about going around the edge of the petals. Do be careful when removing the masking fluid though, as if the paper has a rough surface it can easily lift off with the masking fluid.

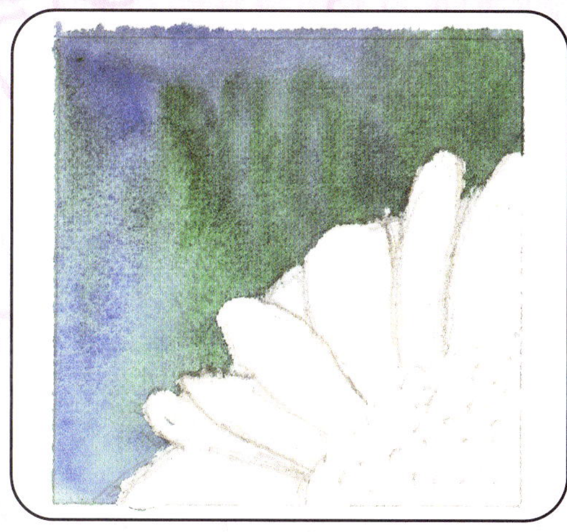

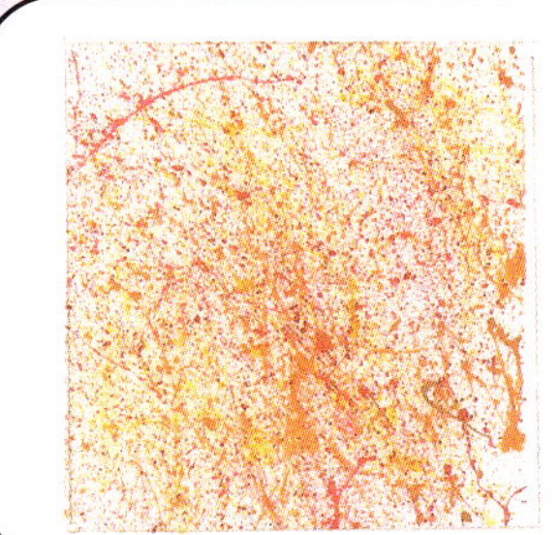

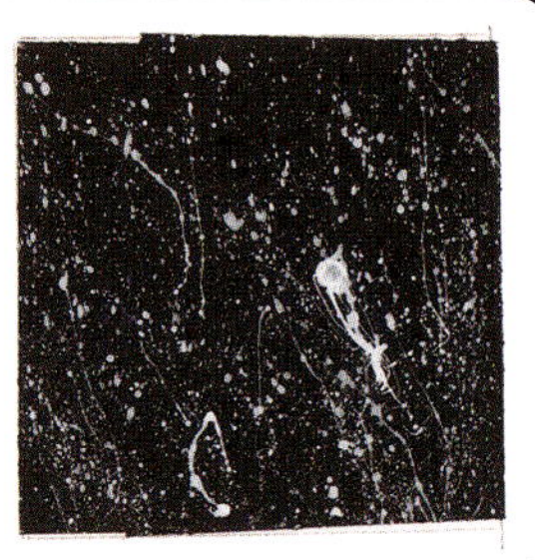

▲ Creating texture

These two examples show how easy it can be to create texture in acrylic using a sponge, some kitchen roll or even tissue paper. If you start off by mixing the darkest colour, dabbing the sponge into the paint and gently dabbing it onto the paper, you can create some wonderful patterns in surprisingly precise ways. Mix your lighter colours and repeat the process until you are happy with the outcome. Always work from dark to light as you will then be able to create the most delicate white highlights on top.

▲ Splattering techniques

Working a splattering technique in acrylic is fun. It can be a little messy, so prepare your work area with plenty of scrap paper to protect your work and other items on the table. Here I have shown one with a light background and one with a dark background, which can look very dynamic – it could be used in the background of a dark faerie illustration. Using an old paintbrush, either flick the paint onto the area from above or hold the brush closely to the paper and flick the bristles with your finger. Use a sturdy brush for this technique.

▶ Dry brush technique

This technique is useful for creating foliage around your faeries. To create a nice soft but solid background, use the wet-in-wet technique and drop a few different tones of blues and greens behind. Blue is a good colour for a background as it recedes nicely. Once this is completely dry, choose a smaller brush, making sure it is clean and dry. Mix up some olive green and some sap green and load a little onto the brush. When painting the foliage, start at the base of the grass and work your way up, lightening the pressure on the brush as you get the the end. Add lighter tones on top, mixing the greens with either a little white or yellow.

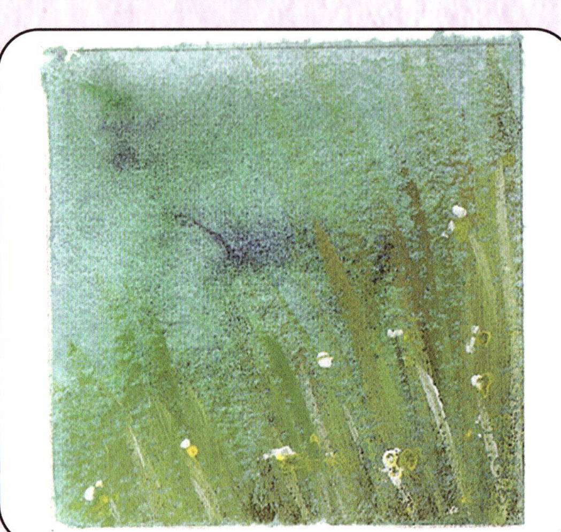

▶ Creating your first acrylic study

Start by drawing something very simple. This daisy, for instance, is a great one to start with. Draw the daisy very lightly using a 2B pencil. If you have any dark lines dab the excess graphite off with your putty eraser. Next, create a wet-in-wet wash in the background. You can use masking fluid on the daisy's petals if required. When the background is nearly dry, add some further grass detail in the foreground. If you paint the grass when it's nearly dry, it will not only blend in with the background a little, but will also give a few hard lines adding detail into the picture. When the background is fully dry you can start adding detail into the flower and stalk. Try to keep the top area of the painting light and warm, and the bottom area of the painting darker and cooler in colours. This will add depth to the overall piece.

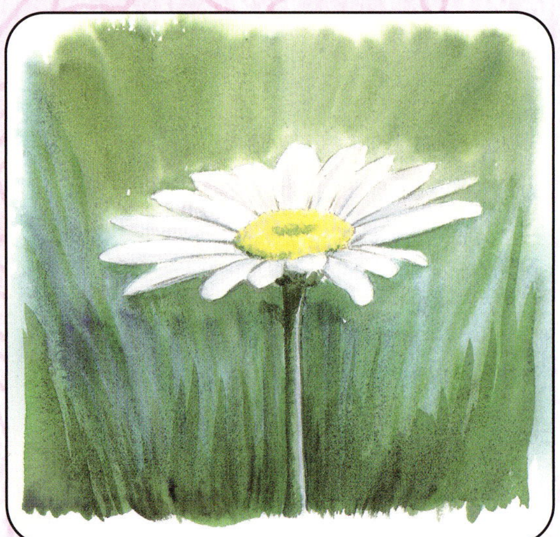

COMPUTER DIGITAL ARTWORK

If you have access to a computer, creating artwork on it is simple – very simple! There are many photo editing programs available, some of which are free to download from the internet, and others that may already be installed on your computer. Most have similar functions and all have 'Help' sections built in, so if you get stuck you can find out how to complete your task.

Experimenting with photo editing programs

There are many things you can do with your original photo even before you start to edit it.

Cropping, resizing and rotating In this photo, a large area to the left has been cropped to focus on the subject. Digital cameras produce large images; resize them smaller so the computer can handle them more easily. You could also rotate the image slightly, as the computer allows us to rotate by degrees.

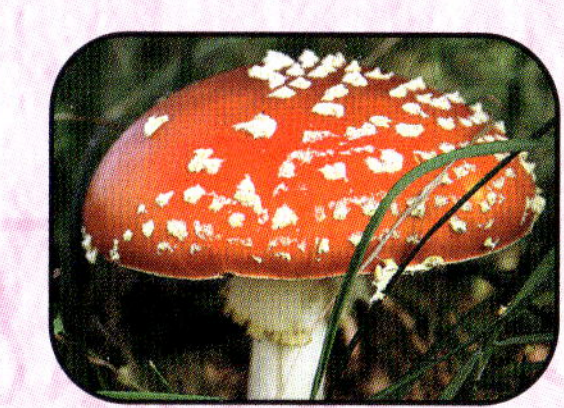

Hue and saturation This image is very different from the original photo and it was created by changing the sliders in the hue and saturation options. The majority of photo editing programs will have this feature or something similar. It enables you to change the colours across the entire photo. Here I have given the image a cold feel. The saturation option will enable you to intensify or lessen the colour of the image.

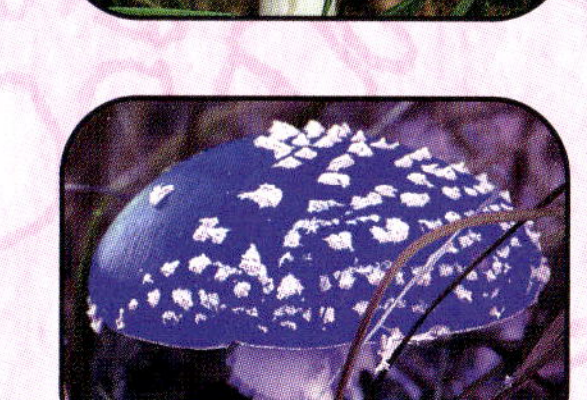

Levels Using a levels function will add contrast and brightness to the photo. As you can see, the image has been made considerably brighter which shows up both the grass and foliage in the background much better, as well as the toadstool itself.

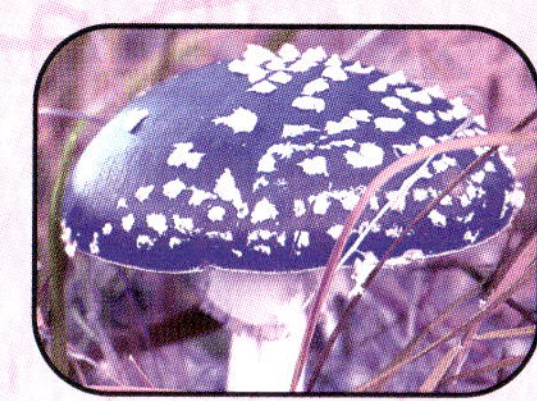

Filters

Filters are available in most photo editing programs and they are wonderful to experiment with. They create an effect across the whole of your image and there are many different ones to choose from. Often you can add more than one effect on top of each other to create your own layers.

Artistic filters Using my original image I played around with the artistic filters and this is my result. I opted for the filter which has given it a watercolour effect. If you wanted to lighten it with the levels and saturation functions, you still could. Within the artists' filters you may have the options of paint daubs and coloured pencil and pastel, among others.

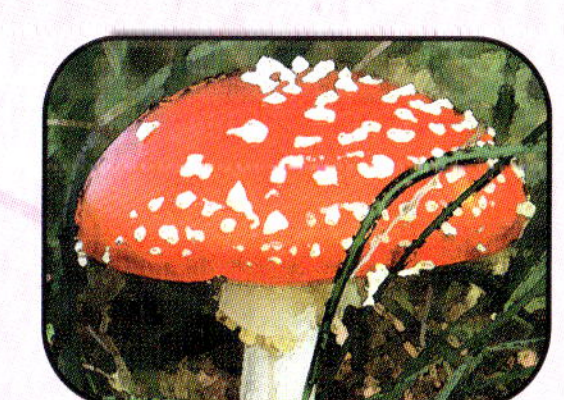

Sketching filters The following image was created using a chalk and charcoal effect. This is more of a sketchy effect and within this category of filters you might find graphic pen, half-tone, and photocopy filters to name just a few.

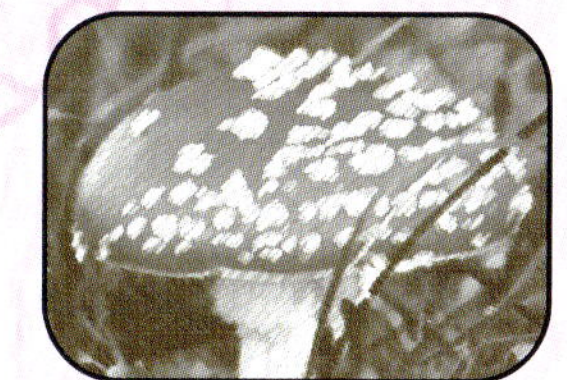

Brush strokes This set of filters are wonderfully vibrant and strong. The particular filter I opted for was 'ink outlines' and you can see the computer has outlined the edges of the image, intensifying the toadstool. You might find filters such as splatter effects and cross hatching within the brush strokes set.

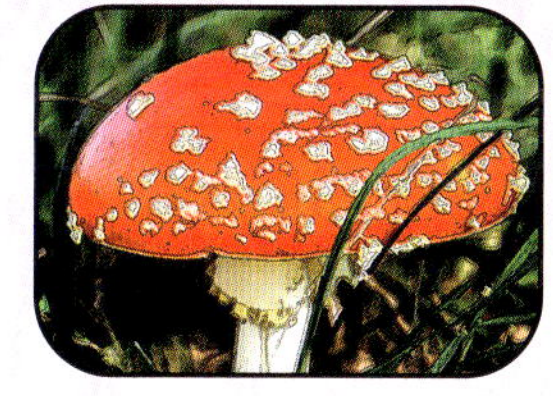

Tablets and pens

There are many advantages to using a tablet and pen instead of a mouse. There are lots of different brands on the market and in a wide price range so there should be one to suit everyone's budget. Using a pen in a photo editing program gives you much more control than a mouse.

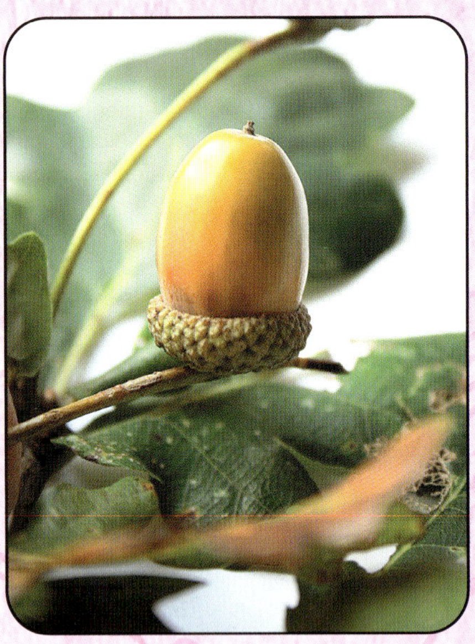

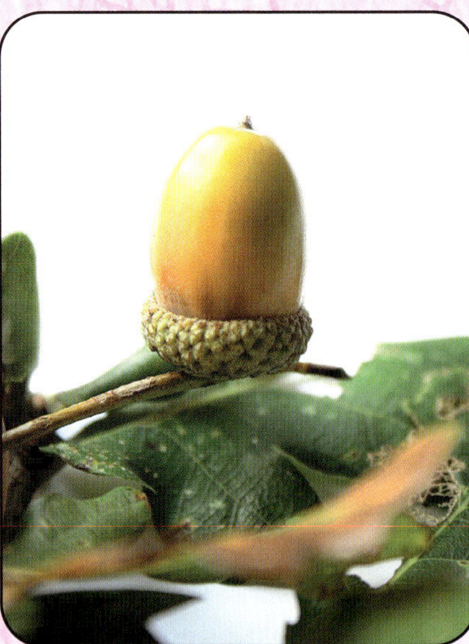

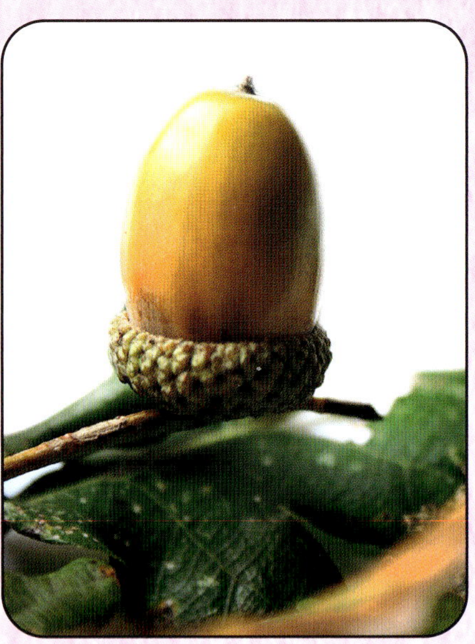

▲ Erasing backgrounds

The three images above illustrate how easy it is to remove an unwanted background from an image. The first is my original image. The second is the image with the background removed. Essentially, you can use the eraser tool to rub out the areas and objects in the background you don't need. The third image is a cropped version, taking away the outer edge so that you can see the subject more clearly and make it the focus of the scene.

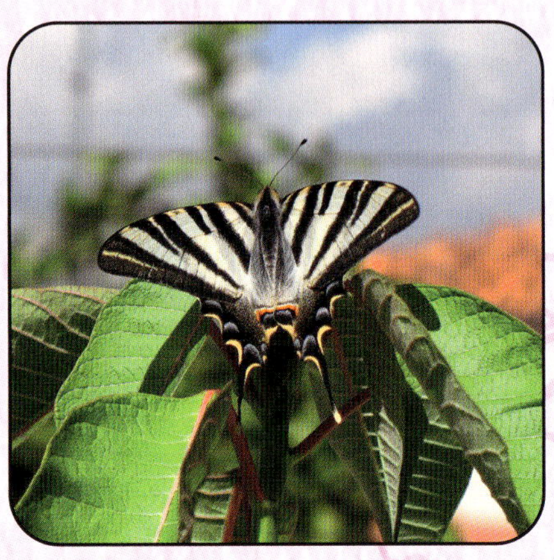

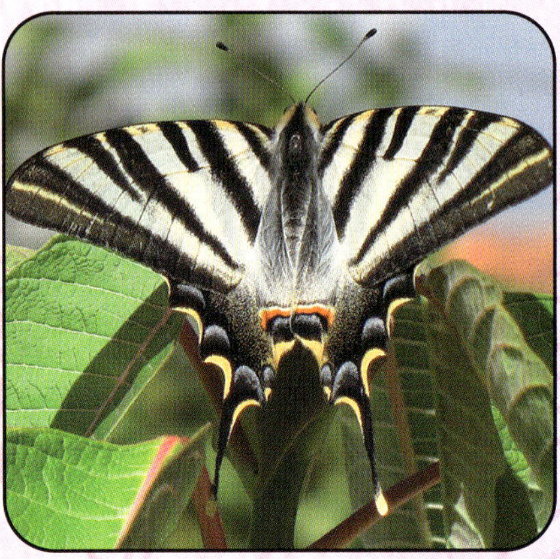

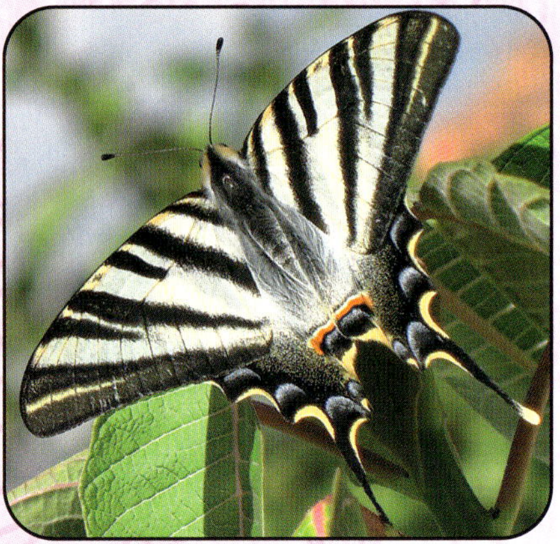

▲ Using cropping for composition

In the next three images I have illustrated how we can create an interesting composition and make the image our own with a little imagination. The first image is the original photo. The subject is quite small in the centre and so the first thing we need to do is crop into the image so that the butterfly is the focus of the scene. Finally, the last photo shows the image rotated. This adds interest into the image, it fills the frame more successfully, adds a sense of movement and gives it that little something extra.

Putting it all together

Let's now create a composition using two photos. The first photo I have chosen is of a toadstool at the base of a tree within a mass of bark and foliage. My second image is a view of trees looking into a woodland scene. These two photos have very different colouring, but let's see if we can join them together.

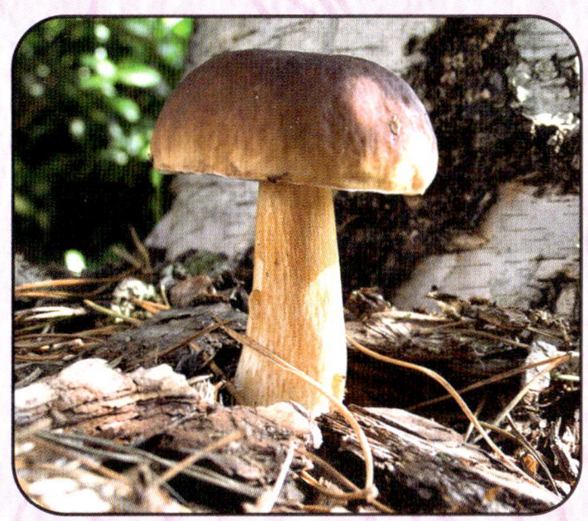

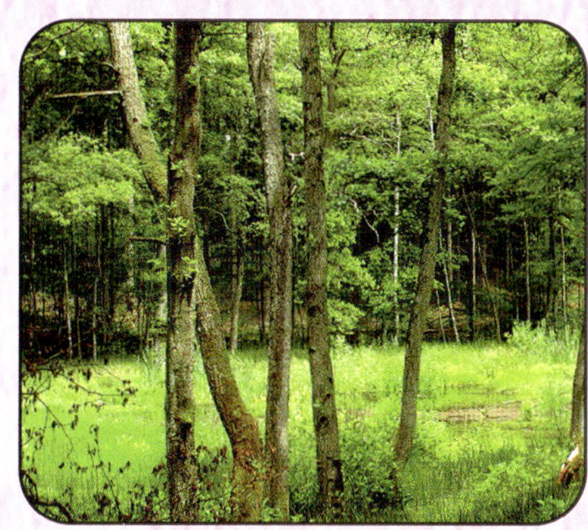

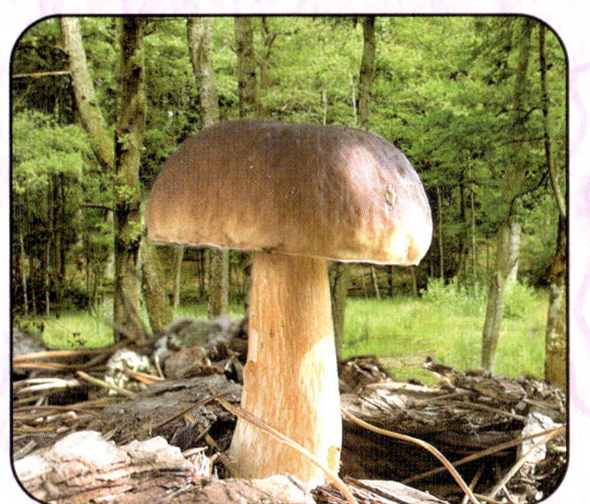

Joining two photos together By placing one image on top of another in your photo editing software you can erase the background from the toadstool, just as we did with the acorn. This will leave you with the woodland behind.

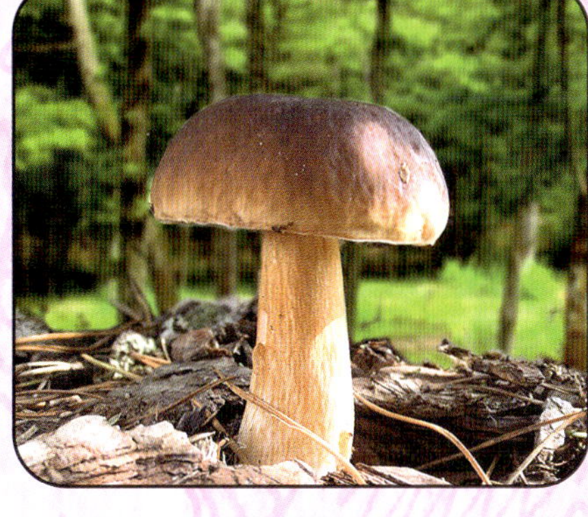

Blurring the background We can now use a filter to blur the background. This will help the toadstool come forward in the scene and the background recede.

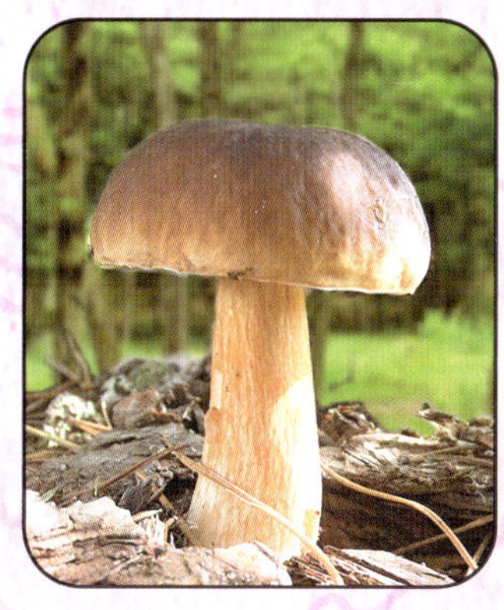

Cropping the image This is a good stage to decide the composition of your final image. Crop the outside of the image to allow the main subject to be the focus. You can also change the image from a landscape to a portrait orientation. Cropping off the sides also brings the toadstool to the fore.

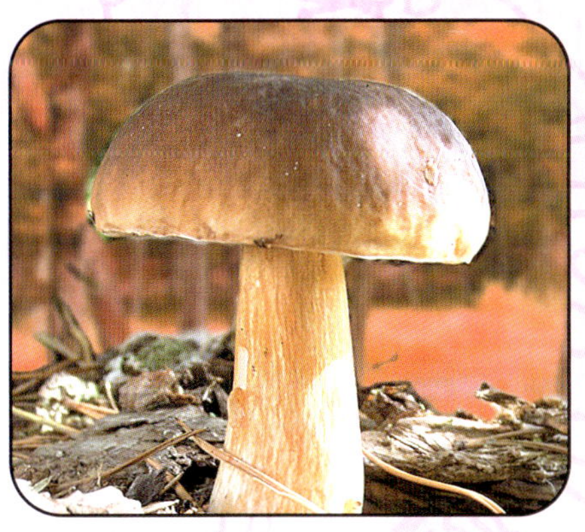

Changing colours We can now bring the background colours more into line with the colours of the toadstool. This is very simple to do within the colour changing sliders in your photo editing program.

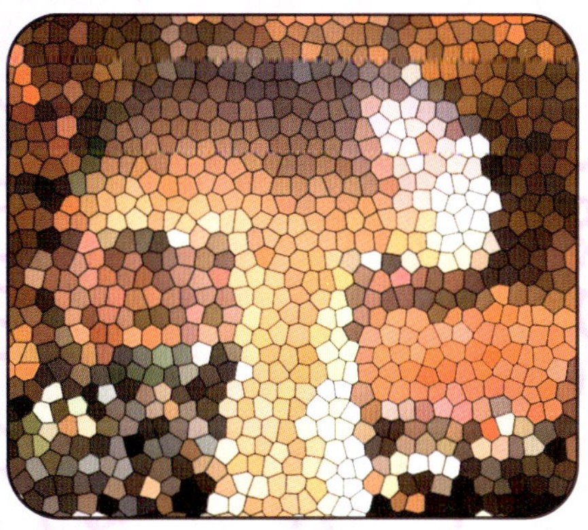

Filters You can either leave your image at this stage, or you can play around with the various filters available within your program. I have used a stained glass effect, which gives a very different result to the original images.

Play around with your photos and follow these guidelines to see if you can create something similar. Experiment and have fun!

Drawing techniques

Learning how to create a three-dimensional solid object with your pencil is imperative for any type of painting. Learning the basics of drawing will enable you to understand how to create form in your work. For instance, if you are drawing a faerie sitting on a toadstool, you need to make the toadstool solid, strong and three-dimensional, otherwise the faerie will tumble off! Using the tonal strips you drew earlier, copy the illustrations on these pages to improve your shading.

THREE-DIMENSIONAL OBJECTS

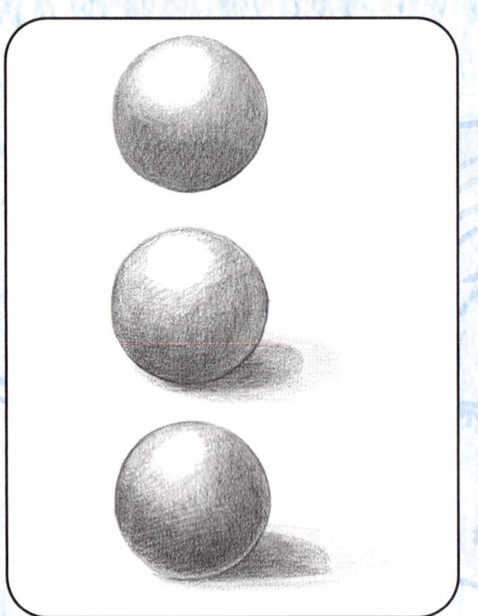

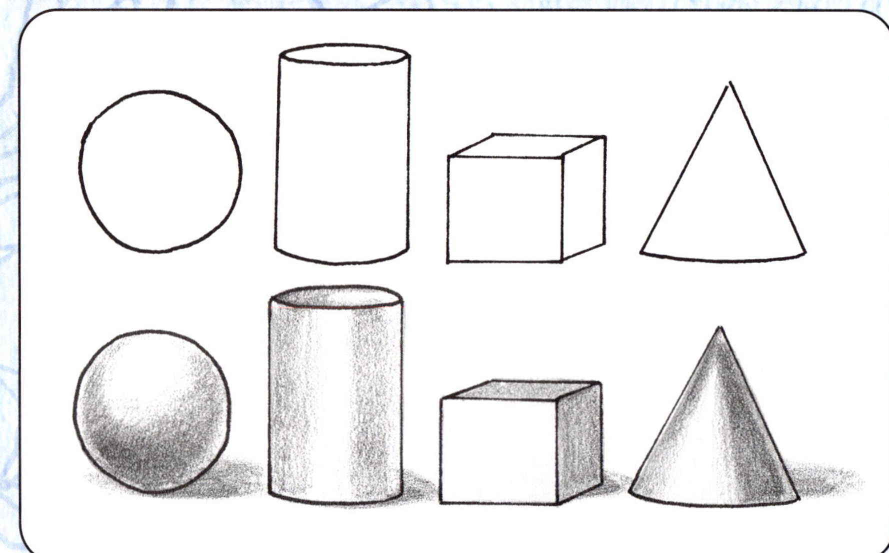

▲ Shading curved shapes

The idea here is to shade within the contours of the object. Shading in a horizontal direction makes the object appear flat. Shading in a curved direction around it creates the illusion that the sphere is round. Light can help: if we leave the top left area of the sphere white and graduate the tones as they go down, we imply that the light is hitting the top of the sphere and the areas below must curve back in as they are in shadow.

The second image is similar but shadows place the sphere firmly on a solid surface. Shadows are usually dark closer to the object and fade out as they go away from the object.

The final illustration shows a reflected highlight; a vital area of light on the bottom of the sphere. It appears on objects that are on a light or shiny surface.

▲ Shading other solid shapes

Trace or draw the outlines above onto paper and see if you can shade them correctly. You are trying to create solid shapes; there should be areas of light, each side of the object should be graduated in tone and they should all have a shadow cast from the objects themselves. Don't forget the reflected highlights. I have shaded the objects above with the light coming from the front of each one. See if you can shade them with the light coming from the top left. How would the shadows fall?

▶ Putting this into practice

Once you have practised the spheres, you can tackle a toadstool. This is basically a sphere and a cylinder together. You can shade it in a similar way as the objects, just add some detail in the foliage and edge of the toadstool. Outline the shape lightly with a 2B pencil. Once you are happy with the shape, start shading and build up the layers. Use softer pencils as you progress, leaving the darkest tones for the final stages.

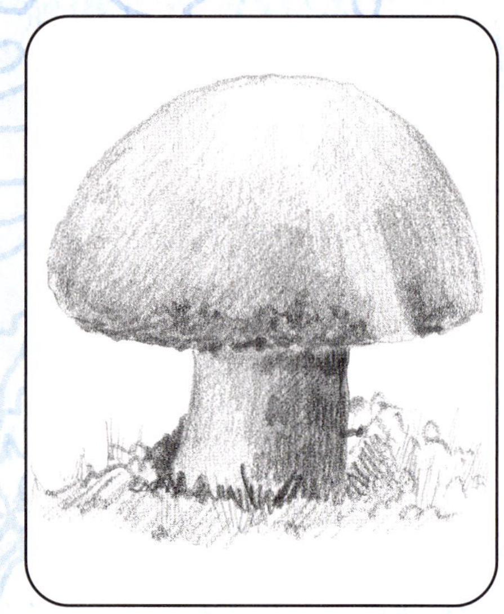

PERSPECTIVE

It is necessary to be aware of a few rules to create an aesthetically pleasing composition. We first need to work out where to place the horizon line, which is the viewer's eye-level.

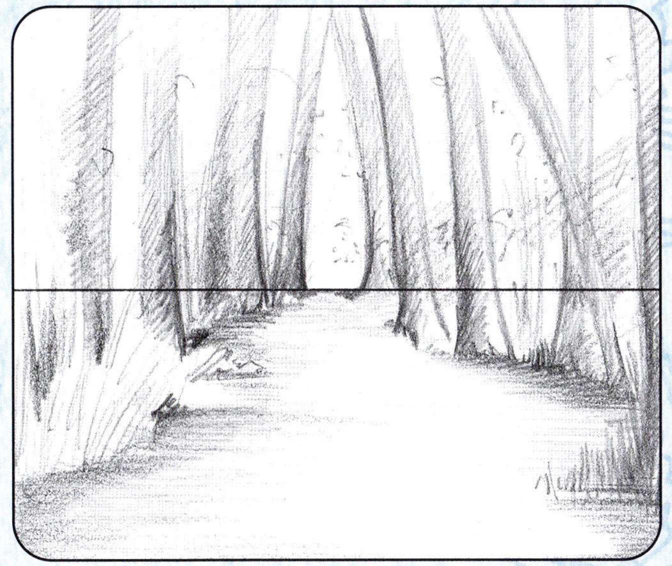

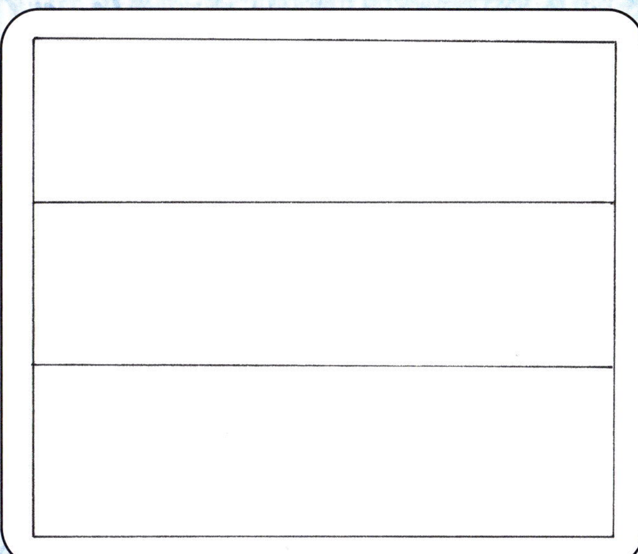

Here a simple woodland scene is shown with the horizon line in the centre of the picture. Although this is an acceptable composition, we can make it more dramatic if we place the horizon line in a different place.

The second diagram shows a square divided by two lines. These lines are in specific places, dividing the composition into what is known as the magic thirds. It is generally considered preferable to place the horizon line on either of these two lines to create a more dramatic picture and make things more pleasing to the eye.

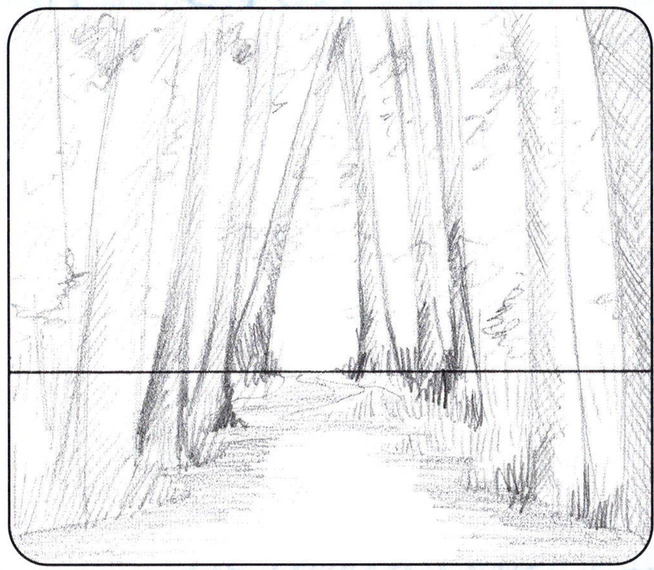

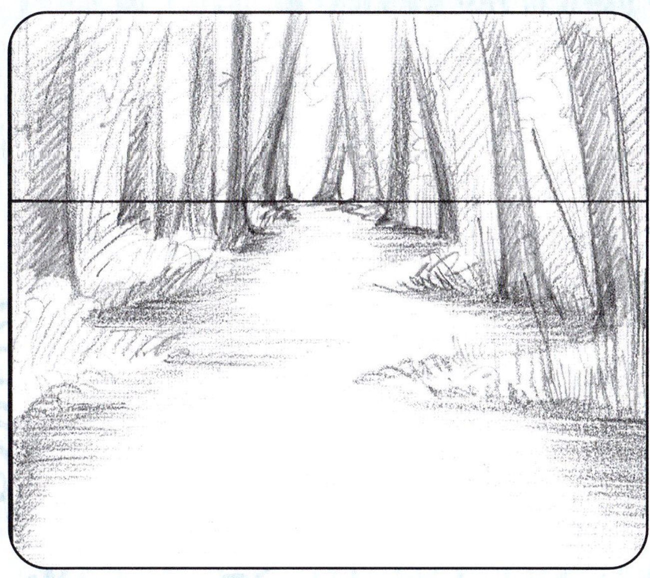

These two illustrations show the same woodland scene, first with the horizon line on the bottom third and then secondly with the horizon line on the top third.

Comparing these two drawings with the first woodland scene, you can see that these are much more dramatic and also allow for more scope if you wanted to place a faerie within the frame.

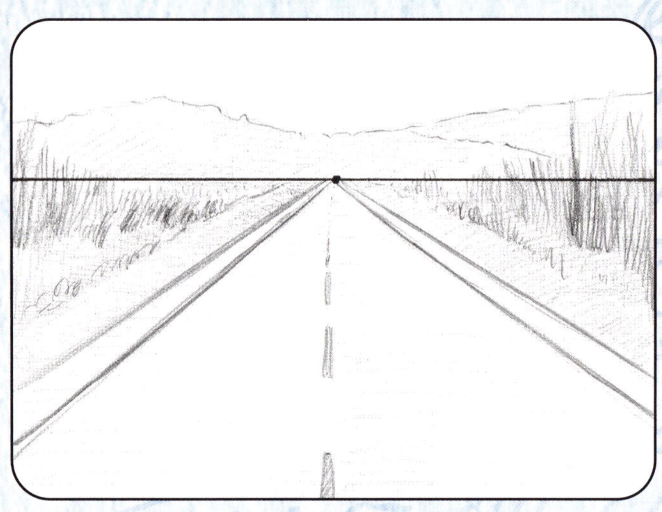

▲ Vanishing points

A vanishing point is the point in the distance at which two parallel lines appear to converge. So in the woodland drawings the vanishing point in all three illustrations would be in centre of the path where it disappears into the distance. The drawing of the roadway illustrates how this works. The point at which the road converges in the distance is the vanishing point. Understanding this concept will help you when creating perspective within your drawings.

▲ Aerial perspective

Aerial perspective, or atmospheric perspective, is the effect the atmosphere has on objects. For instance, if you are looking at a mountain view, the further away the mountains recede, the bluer, colder and lighter they will look. Here the background has been drawn much lighter than the foreground – this creates distance. Things also appear more blurred. If you are trying to make something recede, always draw it lighter, use less detail and, if you are using colour, use more blues and purples in that area.

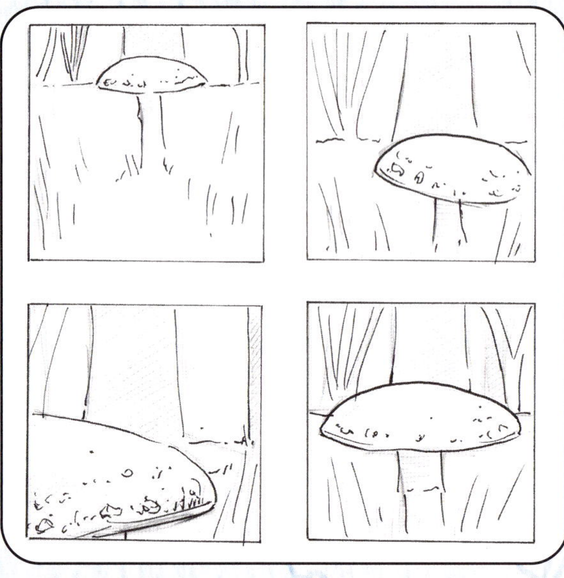

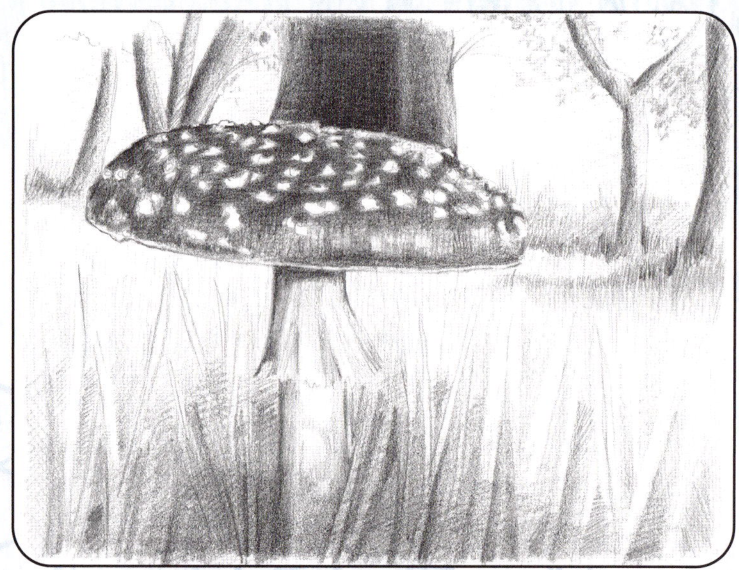

▲ Composition

When you are planning your artwork you need to work out your composition before you start. This encompasses all the things we have discussed here: horizon lines, vanishing points, perspective and aerial perspective. Here the first illustration is a simple line drawing of the basic shapes. I then sketched some designs to help me work out a variety of compositions. I tried the toadstool in the bottom right of the drawing, a closely cropped version with it to the bottom left and one final design with it centred. Sketches like this will help you to ascertain quite quickly if any of the compositions 'feel' right. I opted for the toadstool to be slightly off-centre to the left, in a landscape orientation. The horizon line and vanishing point are on the top third which allows the viewer to concentrate on the toadstool – it is the focus of the composition.

REFERENCE PHOTOS

Artists use reference photos when creating a painting or drawing because it is very difficult to make images up. If you try to draw an object from memory you will often get it wrong, so reference photos are an invaluable resource. You can take them from many sources: magazines, books, the internet or a library and of course your own photos. Collect clippings you feel would work for your artworks and keep them in a folder. You never know when they will come in handy as inspiration.

Copyright

Reference photos are often a necessity, but be careful if any are copyrighted. Any photos in magazines, books, printed material and even some of the photos you find on the internet will be copyrighted. It's not a problem when using them for practice, as long as you don't sell your work, exhibit it or post it on the internet! If you do want to use them, ask the owner's permission beforehand. There are also many websites that provide copyright-free photos, and then you will be sure that you can use them if you want to show your work.

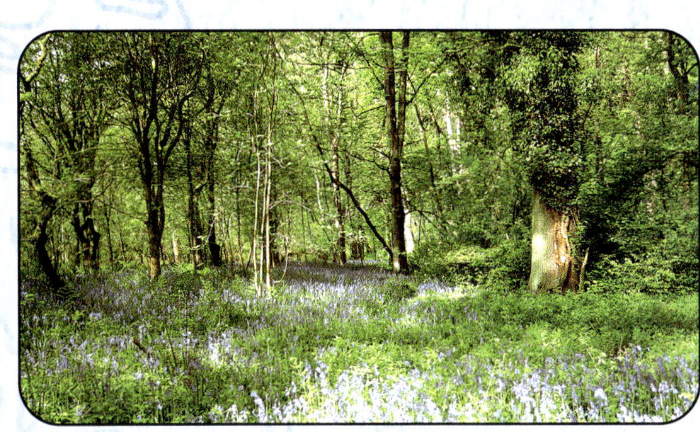

Digital cameras

The best way of making sure you don't breach any copyright rules is to take your own photos. Ideally, have a handy, pocket-sized camera that you can take around with you wherever you go. Digital cameras have plenty of settings for you to play around with, including red eye reduction, anti-blur and anti-shake, and the majority of cameras also have optical zoom facilities so that you can get really close and detailed photos of the subject. You can also invest in large capacity media cards which can hold hundreds of photos at one time, so take as many shots as you possibly can – you never know, that next photo may just be the one you need!

Taking photos for backgrounds

Woodlands are an excellent place to take photos for reference for your faerie drawings and paintings. If you can, try to go early in the morning or late evening as the light at either end of the day produces more shadows and they can create some wonderful effects. Dappled light in summer is a great time to take photos but always have your camera handy and take as many photos as possible. Don't forget the horizon line; when you take the photo, imagine it split into the magic thirds. Try to place the horizon line on either the top or bottom third. You can even try to take some blurred shots for backdrops to your paintings. A blurry woodland scene works really well to help keep the foreground as the main centre of interest.

Taking photos of your family and friends

Photos of people are a must if you want to draw and paint faeries as they give you a basis for your artwork. If you can find some volunteers that will model for you, you can even pose them in classic faerie positions. If they are willing to dress up, even better! Its always best to take photos of your volunteers outside in the sunshine, but always ask their permission first, and try not to take photos of them when they least expect it.

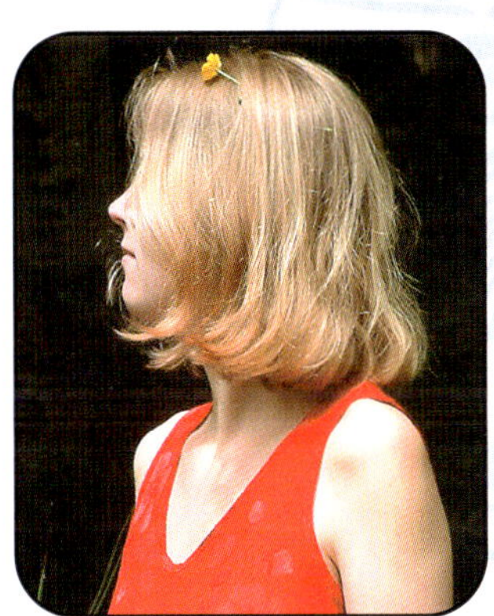

Taking photos of close-ups and textures

Many cameras have a macro setting, to enable you take close-up photos. This is a fantastic way of capturing textures of leaves, bark, stones, grass, moss and foliage either for your faerie to sit on or to be placed around her. If your camera doesn't have this facility you could try getting as close as your camera will allow with the zoom lens, without the whole scene becoming blurred.

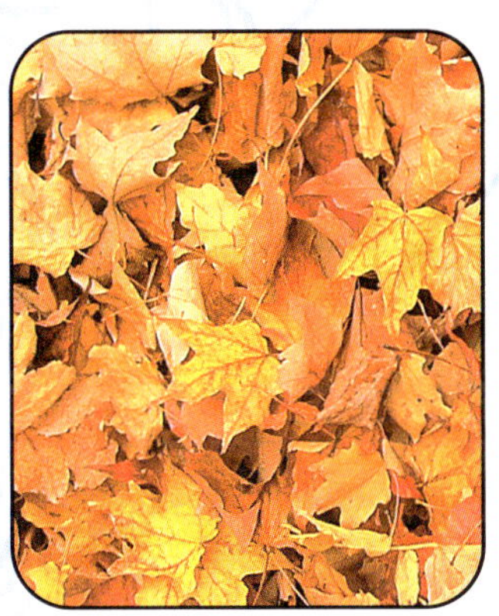

Copying images

If you don't feel confident yet to draw freehand, there are lots of ways of copying an image onto your paper. The following methods will guide you through each process.

TRACING

You can purchase good quality tracing paper from any art shop. However, you can also use greaseproof paper if you have any to hand. This is slightly thicker but can work just as well. Find a picture that you wish to copy and place it on your desk, taping the corners so that the picture doesn't move around. Next cut some tracing paper to size and tape this in the corners over top of your picture.

Now start to draw around the image. You may find you to lose track of which parts you have traced, but you can always check by slipping a white piece of paper between the tracing paper and the photo to see how much you have drawn. Once you are happy with the image on the tracing paper, turn it over and, using a soft grade of pencil – preferably an 8B, shade the entire back of the sheet leaving a good covering of graphite. Once this is complete turn the tracing paper over, lay it onto a clean sheet of drawing paper, graphite shaded side down. Draw over your outline again using a harder grade of pencil. When you are complete you can lift off the tracing paper and the image will have been imprinted underneath.

CARBON PAPER

Stationers and art shops usually sell carbon paper. Using carbon paper is a little like the tracing method, but the graphite has already been placed on the back of the paper for you. Find a picture you wish to copy and tape it on top of your drawing paper. Lay the carbon paper between the photo and the drawing paper, graphite side down. If you don't want to ruin your photo by drawing on it, you can either scan and print the photo, or use a photocopier to duplicate it for you. Draw over your picture, and the image will appear underneath on your paper.

USING A GRID

If you have a particular photo or picture you would like to copy, and you don't want to trace it, the following technique can be very useful. A grid can be a great tool to enable you to correctly position the main points in the photo on your drawing.

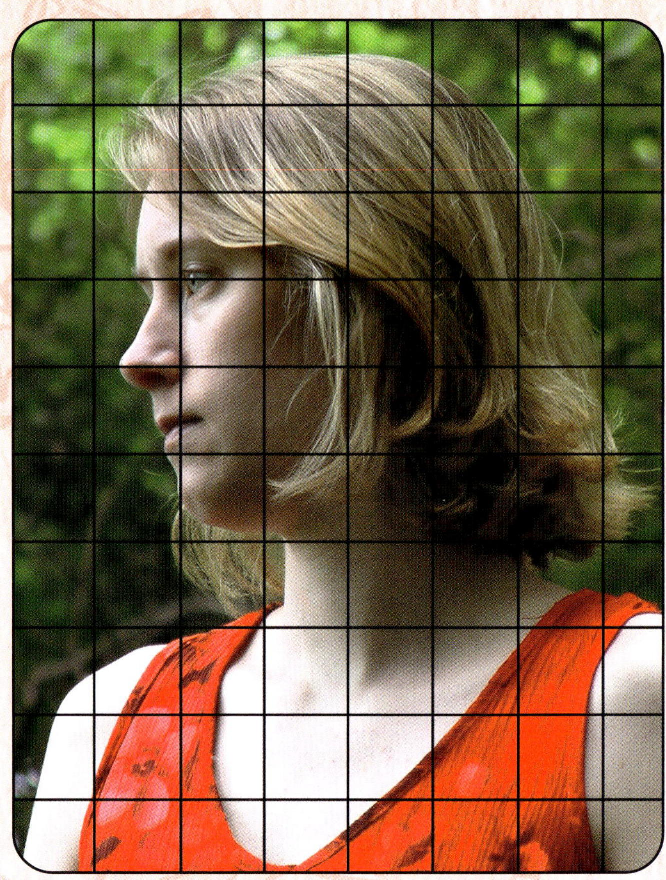

▲ Gridding a photo
Find a photo or picture you would like to copy. You can either draw the grid directly onto the photo, on a photocopied or printed copy of the photo, or lay tracing paper on top of the photo and draw on that. Next, draw the same grid very lightly on your drawing paper, so that the lines can be erased when you have finished. If you wish for your drawing to be larger then the photograph simply make the size of your squares on your drawing bigger.

▶ Copying the image

Copy the image onto your drawing paper using the grid as a guide. Try to look at your drawing as a whole as you sketch, without concentrating too much on individual squares, otherwise your drawing can become a little disjointed. Its important at this stage to get the features and lines in the correct places.

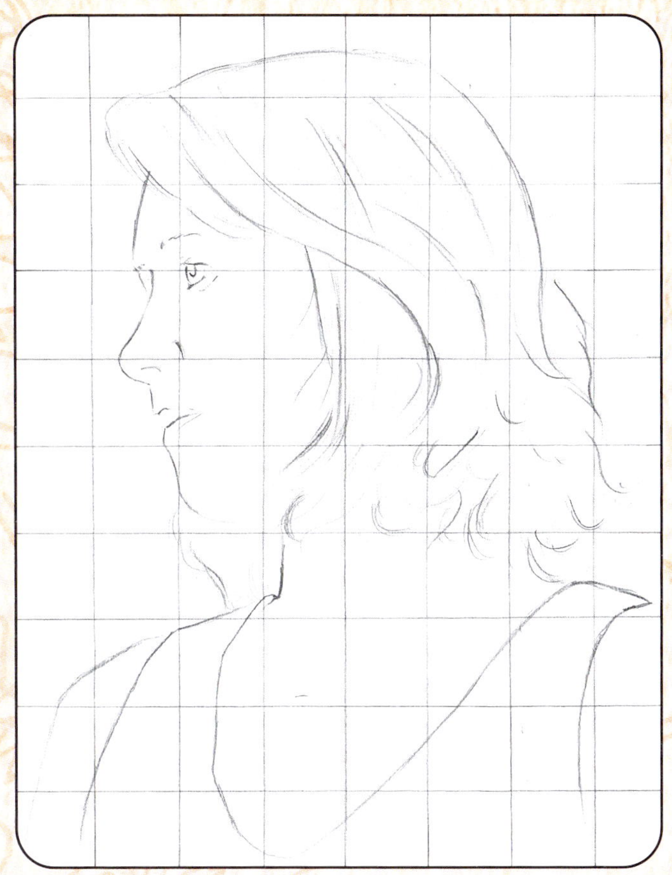

▶ Completing your drawing

Once you have the outline drawn you can start to erase the grid lines. Inevitably you will erase some of your outline, but these can easily be drawn back in. If you have pressed too hard when drawing your grid and you are unable to remove all traces of the grid, as you work up your drawing the lines will gradually be covered up. Don't forget you can use a putty eraser moulded into a point to erase very precise areas.

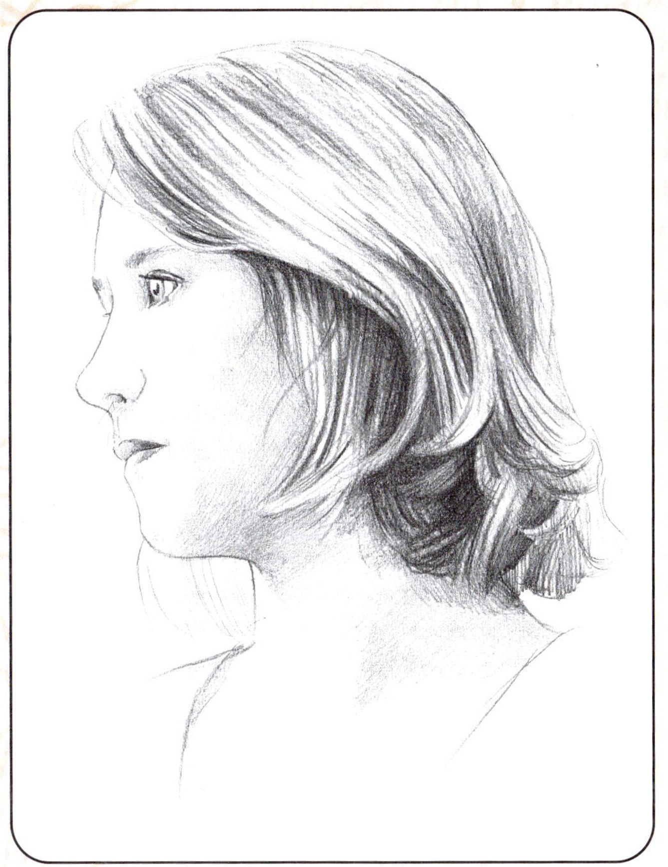

The faerie figure

Before beginning to draw faeries you need to be aware of the correct proportions. We will start by learning about the human form as the faerie figure is similar to a human figure but slightly elongated. This gives them a graceful, ethereal look. Find some cheap paper (copy paper is ideal) and a soft graphite pencil (a 2B is a good grade) to sketch with. Don't worry at this stage about making mistakes, your initial sketches from these pages will be just for practice and you can always erase your lines or start again.

YOUNG FAERIE

▶ Wire frame

To draw a young faerie we need to start with a wire frame or stick figure. This is by far the easiest way to make sure we have all the proportions correct.

The average young human's body is approximately five heads high. This means if we were to draw a human being, we can take the measurement of the head, from top of the scalp to the chin, and fit it into the whole body five times. For an illustration of a young faerie it is a good idea to make them slightly taller, about six heads high.

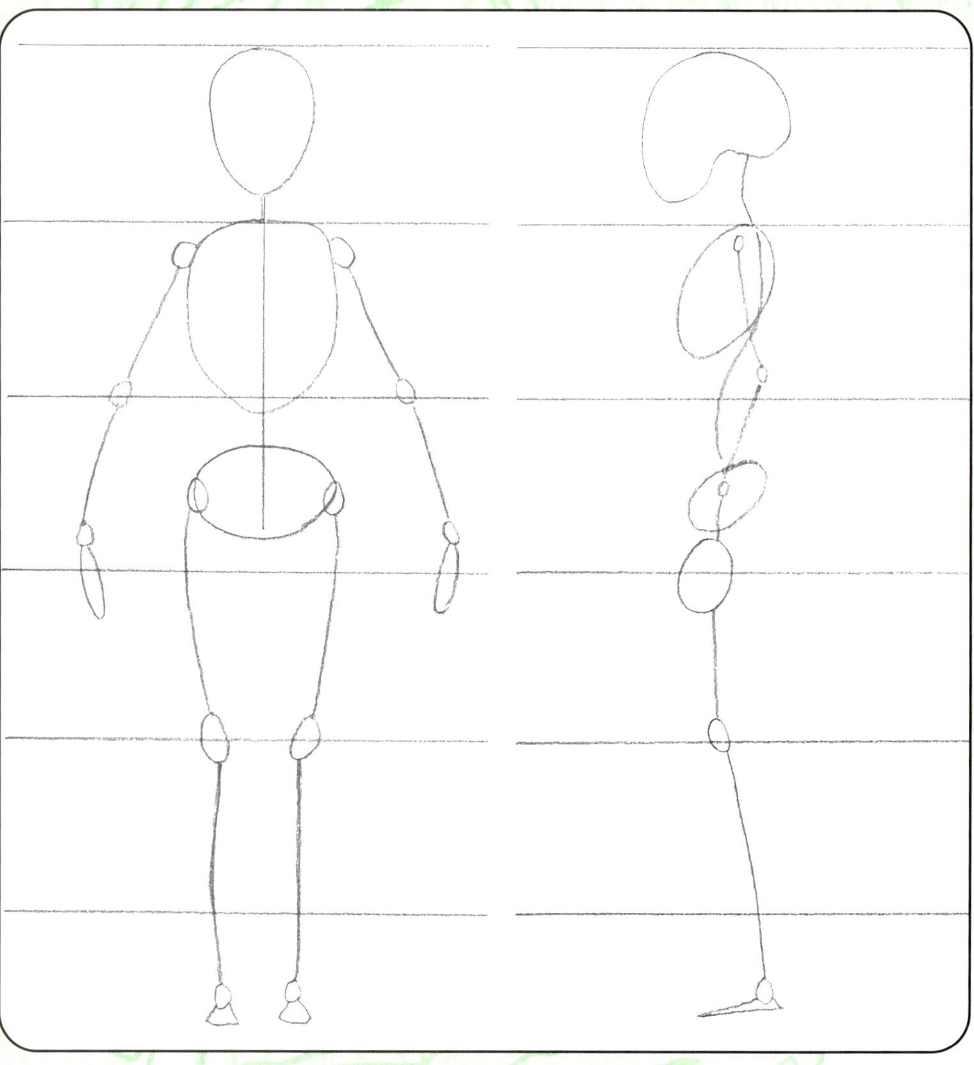

So the first thing to draw will be an oval shape near the top of the page for the head. Draw lightly to start with, as it will be easier to erase if you make a mistake. Once you have drawn the head you can draw some guidelines to help you with the rest of the figure. You can draw horizontal lines as in the illustration to divide up the body into six sections. This will help you draw the chest, pelvis, knees and feet in the correct places.

Next draw a flattened oval for the ribcage and an oval for the pelvis which is approximately halfway down. Now we can draw in the arms and legs, just as lines, and we can even indicate where the joints would be. The knees in particular are important. The elbows fall just below the ribcage and the hands should reach about half way down the thigh. We can then add in shapes for the hands and feet.

The proportions will be the same for the side view, but the shapes will be slightly different. Follow the pattern above to draw the figure in profile, but note the curve of the spine is almost in the shape of an 'S'. The ribcage is thinner and the pelvis is tilted.

▶ Skeleton

Drawing the human skeleton is an excellent way of understanding the structure of the human figure. The illustrations of the young faerie skeleton, both front and side-on, will give you an idea of what lies under our flesh and muscles. Without a skeleton your body would be a jelly-like blob, so it is important to understand it before you begin to draw. The skeleton gives our body strength, rigidity and movement and we need to capture this in our drawings. Even though we can't actually see the bones we must be aware of where they are and how the skeleton is built to enable us to draw a faerie successfully.

Some of the most important features of the skeleton are the joints – the elbows, knees, hips, ankles, wrists and shoulders. We will be drawing faeries in many different positions: standing, sitting, kneeling, flying, jumping, dancing, and even pirouetting like a ballerina. Knowing where the joints are beforehand will help you understand what you are drawing. Using some plain paper and a soft pencil, copy the faerie skeletons in the illustrations and see if you can remember where the joints are and envisage how they will move.

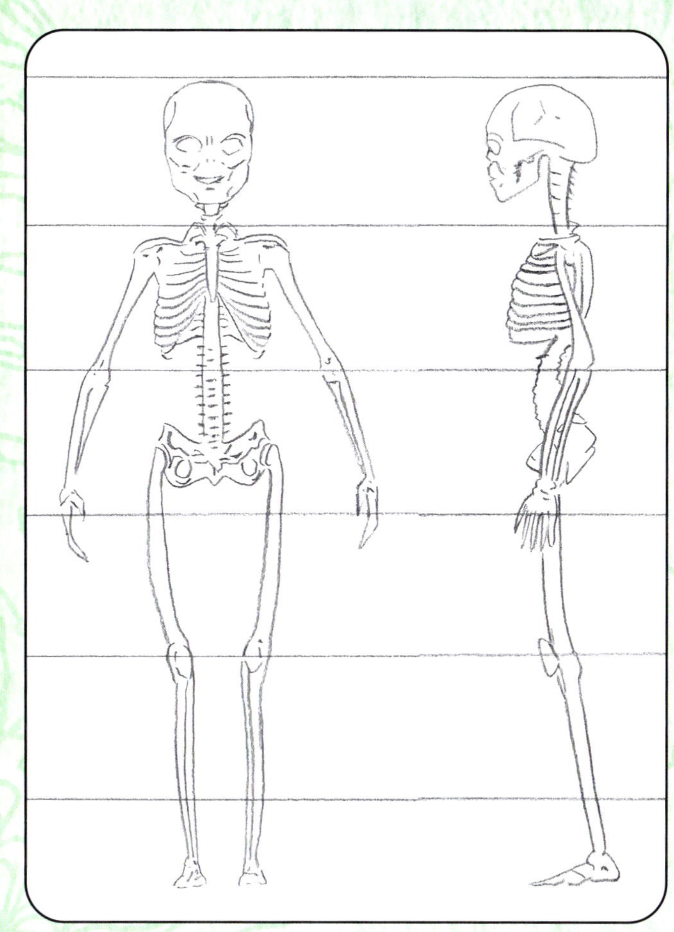

▶ Muscles and flesh

We can now start to add muscles on top of our basic framework and build upon this structure to flesh out our faerie. Bear in mind that the skeletal structure is close to the surface at various points of the body; for instance, we don't need to add very much skin thickness to the elbow as the bone is very close to the surface. You could start a new drawing, or if you have your skeleton and wire frame drawings to hand, you could work on top of these.

At the head, the eye sockets can be added easily, halfway between the top of the head and chin.

We next need to add a neck and work our way around the outer side of the body starting with the shoulder, down to the the elbow and then the wrist and hand, and then up the inside of the arm under the arm socket.

Next draw the sides of the chest down to the faerie's middle and then come out slightly to work around the pelvis. There needs to be a definite protrusion on each side of the pelvis; if you put your hands on your hips, you can feel there is almost a ledge there. Then follow the line of the legs – with the tops wider and tapering in as they get to the knees, out again for the calf muscles and then tapering in again for the ankles. So now you have a basic outline for a young faerie.

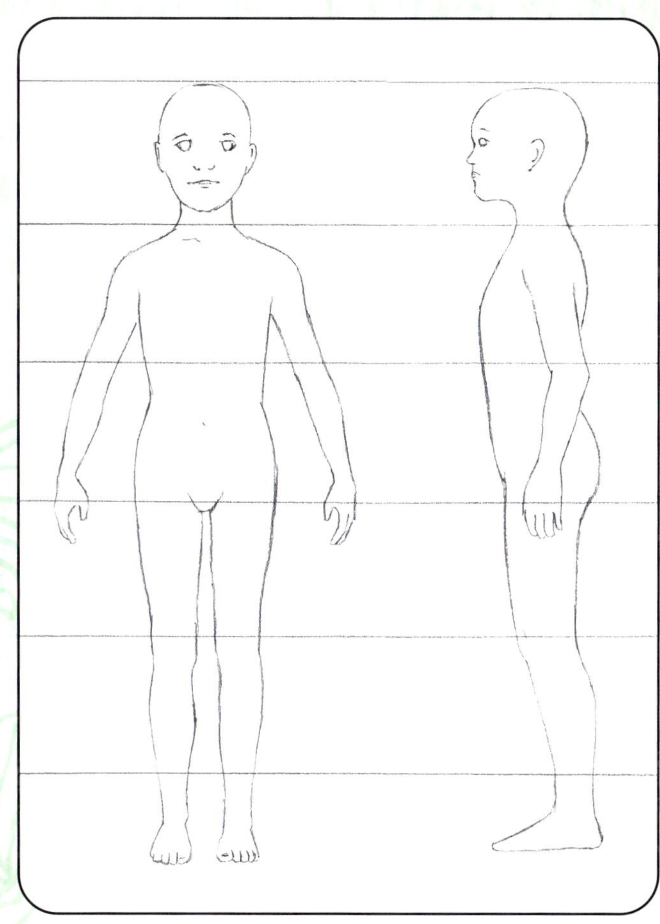

ADULT FAERIE

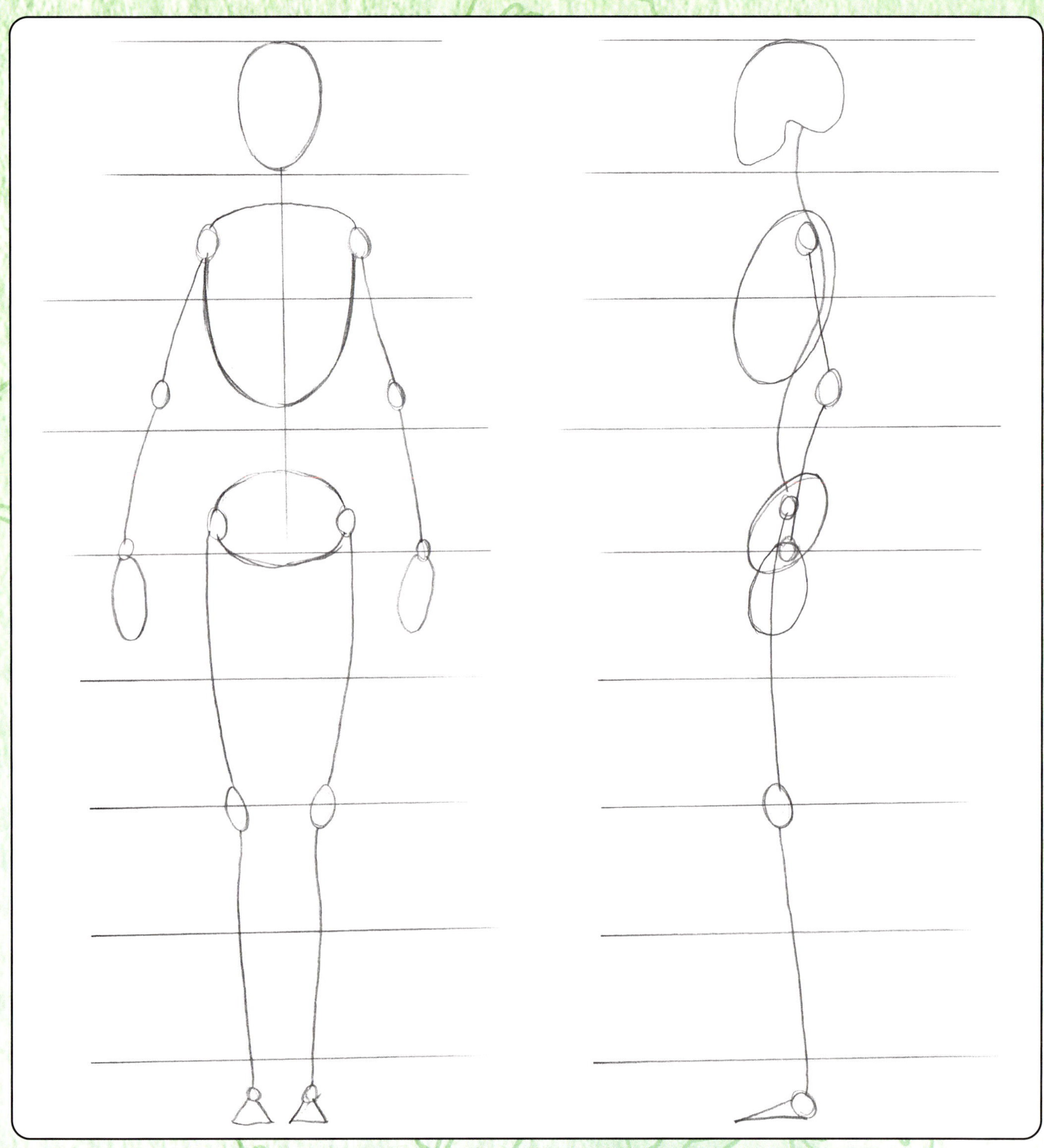

▲ Wire frame

The faerie adult's proportions are slightly different from a young faerie. The average adult human body is about seven heads high. As faeries are also usually taller, these illustrations are about eight to nine heads high, helping to make their forms long, slender and graceful.

Start as for the young faerie, by drawing an oval for the head. Then draw your guidelines in to help you with the rest of the figure: horizontal lines to divide the body into eight or nine sections. This will help you draw the chest, pelvis, knees and feet in the correct places. Draw the rest of the frame so you have a solid-looking structure.

Next draw the side view: the proportions will be the same, but the shapes slightly different. Follow the same pattern as for the young faerie, and take note of the curve of the spine, the ribcage and the pelvis.

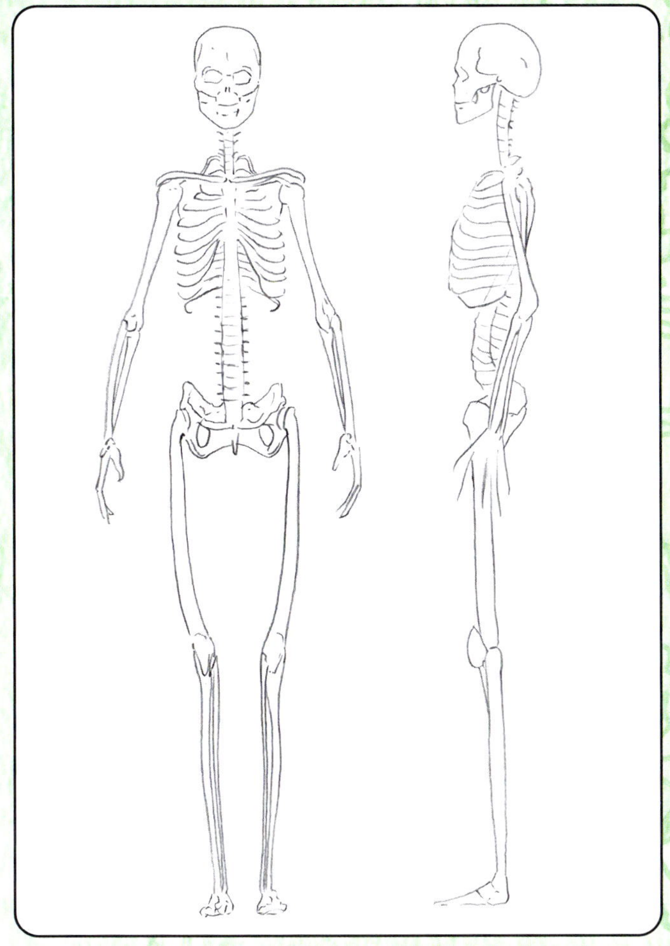

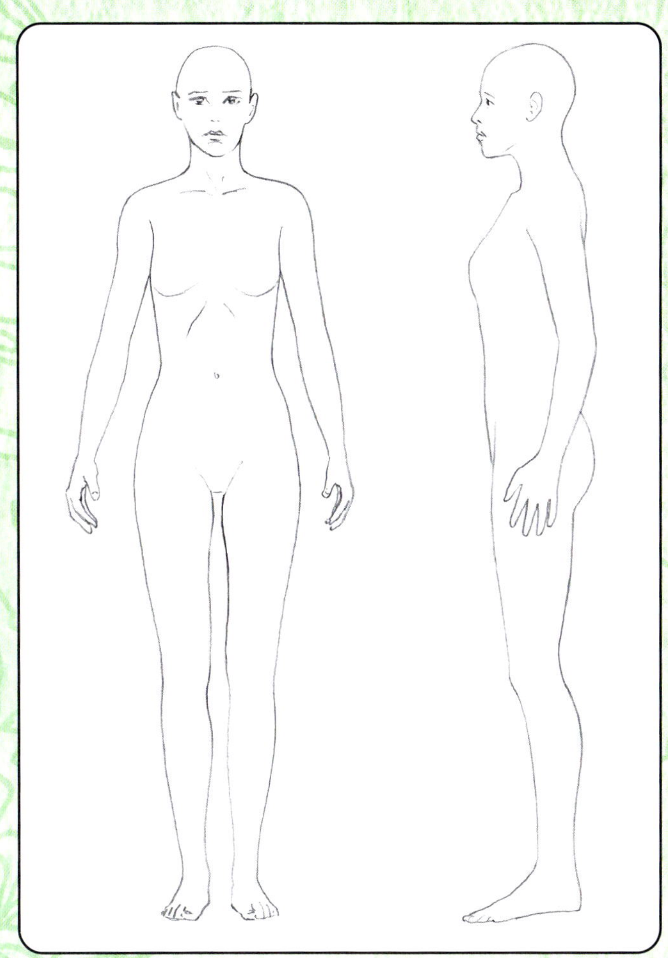

▲ Skeleton

We can draw the adult skeleton in the same way as the young faerie skeleton. Drawing both front and side-on views will give you an idea of what is under our flesh and muscles. Using plain paper and a soft pencil, try to copy the faerie skeletons in the illustrations as you did with the young faerie's skeleton. If you feel you need them, you can draw the guidelines on to help you.

▲ Muscles and flesh

Next we can add the muscles and flesh on top of our basic framework. Flesh out your adult faerie as you did the young faerie. The main difference, apart from being taller, is that you need to give the adult faerie a few more curves in the right places. The hips and thighs should be slightly thicker and wider, the shoulders squarer and you can draw a fuller bust. You still want your faerie to be slim and ethereal so try to make these differences subtly. Once you have completed the outline you can erase your construction lines from both the adult and the young faerie drawing. You can even go over some of your lines again, using a nice soft pencil, and add definition to various areas.

The human form is complex and even artists who practise life drawing for years are still constantly learning. This chapter shows the basic form of the human body and hopefully, once you understand it more fully, you will be able to work on the structures you have studied to create your own faerie figures.

The ideal practice is drawing people from life. Obviously, get their permission first! If you practise drawing every day, your drawings, observational skills and techniques will improve tremendously. Always keep your drawings – don't throw any of them away, even if you feel they have turned out completely wrong. If you can, try to date them and keep them in order of completion. You can then look back at your drawings and see how well you have progressed.

Faerie heads & faces

Drawing a faerie head and face is very similar to drawing a human head and face. The proportions are the same, apart from a few tweaks with the features. The great thing about drawing faeries is that once you have have learned how to construct the basic structure of a human face you don't have to worry too much about getting it perfect: you can use your imagination to give them as much character as you like. The following illustrations will guide you in creating a faerie head and face, for both an adult and a young faerie. Once you've studied the basic form, let your imagination run wild!

YOUNG FAERIE HEAD & FACE

▶ A young faerie's head is different from an adult's: it is much rounder and it will be larger than an adult's compared to its body. Start by drawing an oval, slightly wider at the top than the bottom.

Next, draw three lines like these in the illustration. The top is the brow line, the second is the nose line and the third is the bottom of the chin. The positions of these are the same on every young human figure. Also note that the bases of the ears line up approximately with the nose, so we can now add them in.

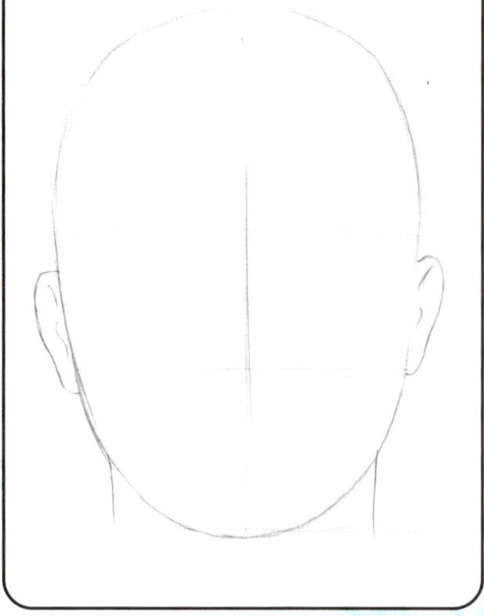

▶ Adding features

The next step is to start adding the eyes. The top line, as we have discussed, is the brow line, so the eye socket will be below this. When drawing eyes, draw a centre circle for the pupil and an outer circle for the iris. We can then set them in an oval shape which will become the upper eye lid and the lower eyelid. Next we can add the nose, the base of which rests on the middle guideline. The lips are placed in the centre between the chin and the nose.

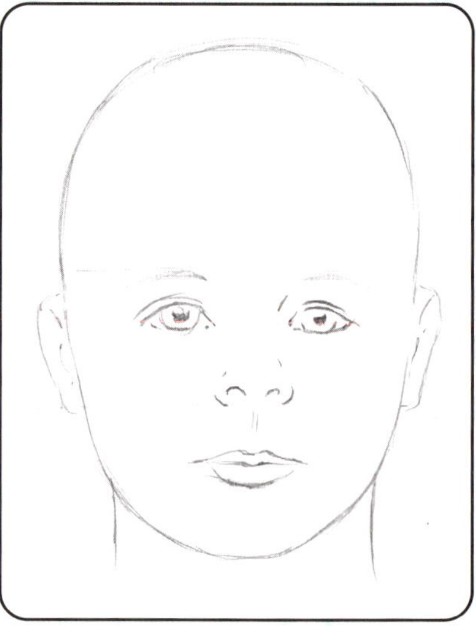

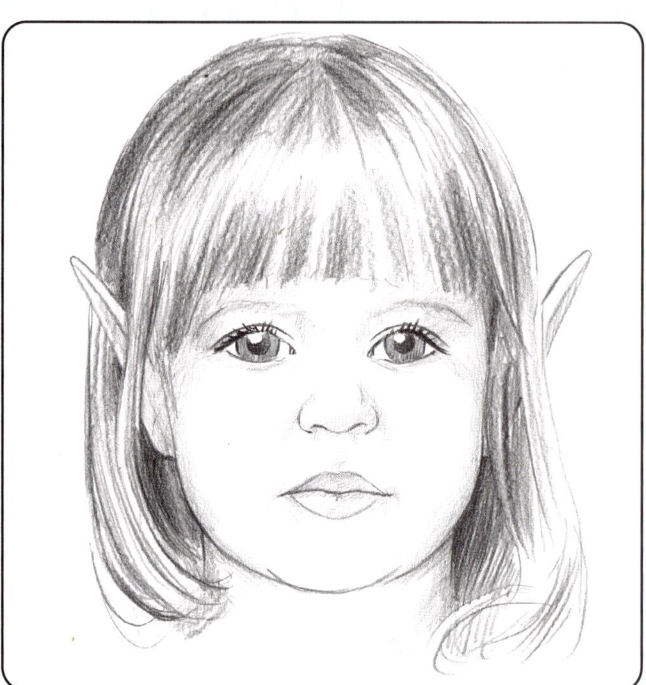

◀ Final drawing

Once you have all the basic features in, you can start shading your faerie and adding detail. The young faerie will have much larger eyes, fuller lips and a more button-shaped and rounded nose than an adult (see opposite). You can give her pointed ears, which can protrude though her hair, and choose whichever hairstyle you feel would suit your young faerie best. Use your 2B pencil to create your initial outline and shading, but try to work your tones up by using a 4B, 6B or even an 8B pencil for the darkest areas such as the eyes and dark shadows. Remember to layer your pencil marks rather than just pressing harder to create a darker tone.

ADULT FAERIE HEAD & FACE

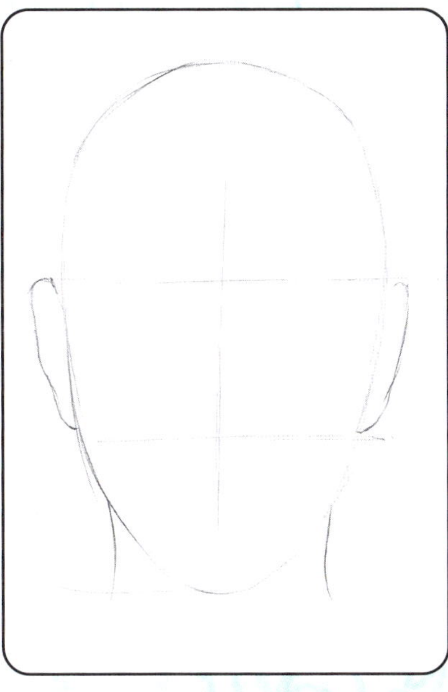

An adult faerie head is narrower and more defined than a young faerie's and we need to be aware of this when drawing our adult faerie. Start by drawing a narrower oval shape, but again it needs to be wider at the top than the bottom. Next, draw the three lines like these in the illustration: the brow line, the nose line and the bottom of the chin. The positioning of these lines is the same on every adult human figure. Finally, you can add the ears which will line up approximately with the base of the nose. You can then go on to add features.

▶ Adding features

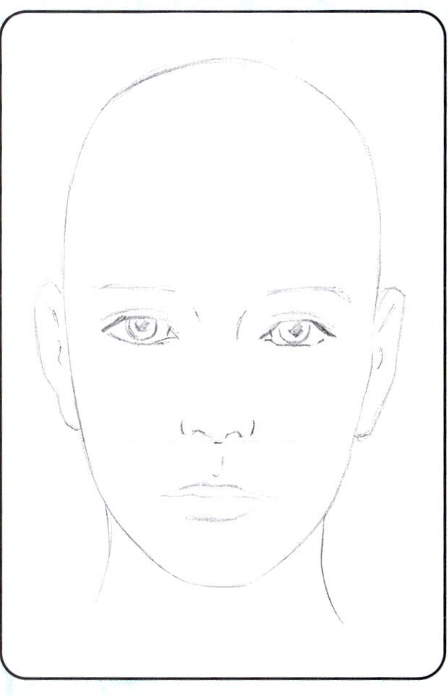

The next stage is to add the eyes, using the brow line to guide your positioning. Once the eyes are in place you can draw an oval shape around the eyes which will become the upper eyelid and the lower eyelid. The nose can be added next, and you can have a more elongated, pointed nose for an adult faerie, the base of which rests on the middle guideline. Finally the lips are placed in the centre between the chin and the nose, and will be longer and narrower than the young faerie's mouth.

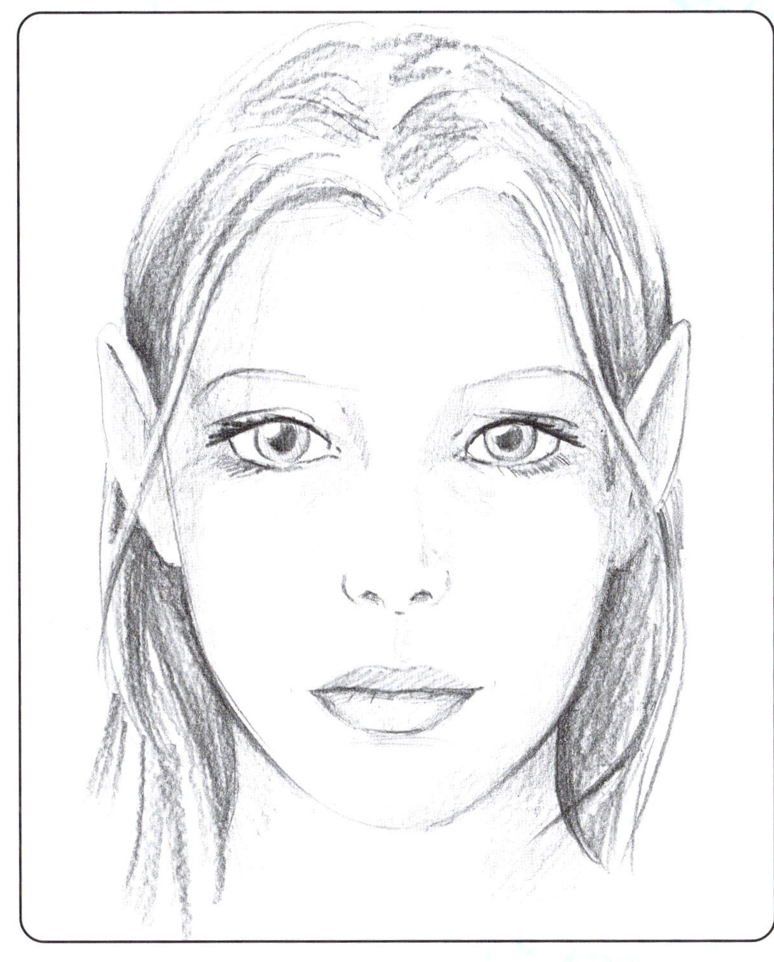

◀ Final drawing

Once the basic features are drawn in, detail can be added to the adult faerie's face to make her look more realistic. The adult faerie will have a slender feel to her face and a more adult hairstyle. She can still have larger eyes than a normal human as this will make her face seem smaller, giving her a more faerie-like feel. To complete your drawing you can give her pointed faerie ears. As usual, it is best to use a 2B pencil for the initial sketching, then shade the main areas with a 4B, 6B or even an 8B pencil.

Faerie features

Each faerie we draw can have a different expression, a different character and look to them. Some will be quite impish, some can be dark and mysterious, yet others can be happy. There are hundreds of different expressions and facial features you can draw. To help you when you are starting to draw faerie features, why not look in a mirror and draw your own features? You can start by drawing your eyes and making them into different shapes. Try to look scared or surprised, happy or sad. Try to accentuate the shapes your eyes make, to make it clear to the viewer how the faerie is feeling. I have drawn a few features on these pages to help you. Why not copy some of these to get you started, then experiment with your own ideas.

FAERIE EYES

▶ The first shape of eyes here are a little bit sly. We can achieve a sly look to the eyes by making them narrow and half closed. This faerie could be peering around a flower to see if anyone is watching. Perhaps she's about to get up to mischief!

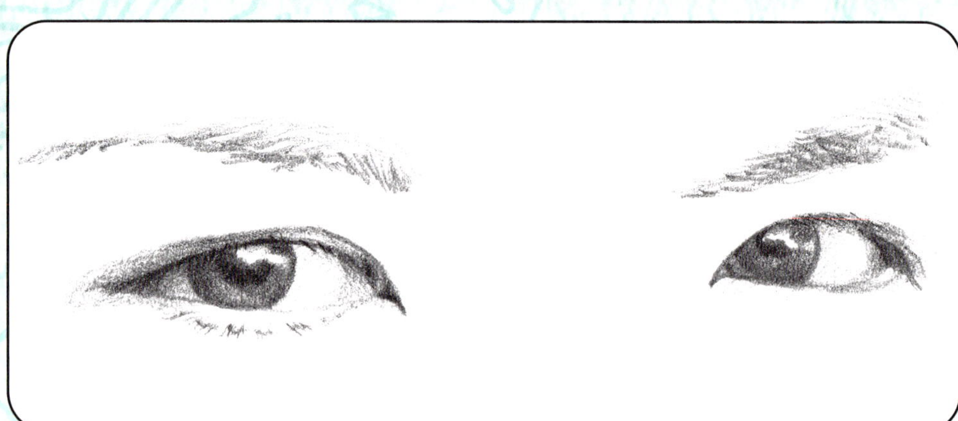

▶ In the second sketch the eyes are a little sad or worried. A good way to create worried eyes is to make them look to one side. Perhaps the winter is arriving, she is surrounded by autumn leaves and worried she isn't going to be able to shelter for the winter.

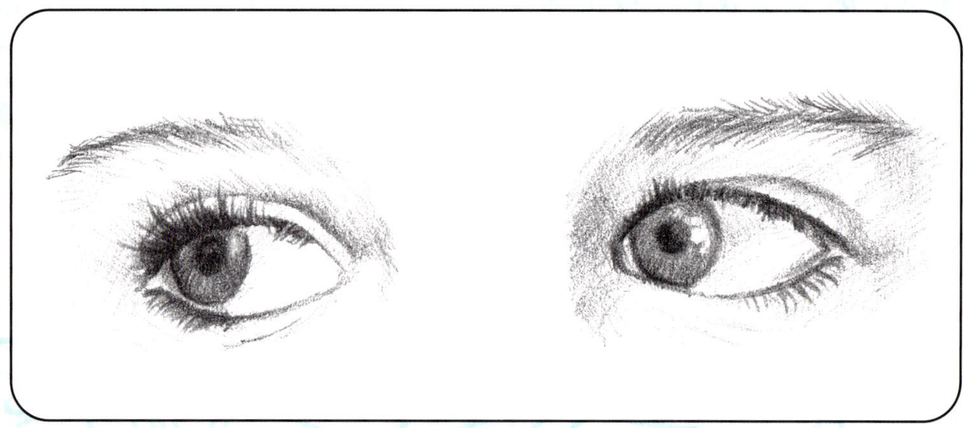

▶ The third set of eyes show a shocked and very surprised faerie! Shocked eyes are really simple to create as we can make the eyes larger and rounded. Perhaps a creature from the undergrowth popped out from behind a leaf and surprised her!

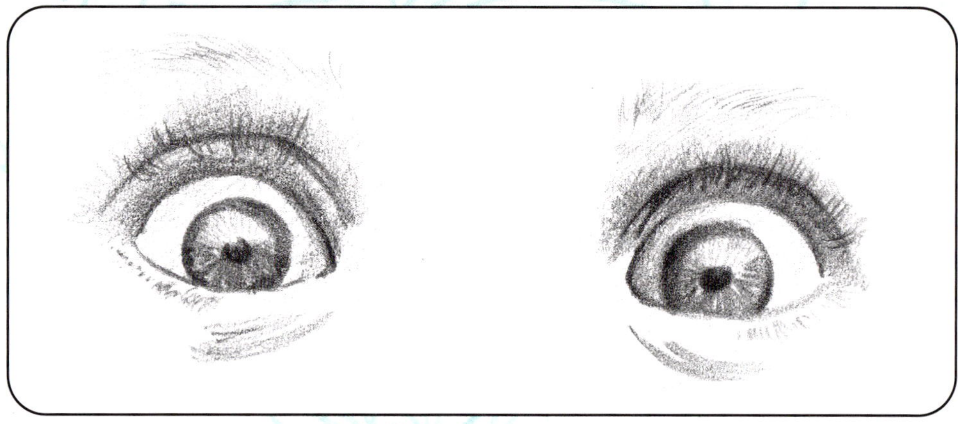

FAERIE NOSES

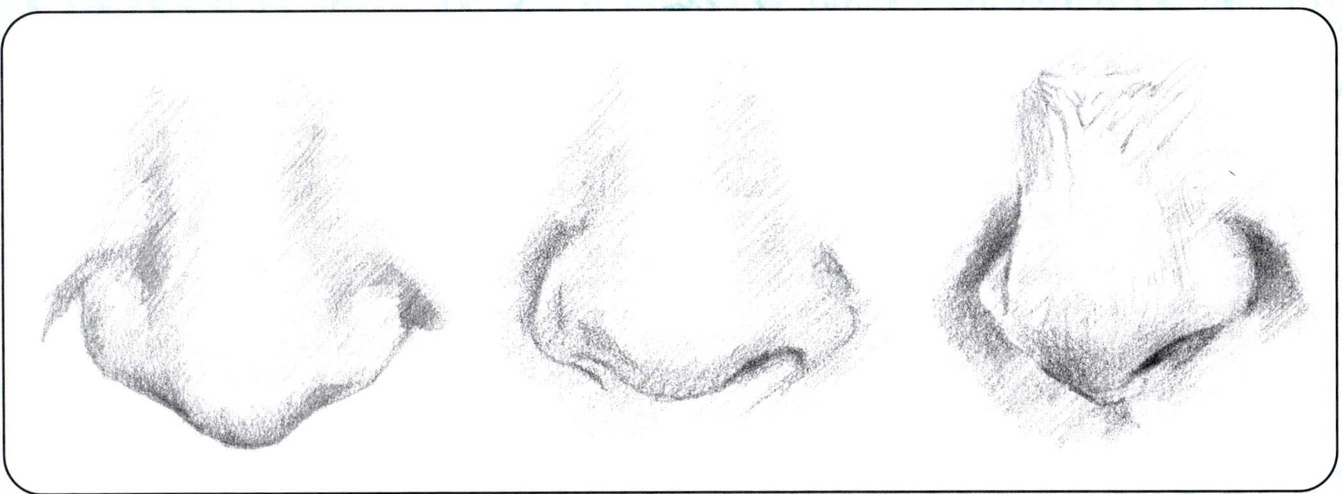

▲ Faerie noses, like human noses, can take on very different forms: a flower faerie or young faerie can have a button nose, an older, darker faerie could have a long hooked nose, or a pointed nose more like a witch's. The first nose is quite flat and would be suited to an adult faerie, and could also be used for a male faerie. The second is a smaller, button nose and is suited to a younger faerie. The final nose is a gnarly wrinkled nose which you might find on an old faerie, a dark faerie or a witchy faerie.

FAERIE EARS

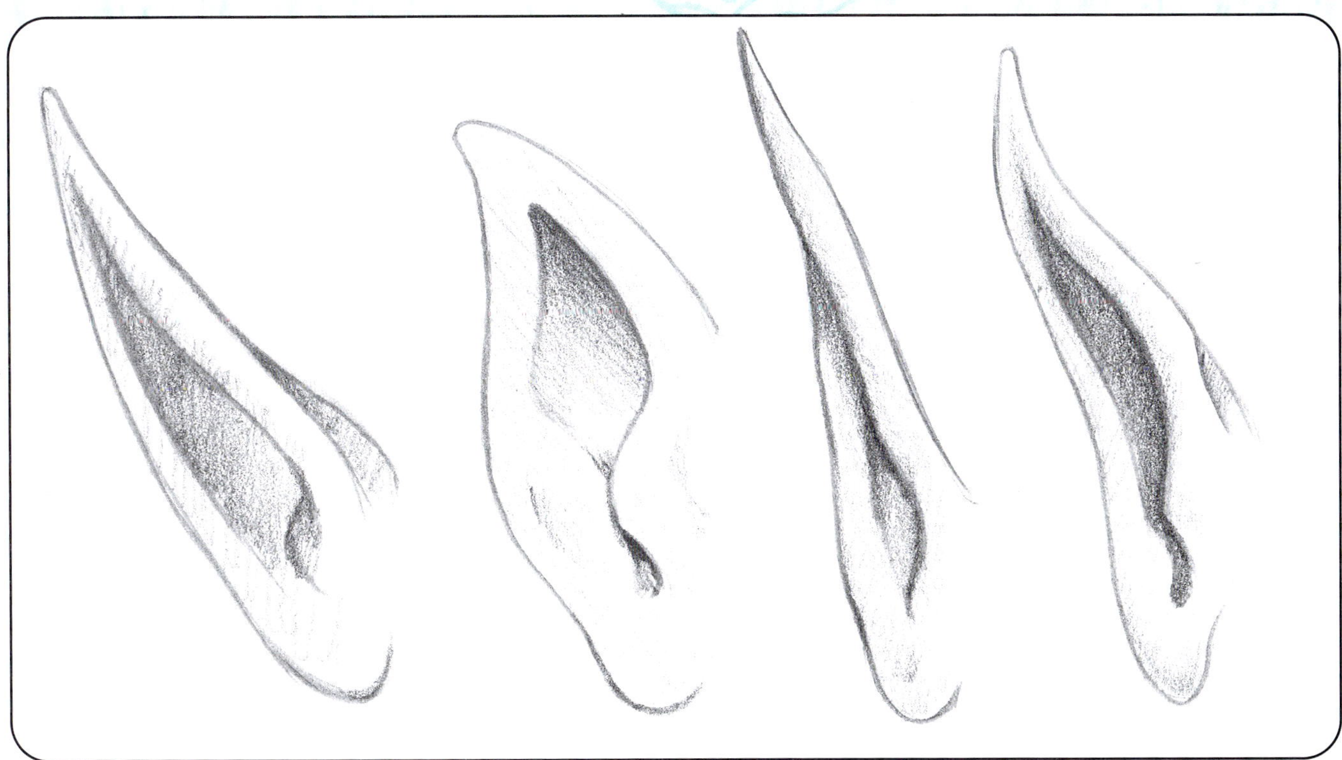

▲ Faerie ears can also be all sorts of different shapes but are generally pointed. There are four examples here. The longer, thinner ears are best suited to ethereal faeries and adult faeries that are graceful and elegant. Younger ears are shorter and thinner and often more fleshy. Once you have the basic shapes to the ears you can add in more detail; they could have earrings, or even tiny flowers in a chain around them.

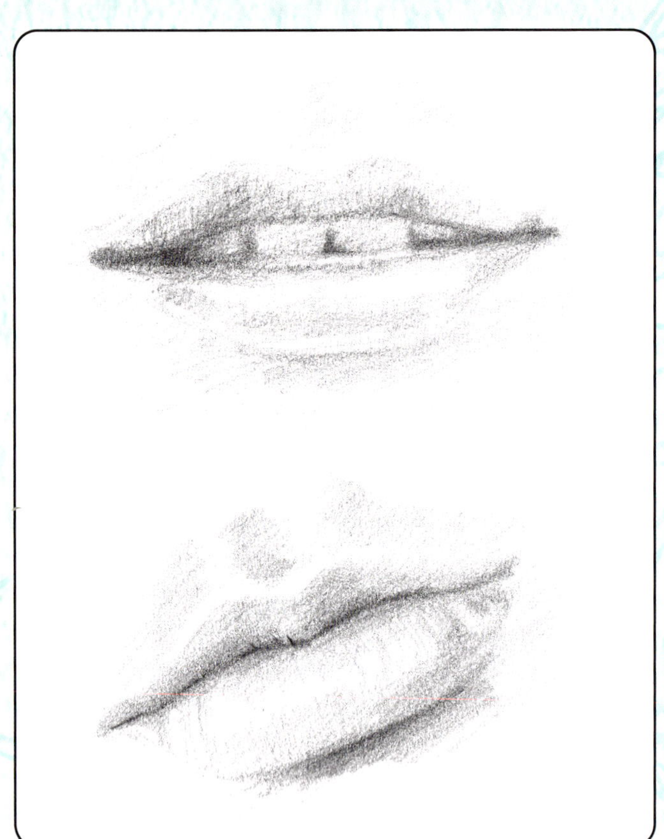

FAERIE MOUTHS

◀ Mouths also hold the key to the character of a face. They can be talking, smiling, pouting, sad, grumpy, scared – there are so many different shapes to choose from when drawing your faeries. Try looking in the mirror and pulling some faces to see how your mouth changes, and then draw what you see. The three mouths here are pouting, smiling and one showing a little teeth. When you are drawing mouths try not to draw the teeth too detailed or in focus, and shade over them with some tone. Unshaded white teeth always stand out too much.

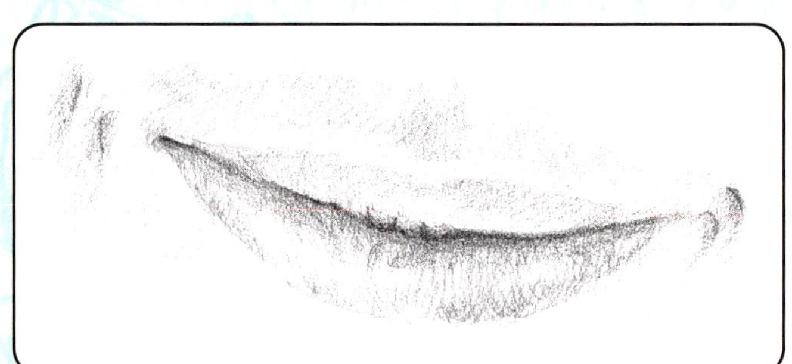

FAERIE HANDS

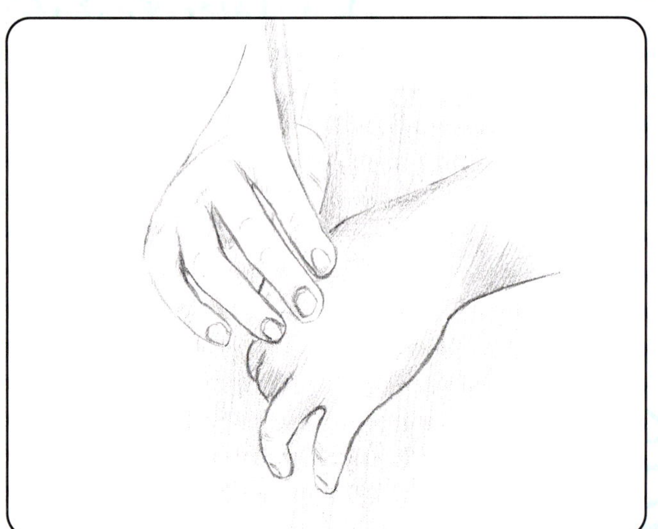

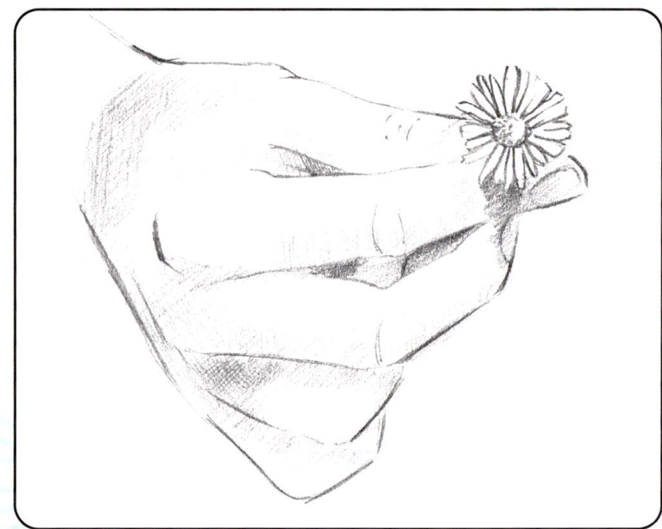

▲ Faerie hands should be dainty. Adults' hands will be slender with long fingers, while those of a young faerie or a flower faerie will be a little more rounded and smaller. Hands are generally quite difficult to draw and so working from photos is often a necessity. If you can get a model to pose for you, take photos of how you want your faerie's hand to be posed and you will find the process a lot easier. Most faeries' hands will show their activity at that moment, for instance they could be holding a stem, a flower, a berry, holding the side of a leaf, clasping their hands together, or to their face, or even holding onto a sceptre if they are a dark faerie. The illustrations here show a young faerie holding the stem of a flower then holding a daisy. You can make the stem or daisy as big or as small as you like. My daisy is relatively small in comparison with a faerie's hands but you may prefer to have the petals hiding a larger area of the hands, making it easier for you to draw.

FAERIE FEET

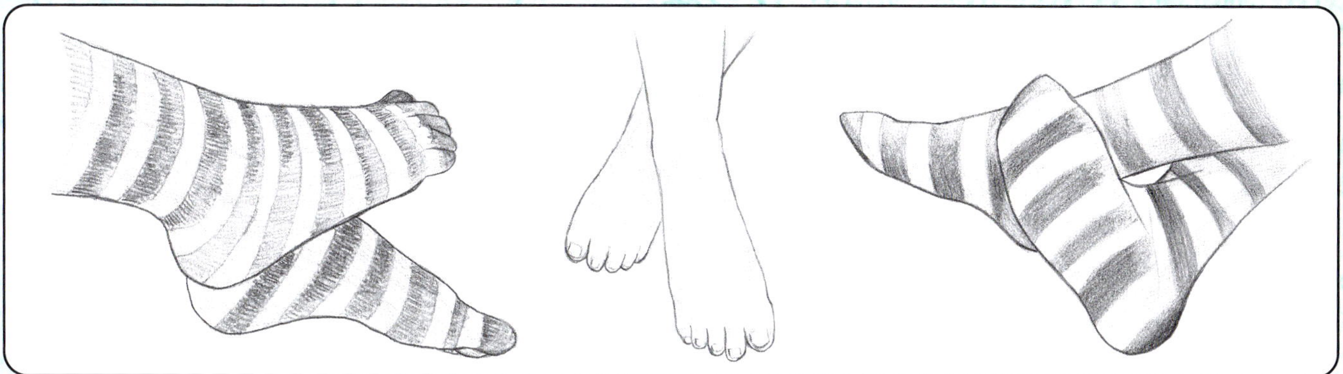

▲ Faeries are often shown wearing stripy socks or tights, making it easy for you to draw the feet. Creating the stripes around the feet helps them to be more three-dimensional, solid and more interesting. The illustrations here show socks, tights and bare feet. You don't have to give them five toes; if you want to create a foot with only four toes, go ahead. After all, faeries aren't human. You can elongate them, or make their toes longer and more slender to help create a more mystical feel. Experiment with all the features, copy the drawings on this page and try to draw your own features from either your reflection in a mirror or photographs.

FAERIE HAIRSTYLES

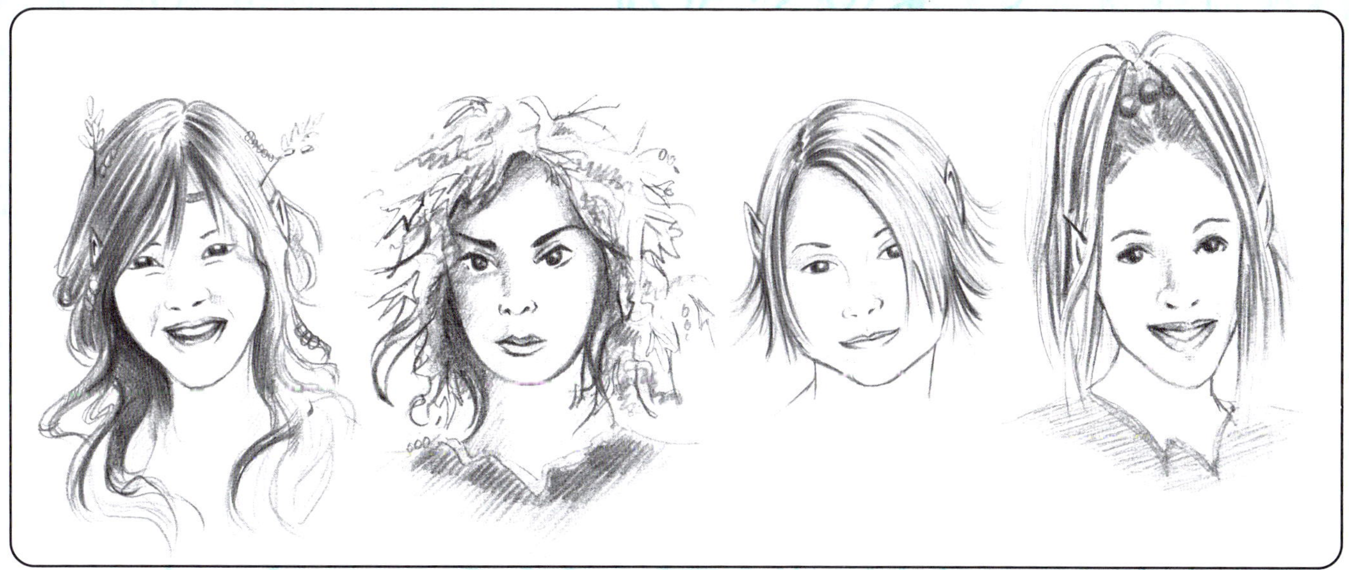

▲ Once you have practised creating different facial features, you will also need to give a hairstyle to match her character and features. The first faerie here is a happy-go-lucky faerie. She has leaf and flower decorations in her hair, which is long and wavy. She is a happy faerie so she is laughing and has shiny, smiling eyes to match.

The second is a woodland nymph. She is quite wild and has messy hair with leaves and twigs sticking out. She tends to scamper around in the undergrowth, so I've given her an unkempt look and feel.

The third faerie is an adult sprite with a wide short face. She has cropped spiky hair and small nose and chin.

The final faerie has an impish feel to her: she has a long face and her hair is tied up in a pony tail high on her head, elongating her face even more. She has berries in her hair for decoration and has a smiling face.

There are plenty of magazines and books where you can find hairstyles and get inspiration to make up your own styles. Don't forget when you are using colour, paint cold and dark colours for naughty and dark faeries and warm light colours for bright and happy faeries.

FAERIE WINGS

Wings are an essential element in the creation of a faerie figure. Using butterfly and moth wings is a good starting point. You can also use other wings, for instance dragonflies and bats wings, or even leaves and spiky unusual flowers. Use your imagination to adapt the natural world and develop an individual look. Try elongating the wings, develop the patterns within them, or change the colours and shapes. For flower faeries and ethereal faeries, use light colours and pretty wings. If you are creating a dark faerie, you can use dark colours and jagged edges. You can work in any of the materials we've discussed, including pastel, pencil, coloured pencil and acrylic. You can even get metallic and glittery inks that will give your faeries' wings a beautiful iridescent feel.

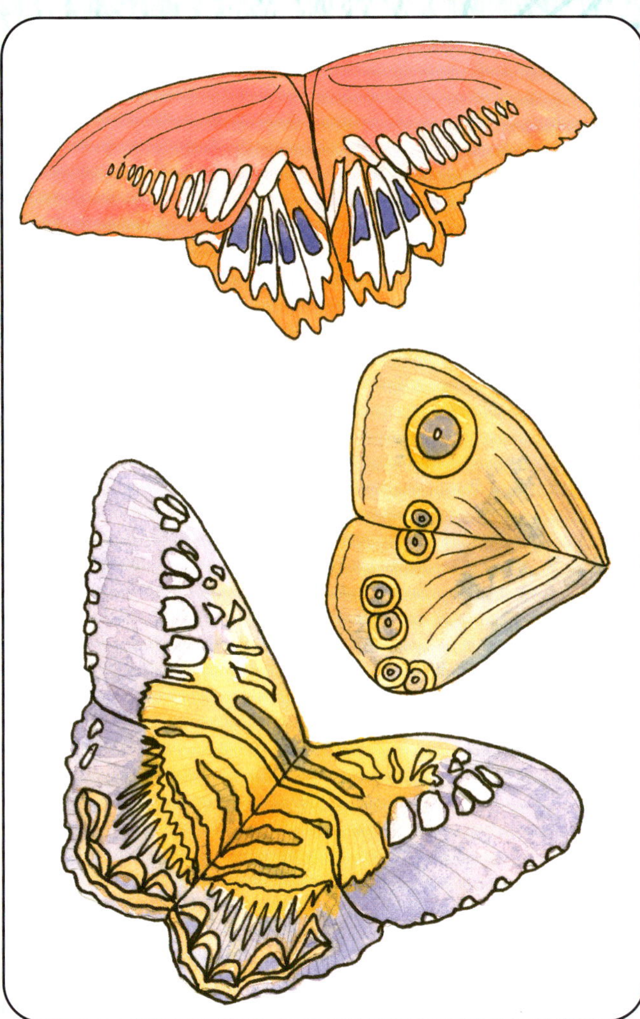

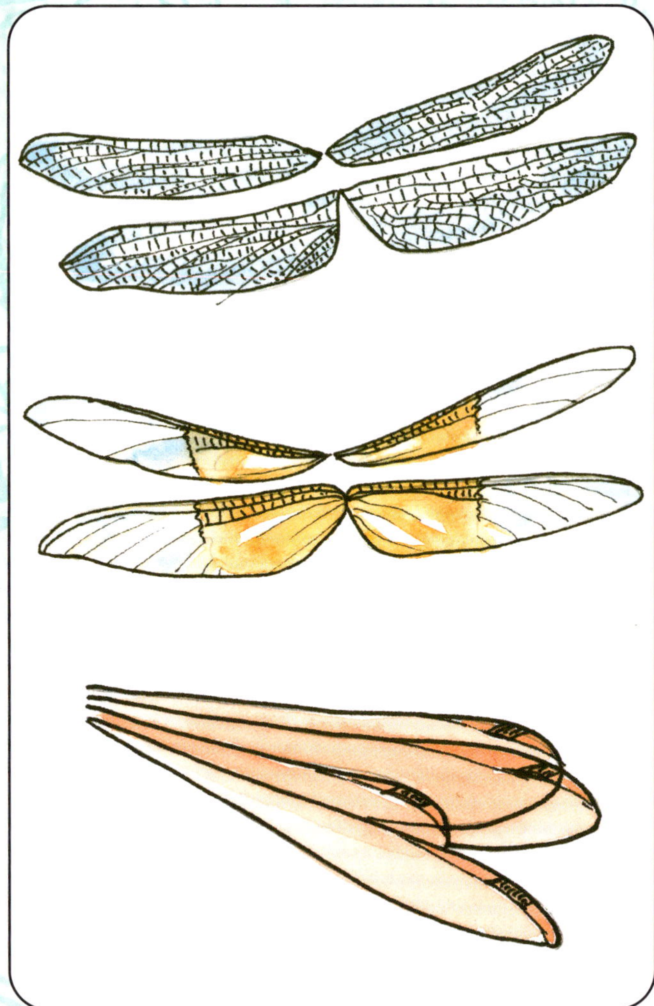

▲ The top illustration is of a moth's wings; you can accentuate the jagged edges if you feel it's appropriate.

Below are a butterfly's wings in profile and spread out – you can tell it's a butterfly because the shape is more rounded than the moth's. Don't forget that butterfly wings are symmetrical, so however you design your patterns on one side, you must mimic them on the other like a reflection.

The wings in profile could be joined to a faerie that is viewed from the side. The wings tend to join between the shoulder blades of a faerie.

▲ Dragonflies' wings can have all sorts of wonderful transparent patterns. The three illustrations here show you how you can decorate the wings whilst keeping a translucent feel. The first illustration shows a full patterned wing with the veins of the wings showing. The second shows a few veins but more colour within the wings themselves. The final wing doesn't show any veins at all making it a more dainty wing suited to a smaller faerie.

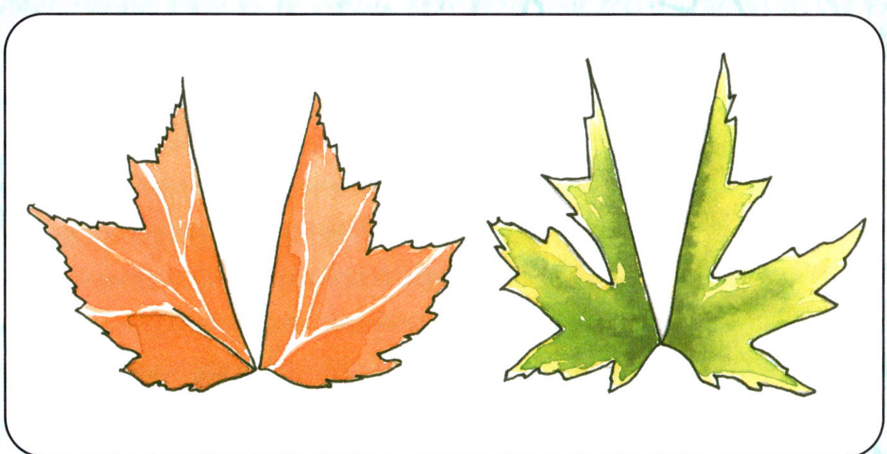

◀ You can also use leaves for wings and the two drawings here show how you could create them. The first leaf wing is rich red in colour, and so suited to an autumn faerie, while the second, more spiky wing is a green colour best suited to a tree nymph or woodland faerie. You can experiment with different shaped leaves and add different colours and patterns.

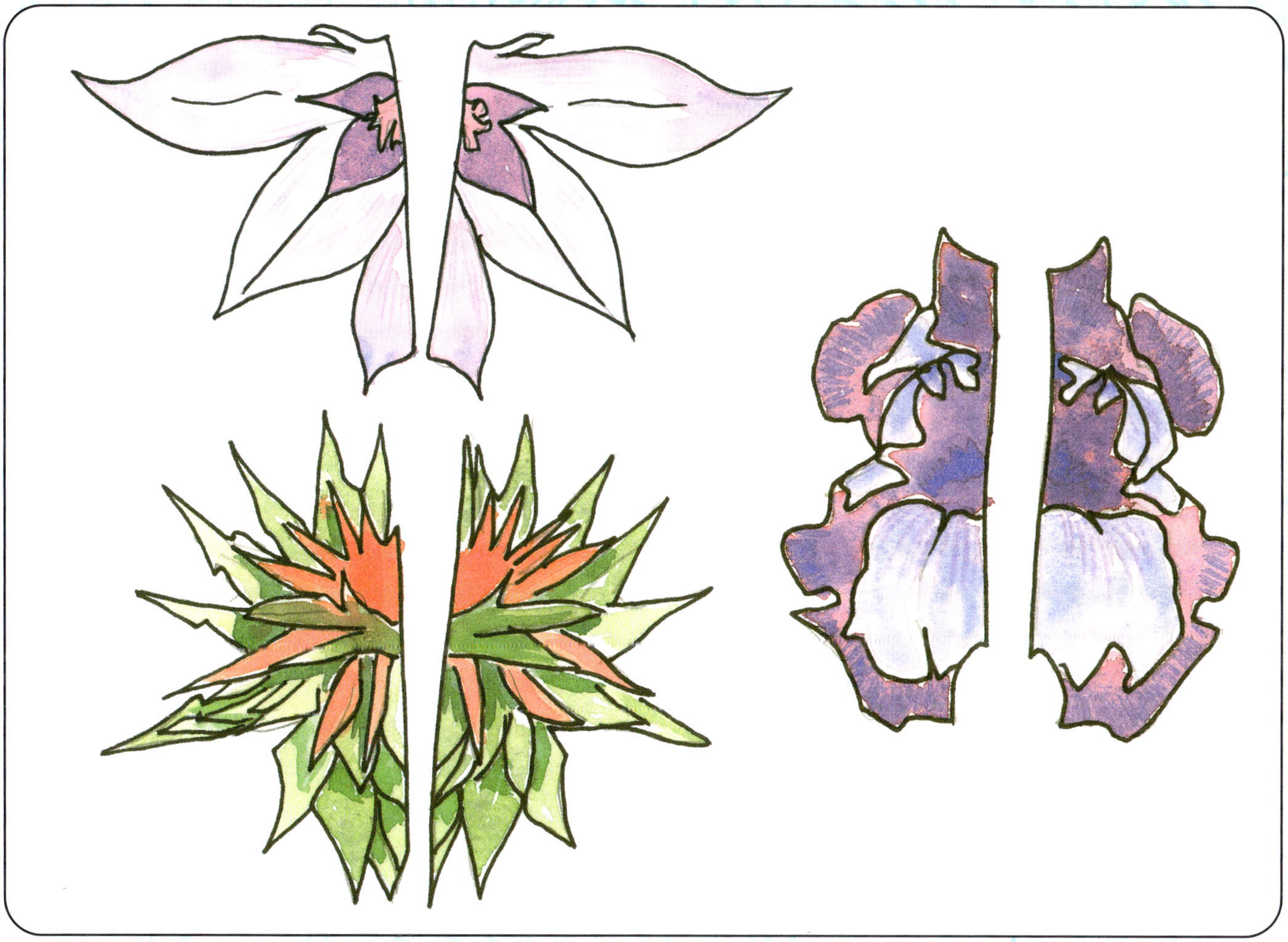

▲ Flowers also work very well for wings. The three illustrations here depict some of the more unusual flowers you can find. If you haven't got any like this in your own garden to copy from, have a look in magazines and books for some inspiration. Orchids, in particular, are fantastic to use for wings, as the top drawing shows. This would be wonderful for a little flower faerie and the purple colours and unusual patterns and shapes work really well. It looks as though it's a very young wing in its early stages of development. The second orchid wing is further on in development, and it is stretched out and much larger in comparison. It is very delicate and elegant. The final wing is based on a spiky flower and could be used for an impish faerie or a dark faerie – or any time when you wanted to depict a faerie getting up to mischief!

Faerie expressions

If you look at any human face, their individual characteristics show in their facial expressions. Similarly, we can create a whole range of expressions for our faeries which will help display their characters and personalities. There are many different types of faeries, and as you learn about each one, you will be able to create a unique face and expression for each of them. The possibilities are endless and, with some imagination, your faeries can all take on completely different personalities with a few minor changes to their features.

If you want to create a specific expression for one of your faeries, why not look in a mirror and try to make the expression you are looking for? You can even draw from your own reflection. Alternatively, if you have access to a digital camera you could ask someone to take photos of you pulling a variety of faces. You could try to look angry, sad, happy, shocked, scared, confused, disgusted or excited. Our faces pull hundreds of different facial expressions every day, so observe people around you and take note of how they are feeling at the time of making the expressions.

Then try drawing a few different expressions, but emphasising your human features to make them more faerie-like. For instance, if you wanted the faerie to be listening intently to something the eyes would be wide and open. So you could simply make your own eyes larger, rounder and more open.

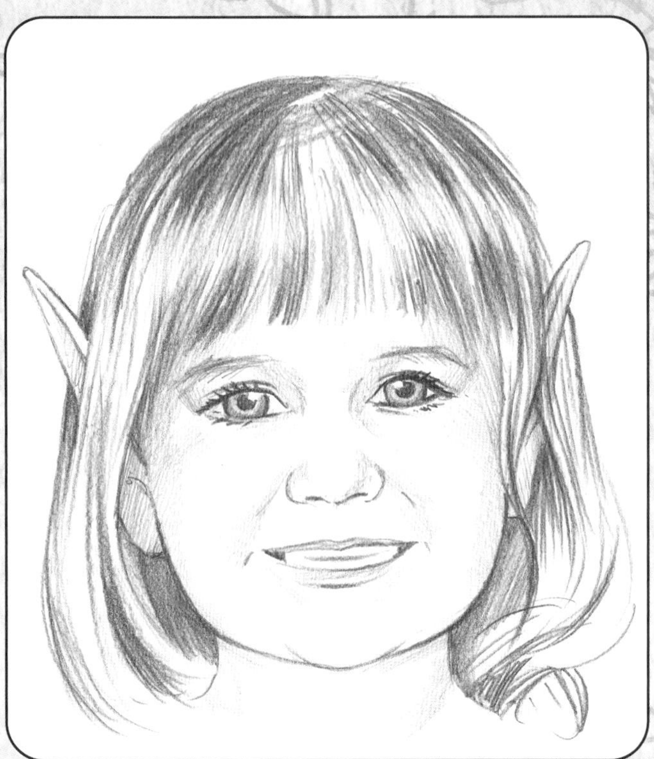

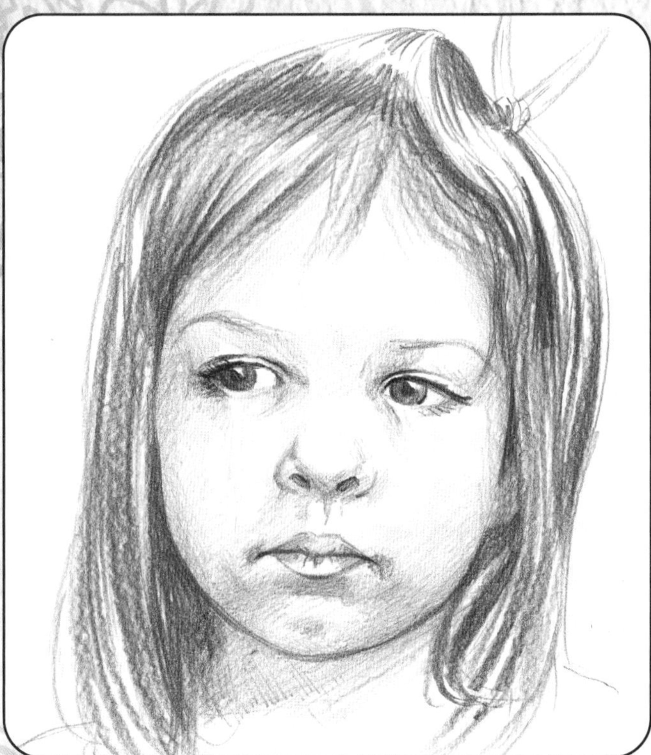

▲ Happy faerie

If you want to create a happy look to your faerie, make the eyes quite large, round and open to show excitement. If you want your faerie to be laughing, the eyes will be narrower, almost upturned slits, and there will be laughter lines around the eyes. Try laughing and looking in the mirror at the same time to see the shape your eyes make. The mouth will be smiling and you may be able to see some of the faeries' teeth. As discussed, it's best to just give an impression of the teeth, rather than drawing each tooth individually.

▲ Sad faerie

Sad faeries can have very droopy features. Their hair can be flat, their ears can be small and narrow and their eyes turned down in the corners. Their mouths can be relatively small and downturned. For added effect you could add some tears or tear stains down the faerie's cheek. Another good way of showing sadness is to have the faerie looking away or to one side, as if she doesn't really want to look at you.

▶ Bored faerie

A good way of showing a bored faerie expression is to place the faerie's head in her hands. Her head can then be downturned, but with the eyes looking up so that we can still interact with her. The eyes should be quite large and round, almost sad-looking. Make the mouth small and don't have her smiling at all. You could even downturn the faerie ears for effect!

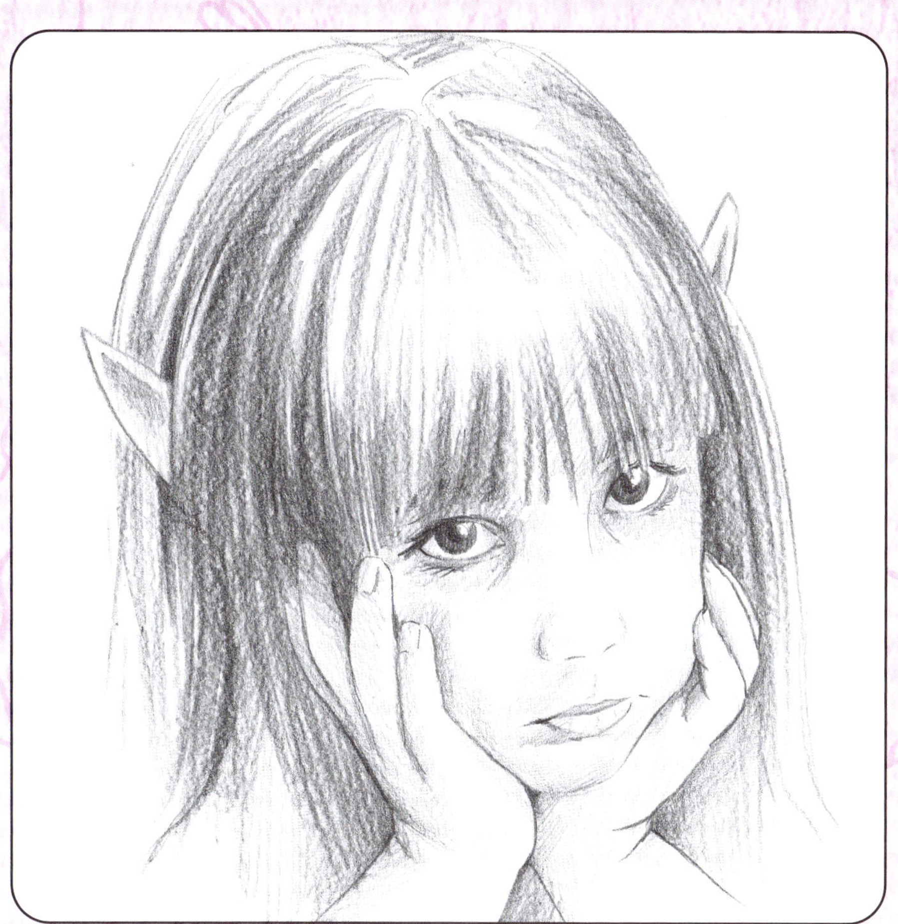

▶ Angry faerie

Angry faeries are lovely to portray as there are so many options. To begin with the brows of the faerie are going to protrude over the eyes and almost come to a point in the centre where the frown will appear. The shape of the eyes is important as they will need to be narrow, and can have a flat upper and slightly curved lower lid. You could play around with really sharp features, like a pointy nose and very sharp pointy ears for a dramatic angry look.

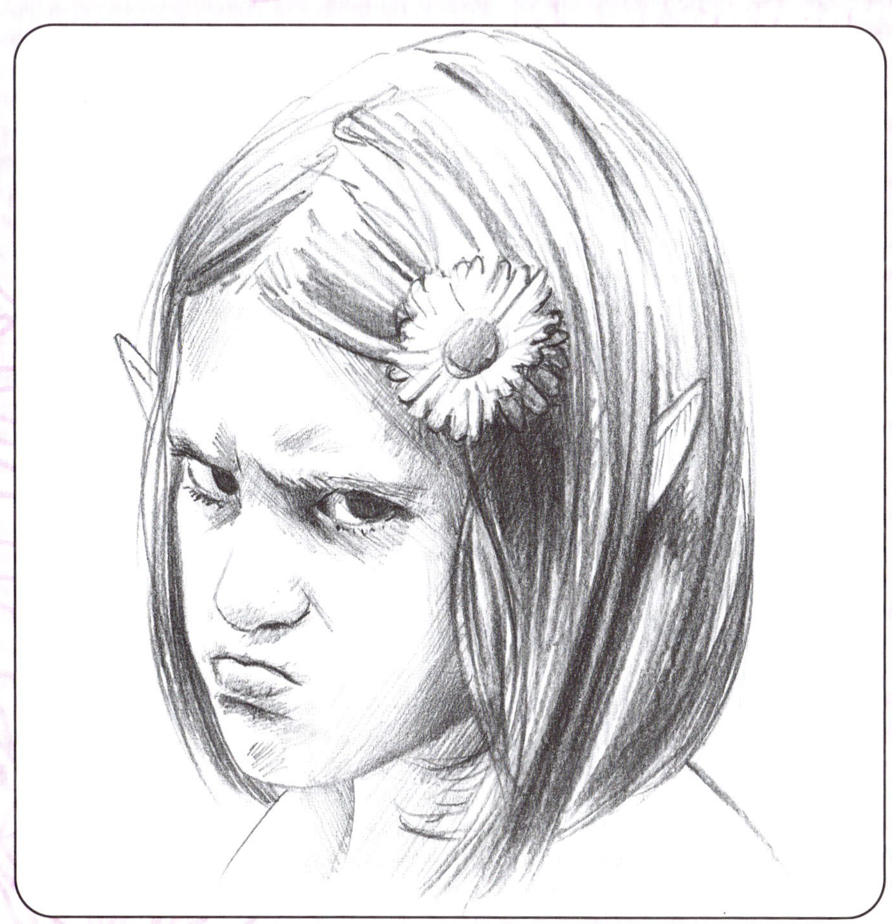

▶ Scared faerie

When portraying a scared faerie the eyes are going to be the most important feature. Look at yourself in the mirror and try to make yourself look scared. What changes about your eyes and mouth? Your mouth will probably turn downwards. Your top lip may be thinner and your overall face shape may be longer. Your eyes would possibly become triangular in shape, narrowing towards the edges of your face, while your eyebrows will be higher and the frown would be high up in the forehead. You could make the tops of the faerie's ears elongated and you could even make her hair a feature. Why not show some of it sticking up in the air as though she has had a fright?

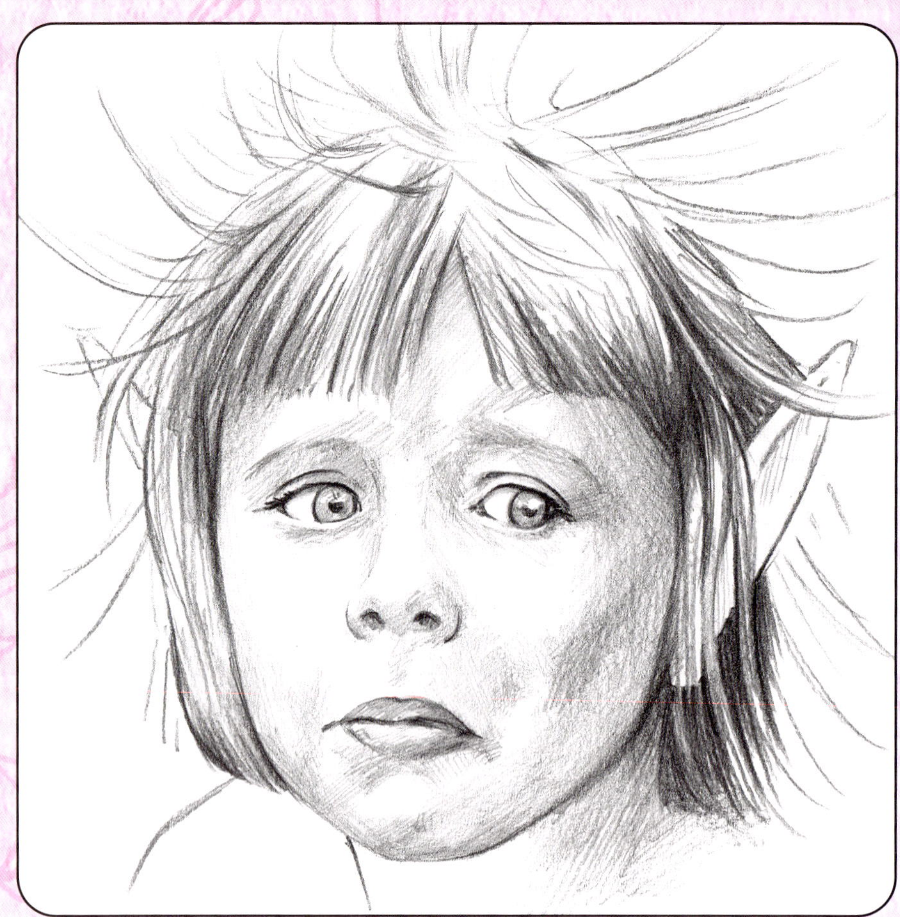

▶ Faerie in thought

A faerie that is thinking or deep in thought could be illustrated in many ways. She could have her finger or hand to her mouth, she could be looking up into the air, or looking inquisitively at an object. This faerie has very wide open eyes looking up in the air. They are oval, and the pupils and iris are quite large. The mouth will often be narrow and probably not smiling.

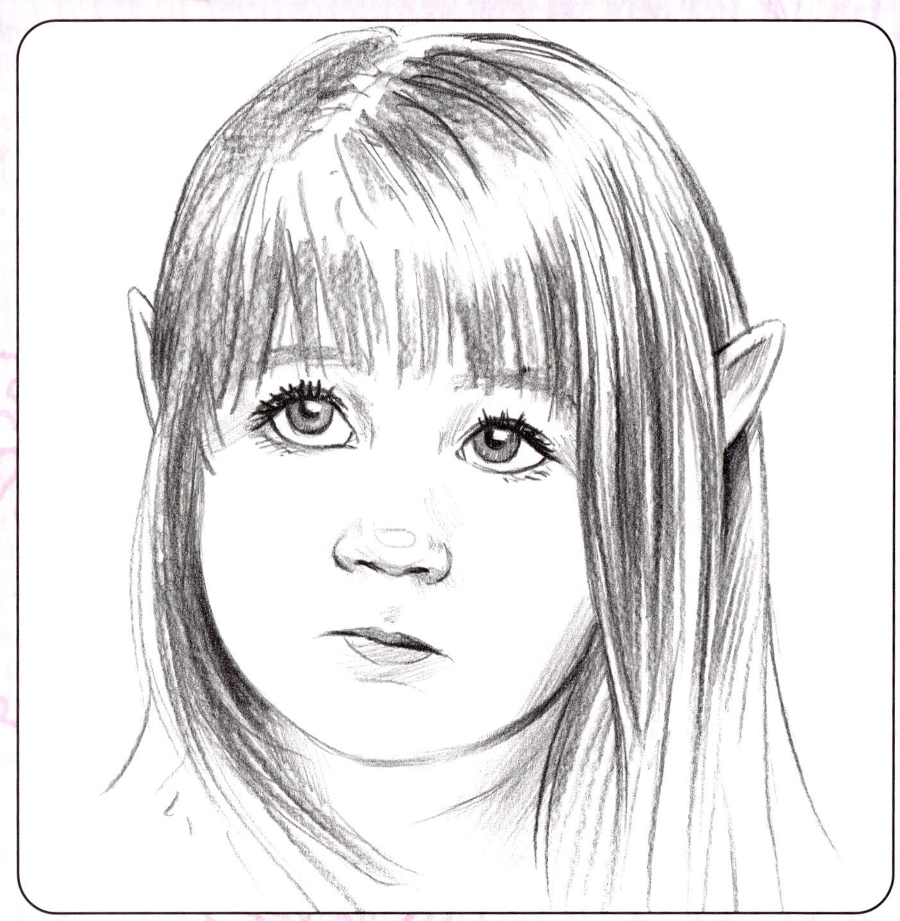

ADDING COLOUR TO CHANGE YOUR FAERIE EXPRESSIONS

The expressions on a face can say so much, but it's not only facial features that we can use to convey character – colour can play a big part in it too. Once you have practised a few different expressions using graphite pencil, have a go at drawing and adding some colour on one of your favourites. The illustrations here show the same pose and the same layout, but these are two very different faeries.

▶ Good faerie

The secret behind creating a happy and peaceful faerie is to use warm colours. Make the eyes large, round or slightly curved and upturned so she looks as though she is smiling with her eyes. The mouth should curve up at the corners and you can even give her dimples in her cheeks. Her hair can be light in colour, anything ranging from light yellows, golden, and even light pinks can look happy. This particular faerie has lots of pretty flowers made into a braid for her hair. The type and colours of the flowers can easily illustrate the time of year or how the faerie is feeling. Summery flowers are always going to exude happiness. The overall feel of this picture is delightfully sunny and warm and the principal colours used are bright yellows, pinks, oranges and pale greens. The whole picture radiates warmth and contentment.

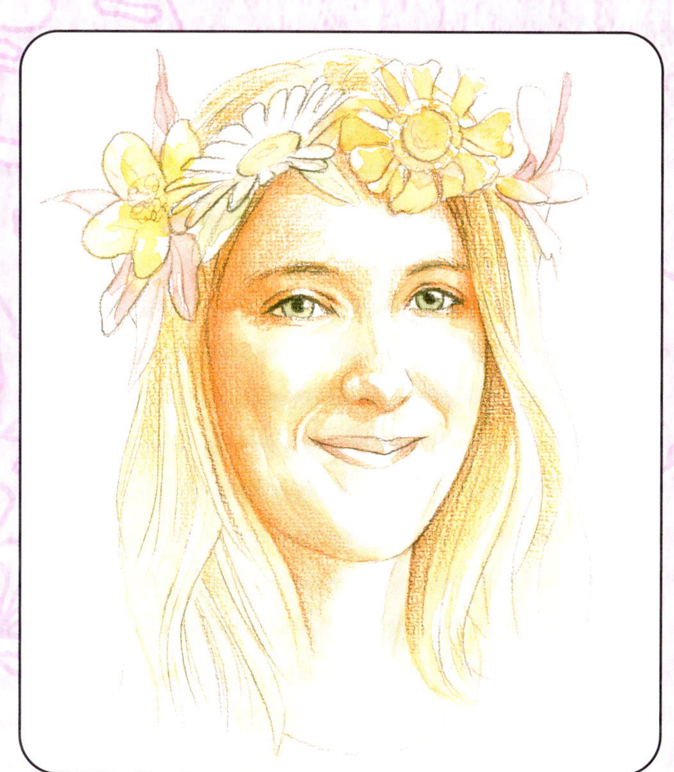

▶ Dark faerie

The same reference photo was used for the dark faerie, but to give her a more dark and intense feel, cooler colours have been used which convey a more wicked side. Purples and blues are perfect colours for the hair, and if we use cooler colours for the flowers they look wintry and cold. To give your faerie a more unpleasant feel, make her face thinner with more angular chin, as this helps to give her an untrustworthy look. The eyes of a dark faerie can be any cool colour ranging from blue to purple and even black. If you tilt the eyes so that they point up slightly at the outer corners and down on the inner corners, with slanted eyebrows, this will give an impression of frowning. Finally try to give your faerie a more pointed nose, almost witch-like and you will end up with a dark faerie based on the same photo as the happy faerie!

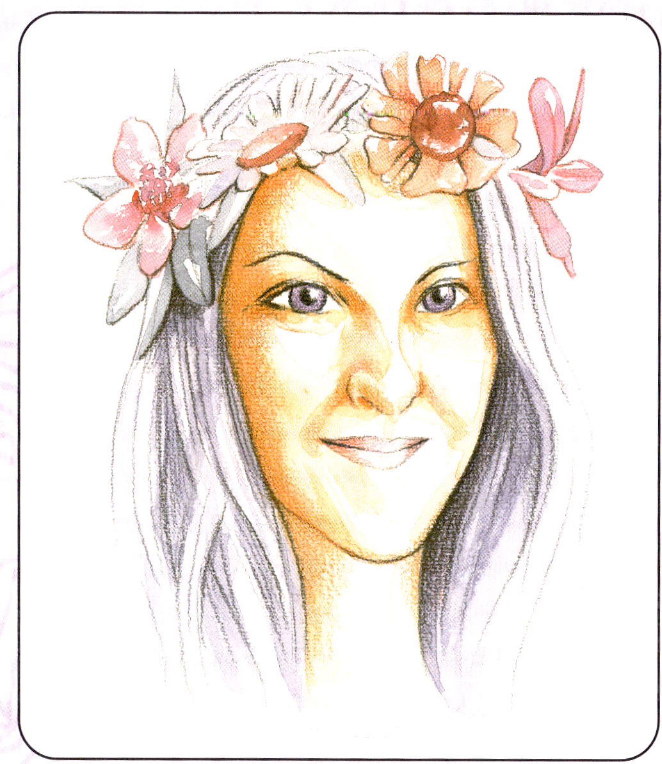

Faerie poses

There is a range of typical faerie poses that artists use. Whether you have someone to take photos of yourself in a faerie-like pose or you use photos in magazines, books or from the internet, try to capture a typical pose. The most popular and easy-to-draw faeries are those sitting on leaves or toadstools, perching on a fallen tree trunk or balancing on the soft petal of a flower. When you have chosen a basic pose you can use your imagination as to where you would like them to be. Just like with their expressions and faces, you can use the same pose to create endless different faeries by varying their clothes, settings and expressions.

CROUCHING FAERIE

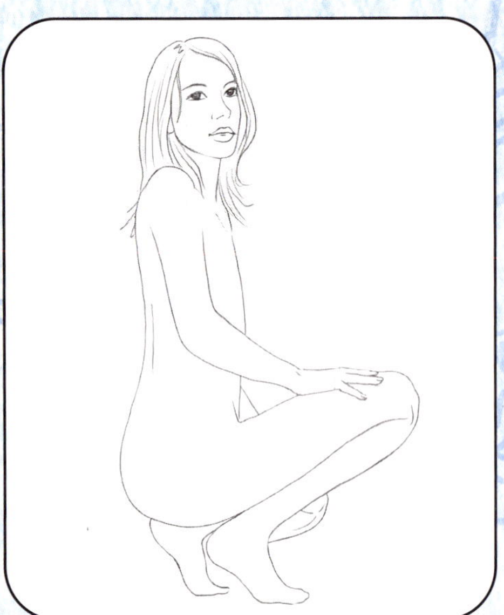

◀ This is a good faerie pose as she is daintily balancing on her toes, her hands are rested on her kness and her body is straight. We can quite easily find lots of different clothes to dress her in, find many different surfaces to balance her on, and accessorize her as much as we like. Think about what image you want your faerie to have, for instance you could create one faerie for each season; a cold frosty one for winter, a bright happy excited one for spring, a lazy warm feeling for summer and a rich glowing orangey brown for autumn. Even if you draw your faerie in graphite pencil only, you can still create a feeling of warmth or coldness in your shadows and the depth of tone. Why not trace this faerie pose and make your own version of her?

▶ Summer and autumn faeries

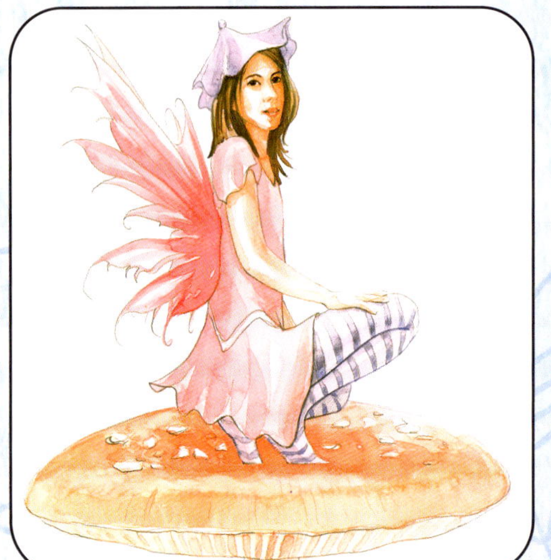

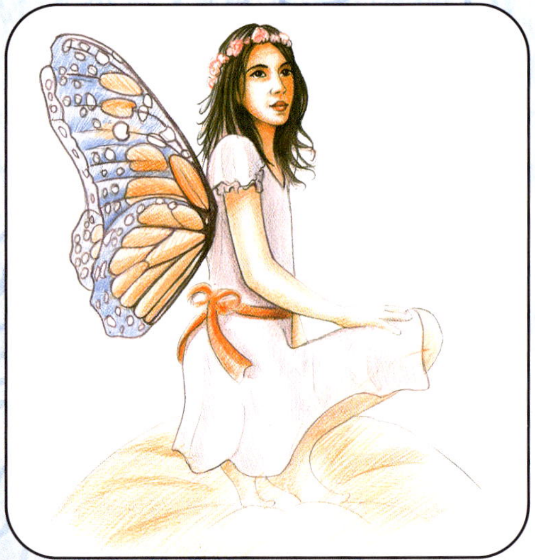

These show how the crouching pose can be turned into a summer and an autumn faerie. The summer faerie, sketched in graphite pencil then painted in watercolour, has bright red wings, full of warmth. She has a matching corset and stripy tights, and is perched on top of a Fly Agaric toadstool. These are fantastic for faerie paintings as their rich red colour and white spots are perfect for creating a warm painting.

In the second version the pose has been used to create an autumn faerie. It was sketched out in graphite pencil and then shaded in coloured pencils. She is perched on top of a pumpkin, which gives us a lovely warm orange-brown base. She has been dressed in a simple pretty dress with an autumnal orange bow to match the delicate blossom in her hair. Large wings have been chosen for this faerie and warm browns, oranges and ochres have been used to emulate the autumn leaves.

SITTING FAERIE

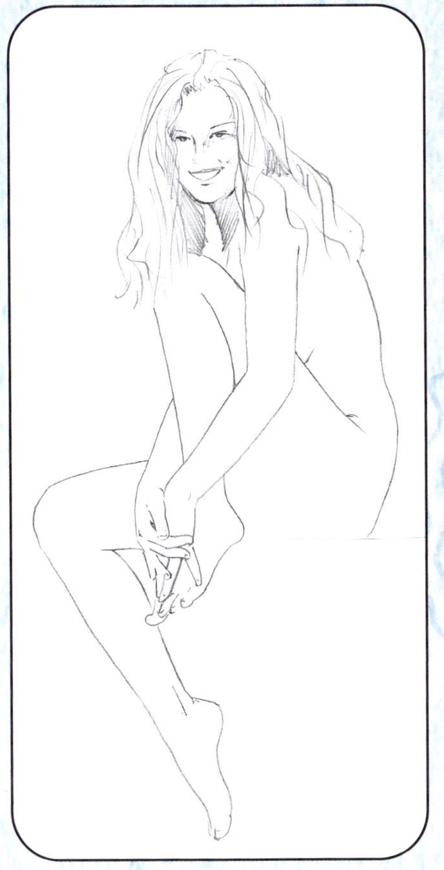

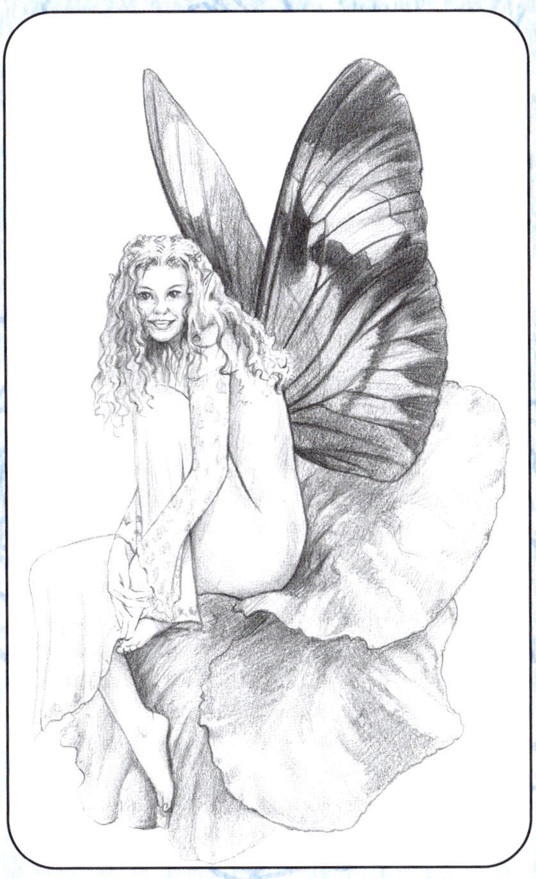

◀ Petal faerie

This faerie has been drawn in graphite pencil and she is sitting in the centre of a large flower. The faerie is wearing a long flowing dress and its crinkled edge resembles the edge of the petals. If we were to illustrate this in colour we could use similar colours for the flower, dress and the wings. The butterfly wings also echo the wrinkles and folds in the petal, and this, coupled with her long wavy hair, brings this faerie and her surroundings together as one.

▲ A faerie in a sitting pose is another typical and popular stance for a faerie. It's also one where the faerie can easily be placed on any surface or object found in nature. We could sit this faerie on many different objects – for example, a whole variety of flowers, any kind of greenery including leaves, stems, stalks, grasses and even brambles. We could sit her on a fallen tree trunk or a stone by a stream; we could even sit her on an old gnarled tree root in a hedgerow. The possibilities are endless. This faerie is also easy to clothe and accessorize. You could even adapt the faerie to her surroundings so that she is camouflaged: if your faerie was sitting on a daisy you could give her fair hair to match the centre of the flower, a white petal dress, green shoes and hair accessories. The choice is yours!

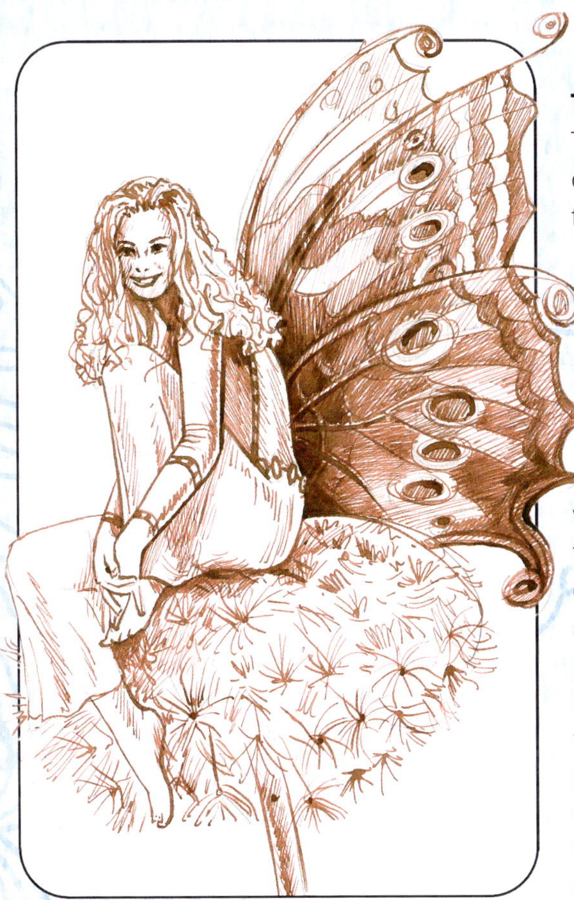

◀ Meadow faerie

This faerie is swaying on a dandelion in the middle of a field in the summer months. She has been drawn in pen and ink, giving some movement to the picture. The viewer can imagine her in the open meadow fluttering from flower to flower. The butterfly wings have been chosen for their swirling patterns and circles, adding to the flow and movement of the picture. Use your imagination and enhance the wings – add swirls, patterns or change their shape. Don't forget though that each wing must be a mirror image of the other!

Clothes & accessories

Designing faerie clothes is great fun. Faeries can wear anything, so magazines can be a good resource. They also wear clothes made from the natural environment. So they may have hats made of petals, dresses made of leaves, shoes made of berries, parasols made from daisies – the list goes on! Study the shapes of flowers and leaves and work out how they could become a faerie outfit. This page should give you some ideas of how you can put together your own faerie collection.

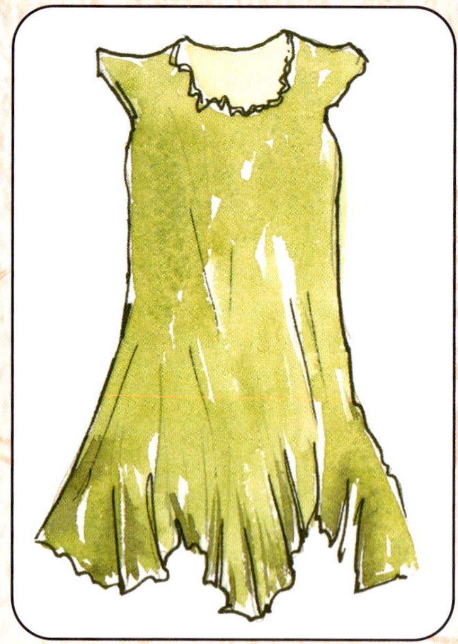

CLOTHES

◀ Leaves can be a good place to start when designing faerie clothes and this is a good example of how a faerie could tailor a simple dress from a large leaf. The edges of the dress are uneven to show a natural jagged edge. It has been painted an olive green but it could easily have been an autumn red, yellow or a bright spring green.

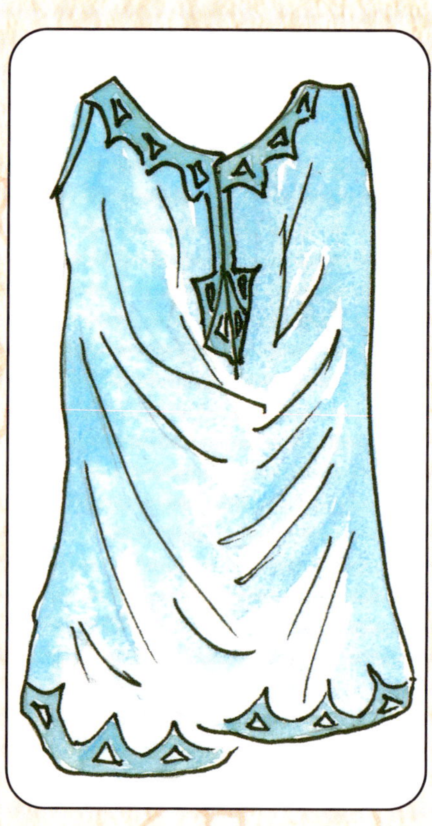

▶ Water faeries and faerie nymphs always wear shimmering blue colours as they live near lakes and rivers. This tunic has been painted cobalt blue and the flowing lines in it emulate the ripples in the water. You can also add patterns on the clothes as this adds interest in the piece.

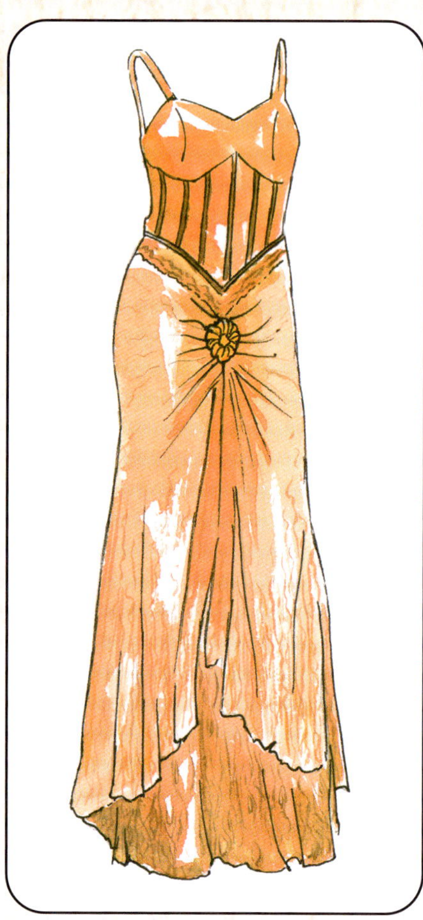

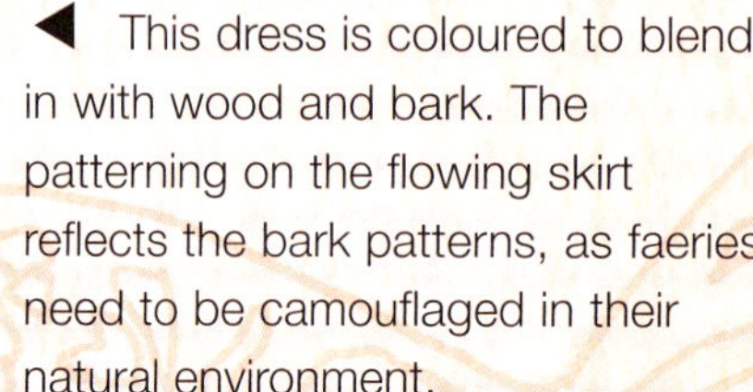

◀ This dress is coloured to blend in with wood and bark. The patterning on the flowing skirt reflects the bark patterns, as faeries need to be camouflaged in their natural environment.

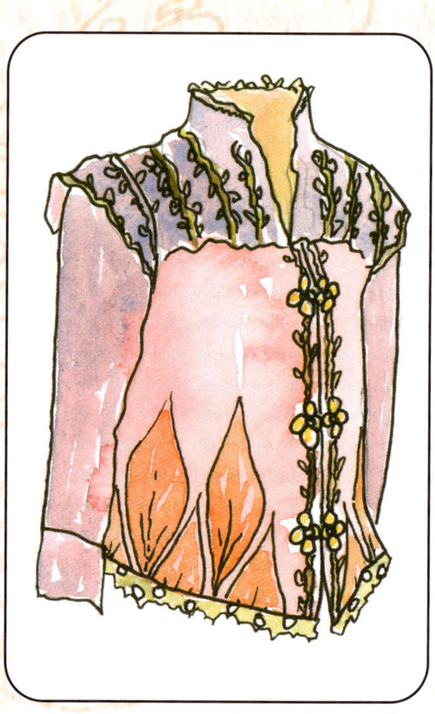

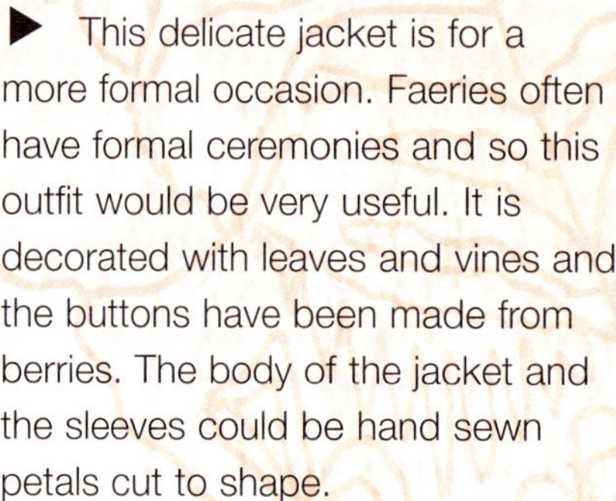

▶ This delicate jacket is for a more formal occasion. Faeries often have formal ceremonies and so this outfit would be very useful. It is decorated with leaves and vines and the buttons have been made from berries. The body of the jacket and the sleeves could be hand sewn petals cut to shape.

▶ Some young faeries like to be fashionable and so creating up-to-the-minute designs for them can be fun. This skirt is short and chic, and camouflaged too. The petals and leaves hanging down add interest to the piece and the colours mean that a faerie could hide in the undergrowth without being seen.

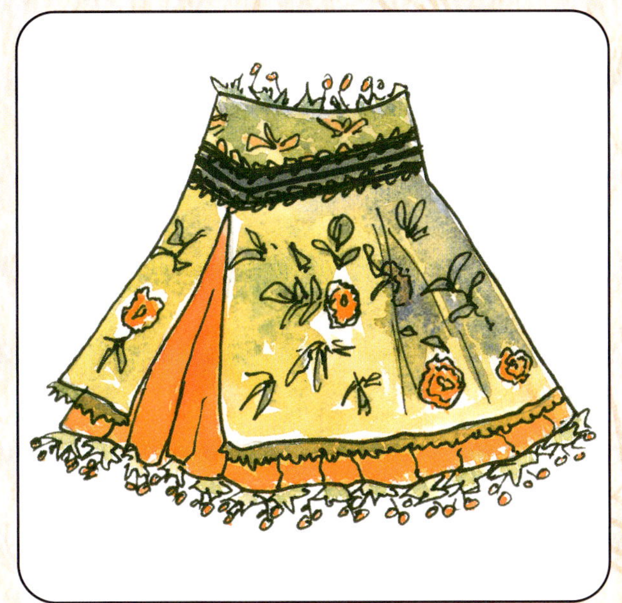

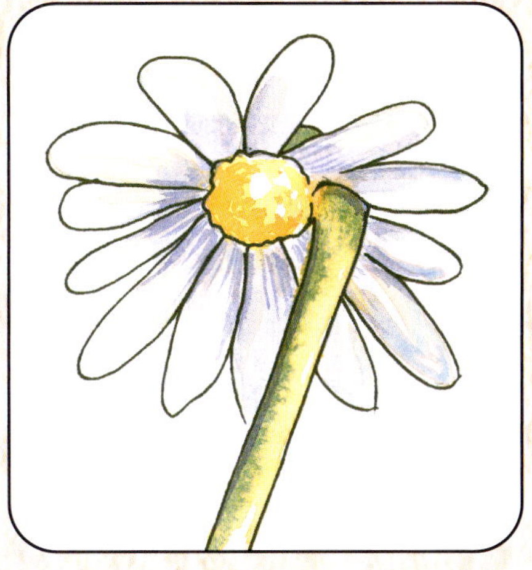

▲ This daisy has been turned into a parasol for flower faeries to shade themselves from the sunshine or rain. The stalk has been bent forward and pulled through the petals so that they can hold onto it and the flower shades them when they need it.

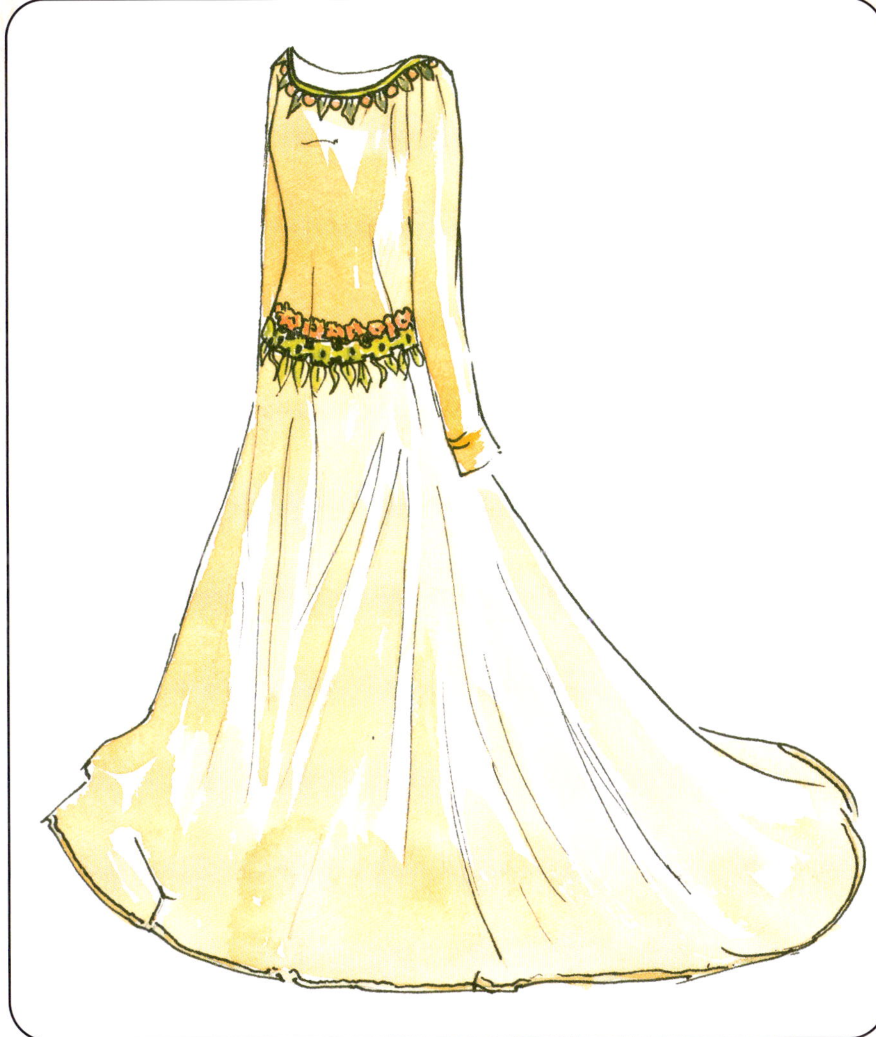

▲ This long flowing dress is for an elegant ethereal faerie. The small flowers and vines around the waist and the neckline add pretty detail, just enough for a beautiful, graceful faerie.

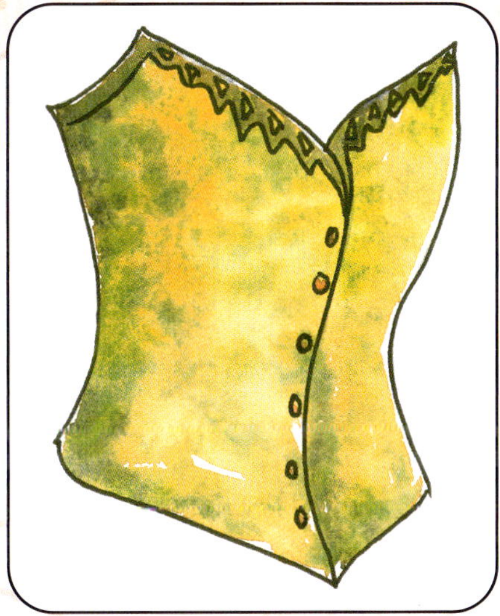

▲ Bodices and corsets are suited to dark faeries, and this corset has leaf patterns created by a wet-in-wet wash in greens and oranges. You could try many colours: this one would camouflage a faerie in a woodland scene. If you were painting a dark faerie in a night-time scene you could create a very dark blue corset and even add some salt into the paint while it's drying for a starry patterned effect.

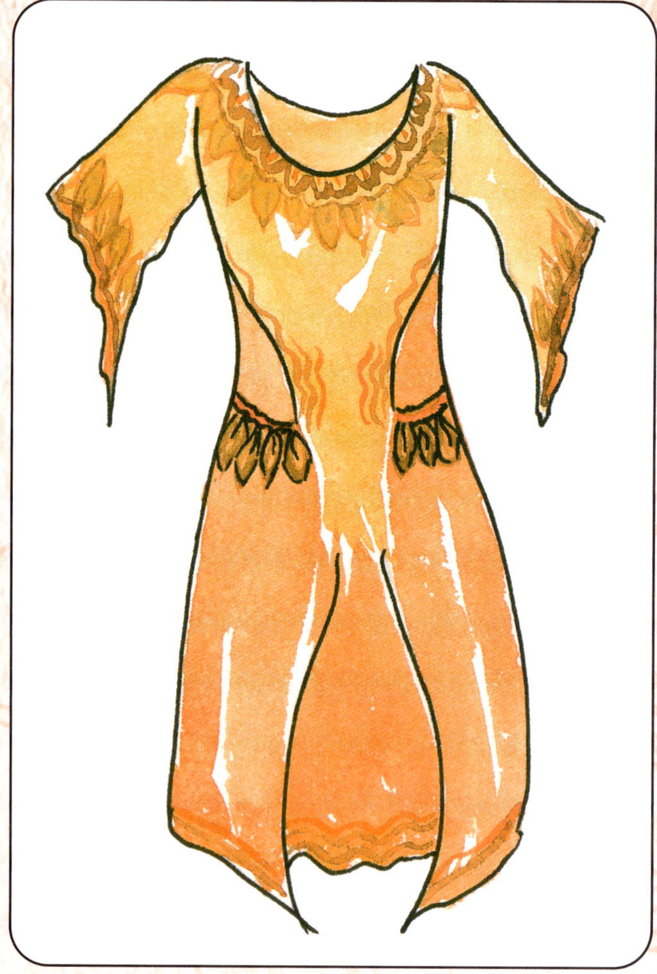

▲ This dress will camouflage faeries in the autumn, so the faerie can dance around the woodland without being seen. It can be held together by tiny grasses, and delicate leaves are used to decorate the neckline and sleeves.

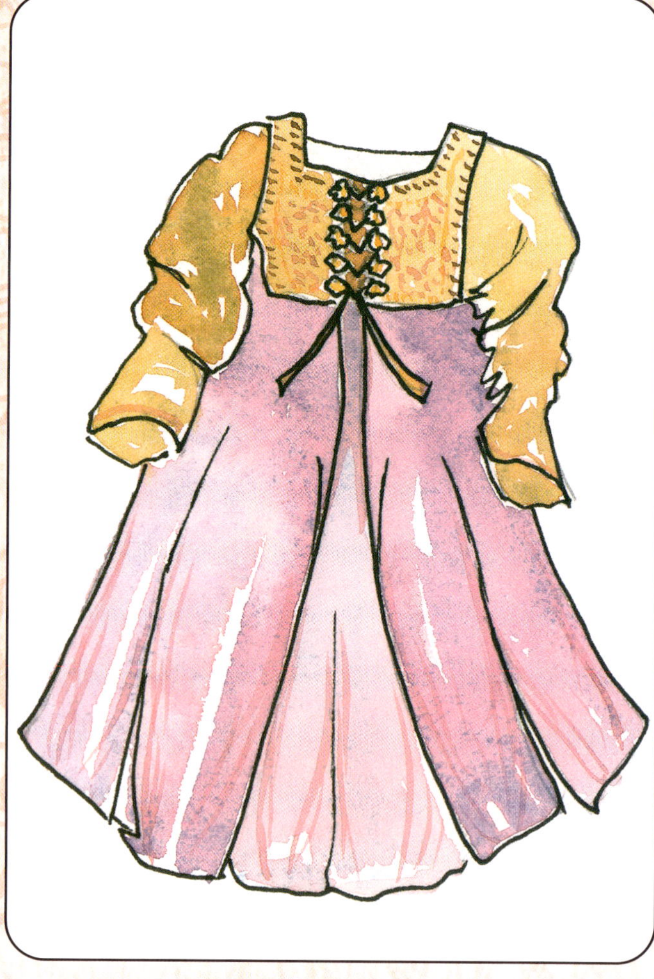

▲ This dress has a Victorian feel to it. Clothes of the Victorian and Georgian era really suit faeries and this one is perfect for a very young sprite or dryad.

FAERIE SHOES & ACCESSORIES

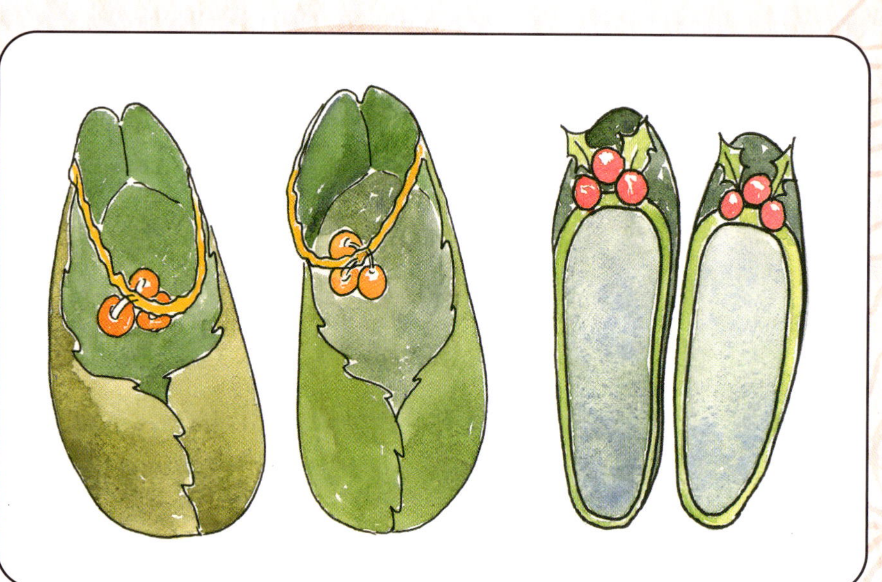

◀ Faeries often wear shoes fashioned from leaves and petals. The first illustration here shows how a single leaf can be folded over with a vine and some berries used as a tie. The second illustration has a seasonal feel, decorated with holly and berries.

▶ Stripy socks are a must for many faeries and you can have endless fun designing the different colours and stripes on socks and tights for your creations to wear.

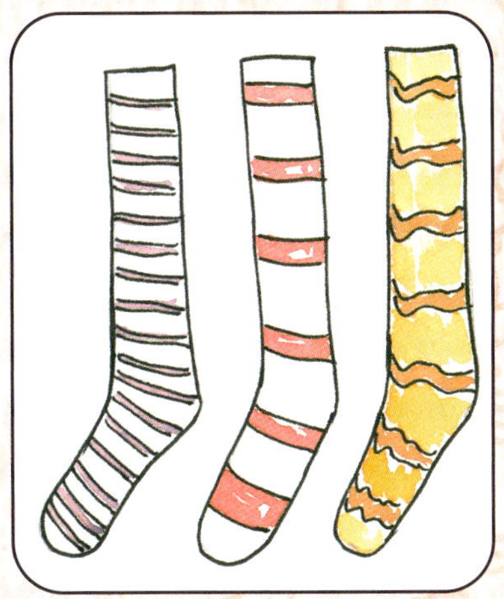

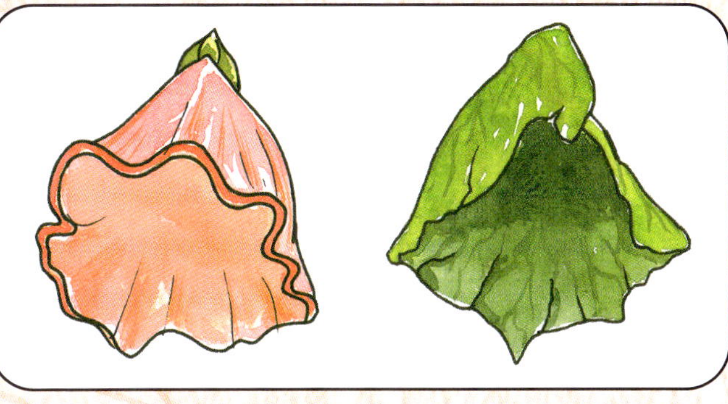

▲ Young faeries and particularly flower faeries often wear hats. These illustrations depict one made from a petal and one from a large leaf. The leaf curls around and sits on the head of the faerie to protect her from the rain and cold. In the summer faeries have lots of choice as to which flowers they would like to use as hats. Flowers in a bell shape are the most popular; this one is a petal from a foxglove. Bluebells and snowdrops are also excellent to make into hats.

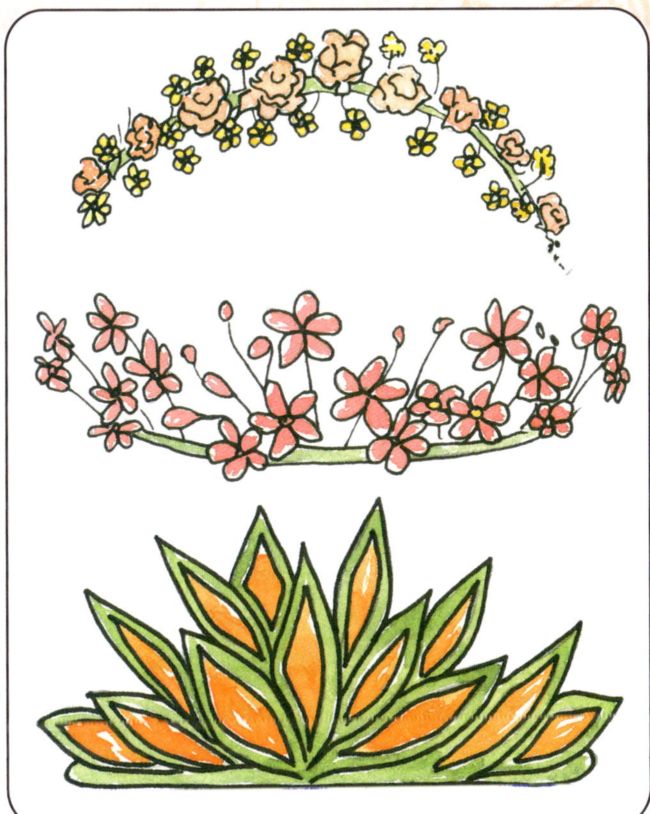

▲ Faeries adorn themselves with all kinds of decorations, jewellery and headdresses. Study the smaller varieties of grasses, mosses and flowers as they can be a great source of inspiration for small faerie accessories. The first illustration here shows how you can create a headband for a young faerie using pink flowers and a vine to keep them in place. The second is of a tiara with deep red flowers; this could be used for either an adult dark faerie or an ethereal faerie. The crown has been made from leaves, whose centres have been cut out and orange petals sewn in their place so that they are translucent. A faerie seen wearing this crown would have to be very important in the faerie realm.

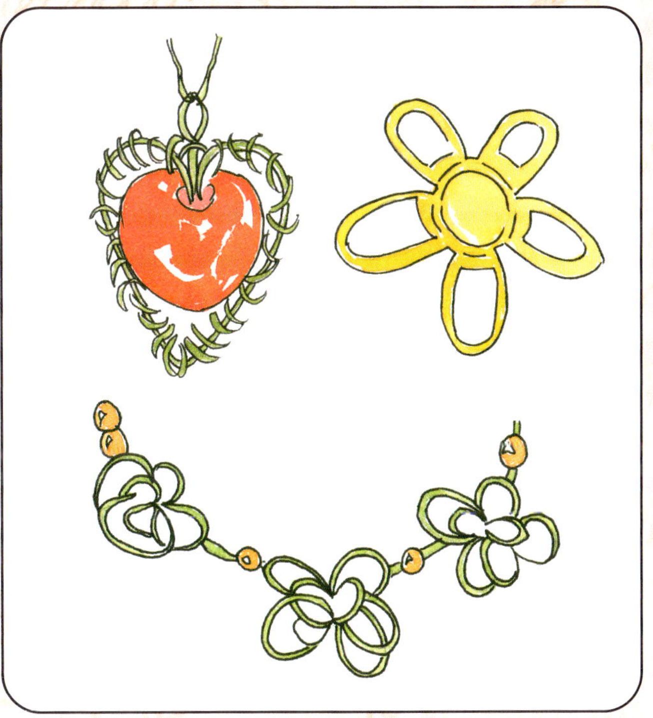

▲ Jewellery is favourite adornment and many of a faerie's treasures are made from the natural items found in their environment. This heart-shaped pendant is made from grasses and a red berry in the centre. The bottom necklace has been made from fine quality vines and orange berries, delicately curled to give extra detail. The drawing of a daisy-shaped piece is suitable for a young flower faerie. It's bold and simple and not easy for them to lose when playing in the hedgerows!

Creating different faeries

There are many different types of faeries in the faerie kingdom. In general, faeries are all usually described as more or less human in appearance and as having some sort of magical ability, such as flying, casting spells or foreseeing the future. Each type of faerie is different in character and form, from where it lives to the clothes it wears. Each is often associated with a particular place or area, such as the flower faeries, the woodland faeries and water faeries. The following pages illustrate six different types of faerie and explain a little about each one's habitat, background and how you can create a similar drawing or painting of that faerie.

NYMPH

Nymphs are considered to be very shy creatures: beautiful and graceful, they protect all the natural woodlands, rivers and streams.

In this illustration we have a nymph standing in a shallow pool of water, possibly on the edge of a fresh water stream. She would be naturally surrounded by woodland and foliage. We can see that she is pulling at a vine, almost hiding her face behind the leaves. She is a shy creature and avoids any sort of confrontation, although she will be guarding her natural habitat.

She has been painted in watercolour which gives her an intangible air, the olive colours in her flowing dress allowing her to blend in easily with the trees and leaves. Her wings are translucent and are cool in colour so that they recede and almost disappear into the background if needed.

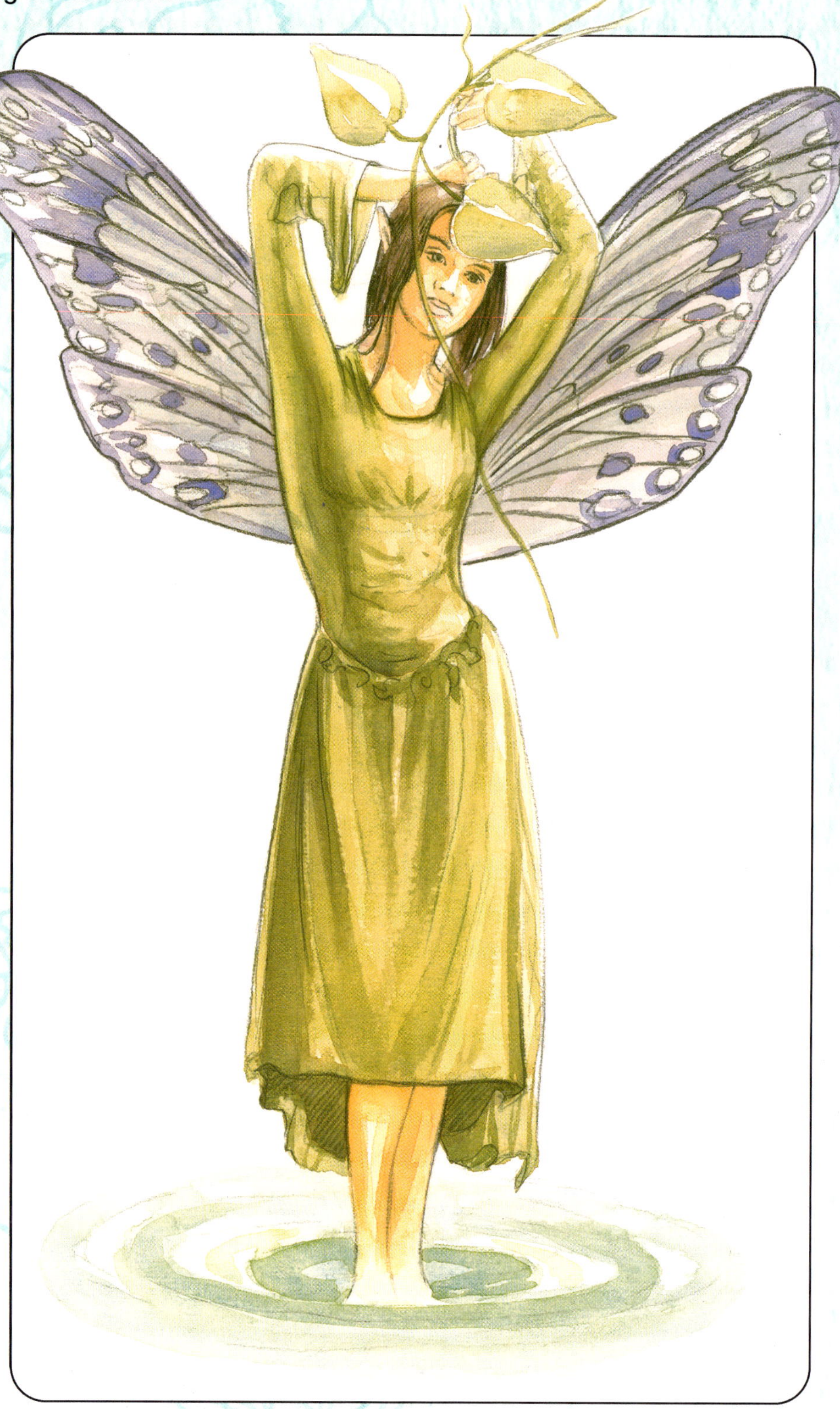

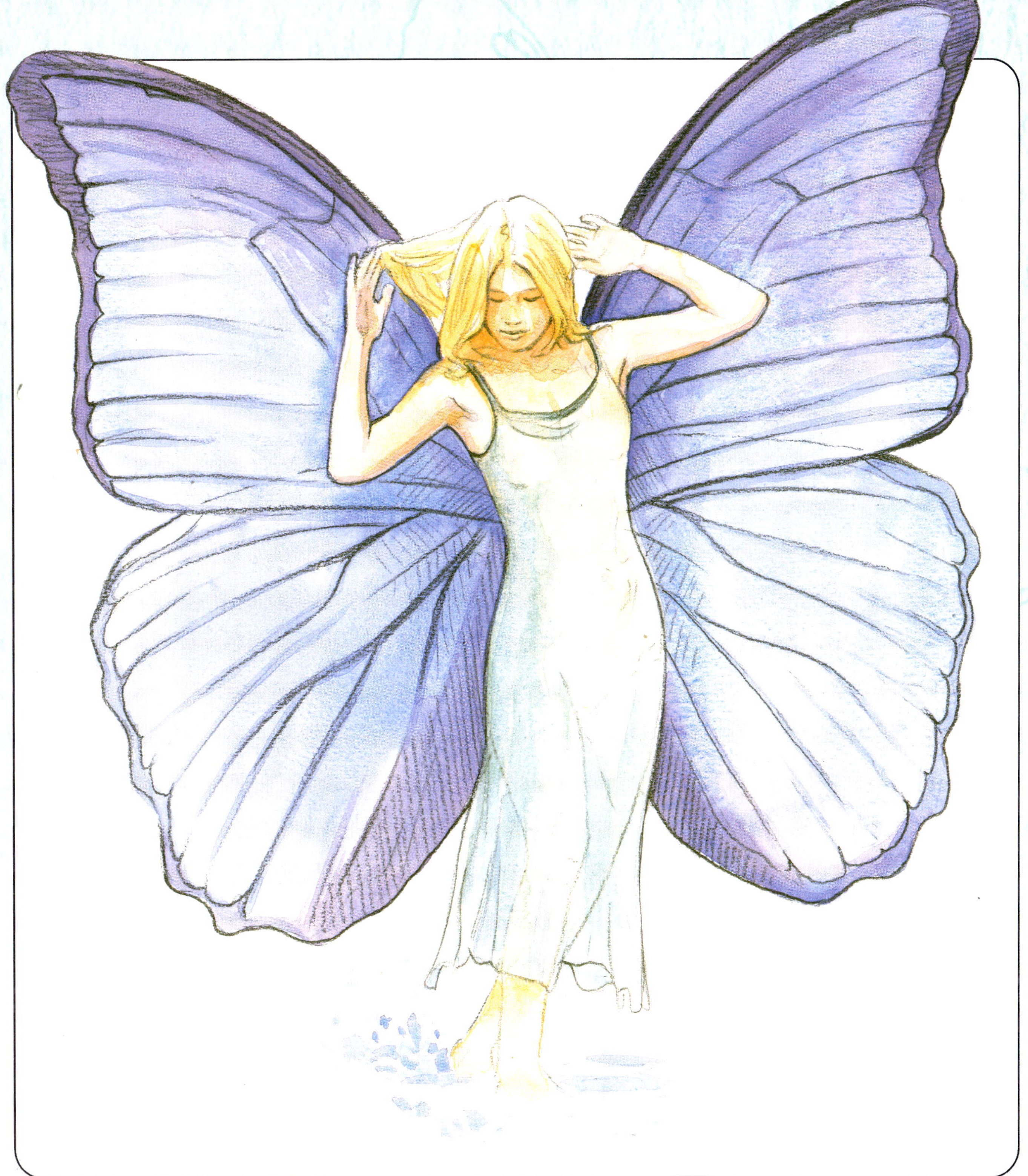

WATER FAERIE

Water faeries, also known as water sprites, are said to protect all bodies of water, from the largest oceans to the smallest stream. They are said to be able to breathe both water and air, and are mostly harmless unless threatened. They can camouflage themselves in the water, and if a human pollutes their waters, they can take on a different form to retaliate. They might appear to you ugly and terrifying, or shower you with a storm. If, however, you are kind to them they may appear to you as in this illustration – a beautiful, ethereal, fair-haired beauty.

This water faerie is splashing in the cool water on a summer's day. It is painted with watercolour, the perfect medium for a water faerie. She is wearing a long flowing dress the colour of cobalt blue. Her large butterfly wings reflect the water beneath her and keep her cool in the warm sunshine.

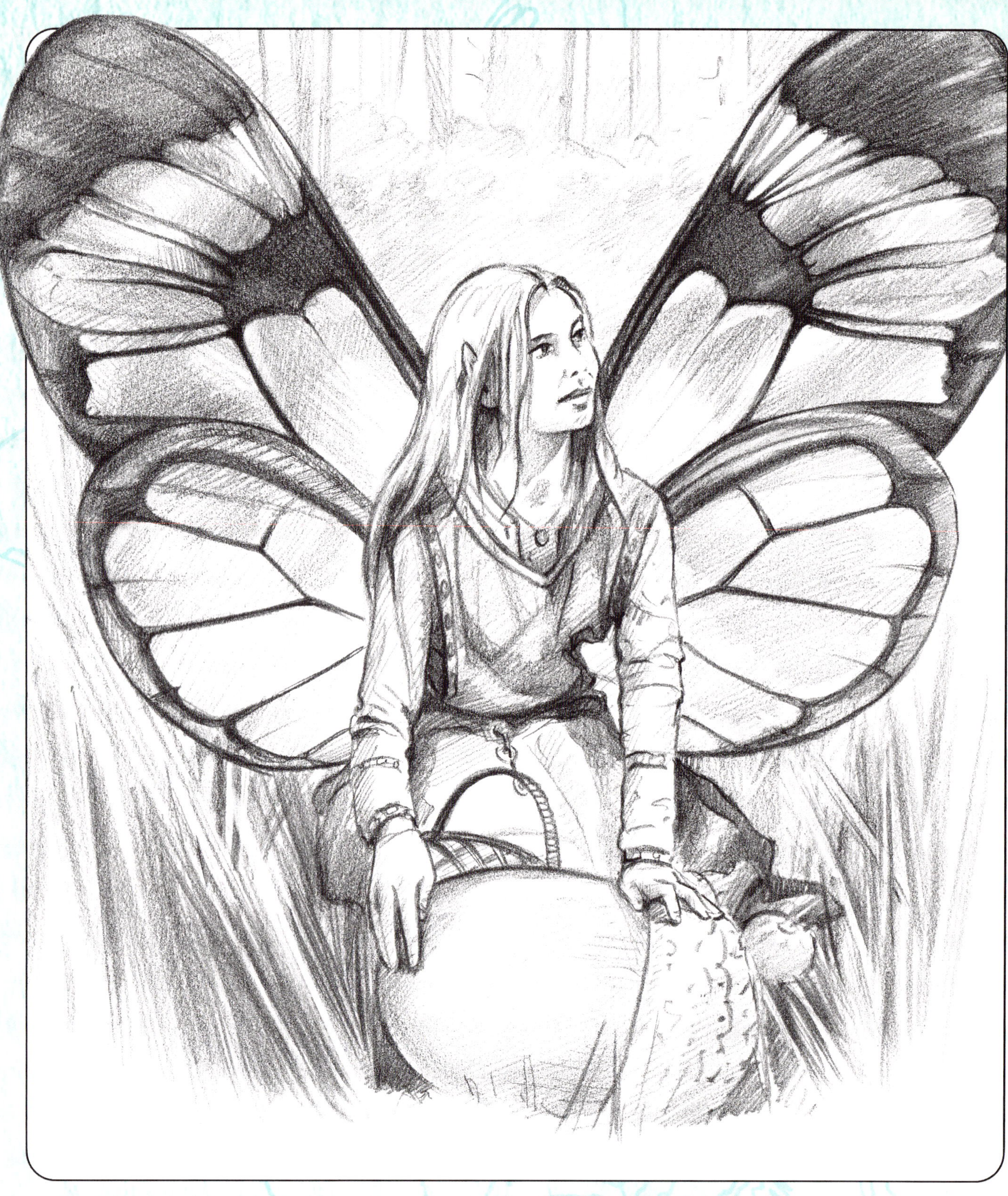

DRYAD

Dryads live in far-away, forgotten forests where prying eyes can't find them. They are essentially tree nymphs; each dryad is connected to just one particular tree in its lifetime and when that tree dies, the dryad dies with it.

This illustration is of a nymph protecting the fruit of her tree. She is guarding her oak tree and will often be depicted as being part of or as one with the tree, sometimes only with her face visible. The faerie depicted here is warm-hearted and friendly and her soft wings, translucent in places, shine in the dappled light of the woodland. Tree nymphs leave their trees in the evening to dance in the woodland clearings along with other tree nymphs in the moonlight.

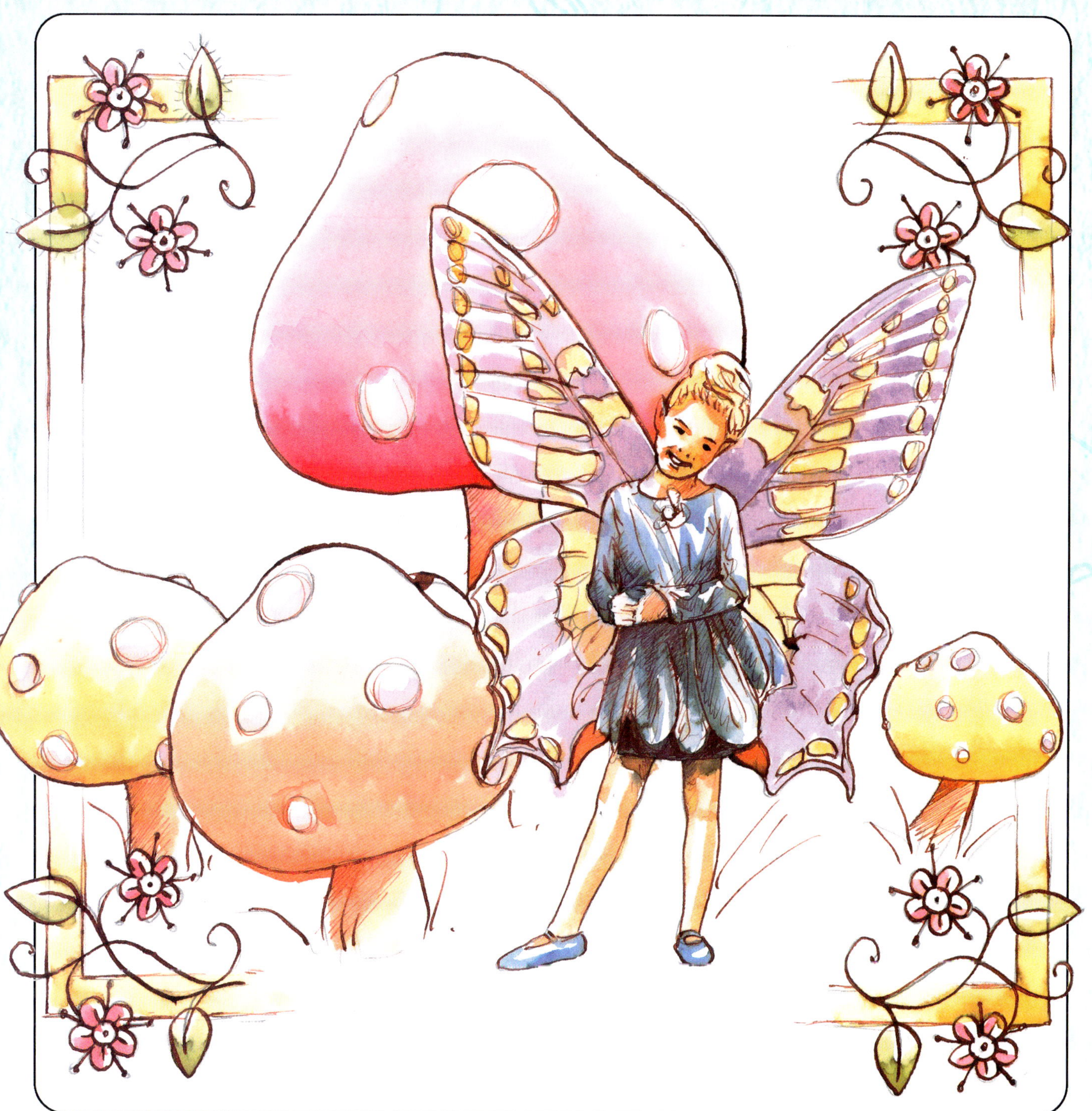

SPRITE

Sprites are small elf-like creatures and live up to their name – sprightly, lively and happy. They are known for changing the seasons between autumn and winter and bridging the gap between the mystical world and our human world with a rainbow.

With this in mind I painted this little sprite in a lovely, colourful scene with pretty toadstools and flowers. The sprite has large, patterned, swallowtail butterfly wings which mimic her blue petal dress and shoes.

This illustration was drawn in pencil, and lined over using sepia pen and ink and then a watercolour wash was added. The border adds just that little bit of extra decoration to the scene with the motifs of flowers, leaves and vines. You can experiment with many different types of borders around your work, or do as I have done here, overlapping the edges to bring the border and picture together. A sprite's face is always going to be dainty and here I have given her a happy-go-lucky character with a broad smile and small nose. Everything about sprites is dainty, small and slender, so keep this in mind when you are drawing your own versions.

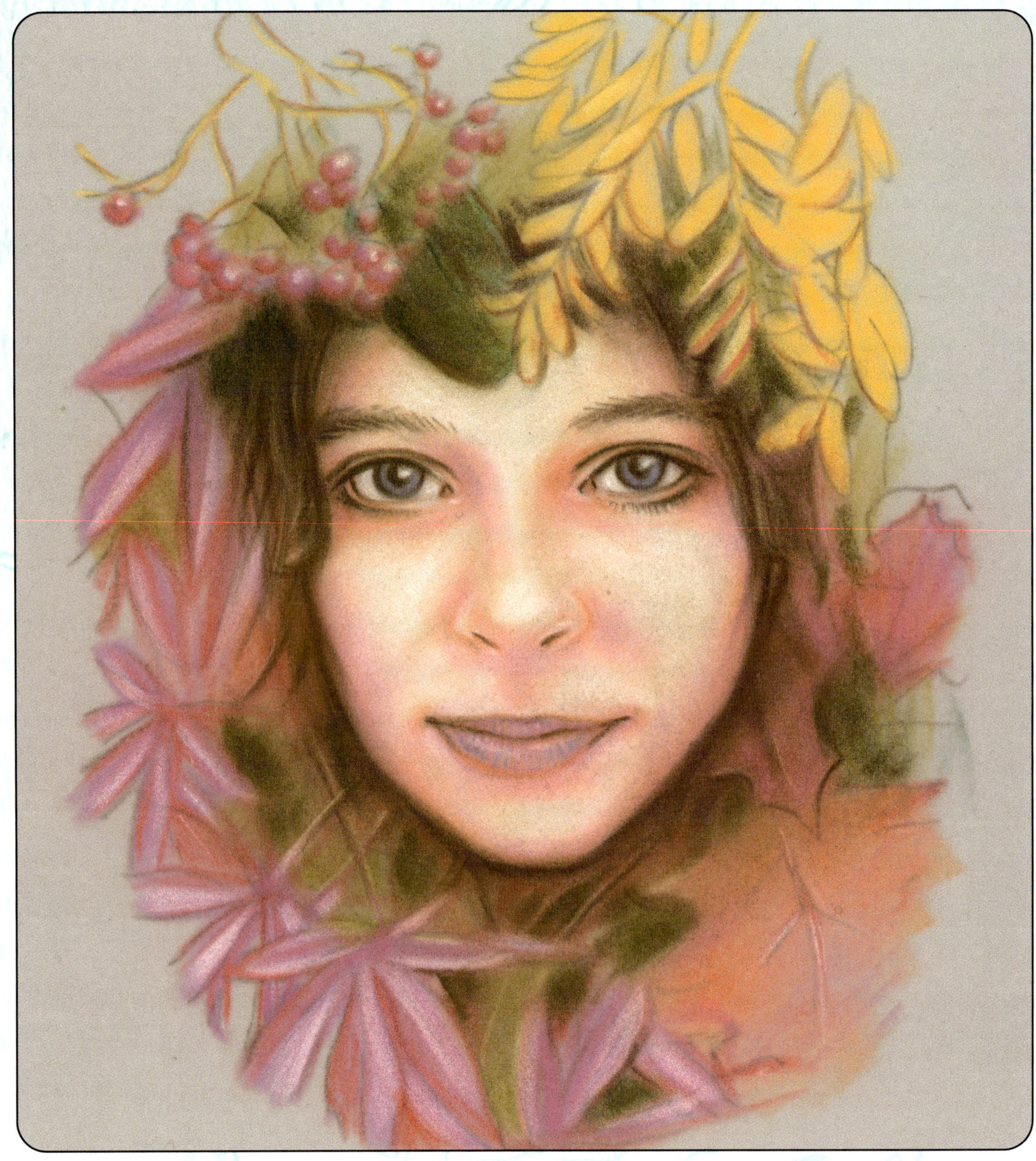

ELEMENTAL FAERIE

Elemental faeries are part of the four elements that make up the world around us – fire, water, air and earth. They each have characteristics identifying them with the element that they embody with their incredible powers. This illustration depicts a face peeping though the foliage and leaves, which distinguish her clearly as an Earth faerie. She protects plants and trees and is at one with them.

The Earth faerie drawing was created in pastel sticks and pastel pencils on soft velour paper. I sketched out the face and arranged some foliage around it in an oval to create a vignette. Creating this type of composition makes a drawing more dramatic as it really feels like the faerie is peeking though a dense amount of foliage. The colours are important, as the deep red tones and warm ochres and yellows frame the face, and her skin and eyes glow with radiance.

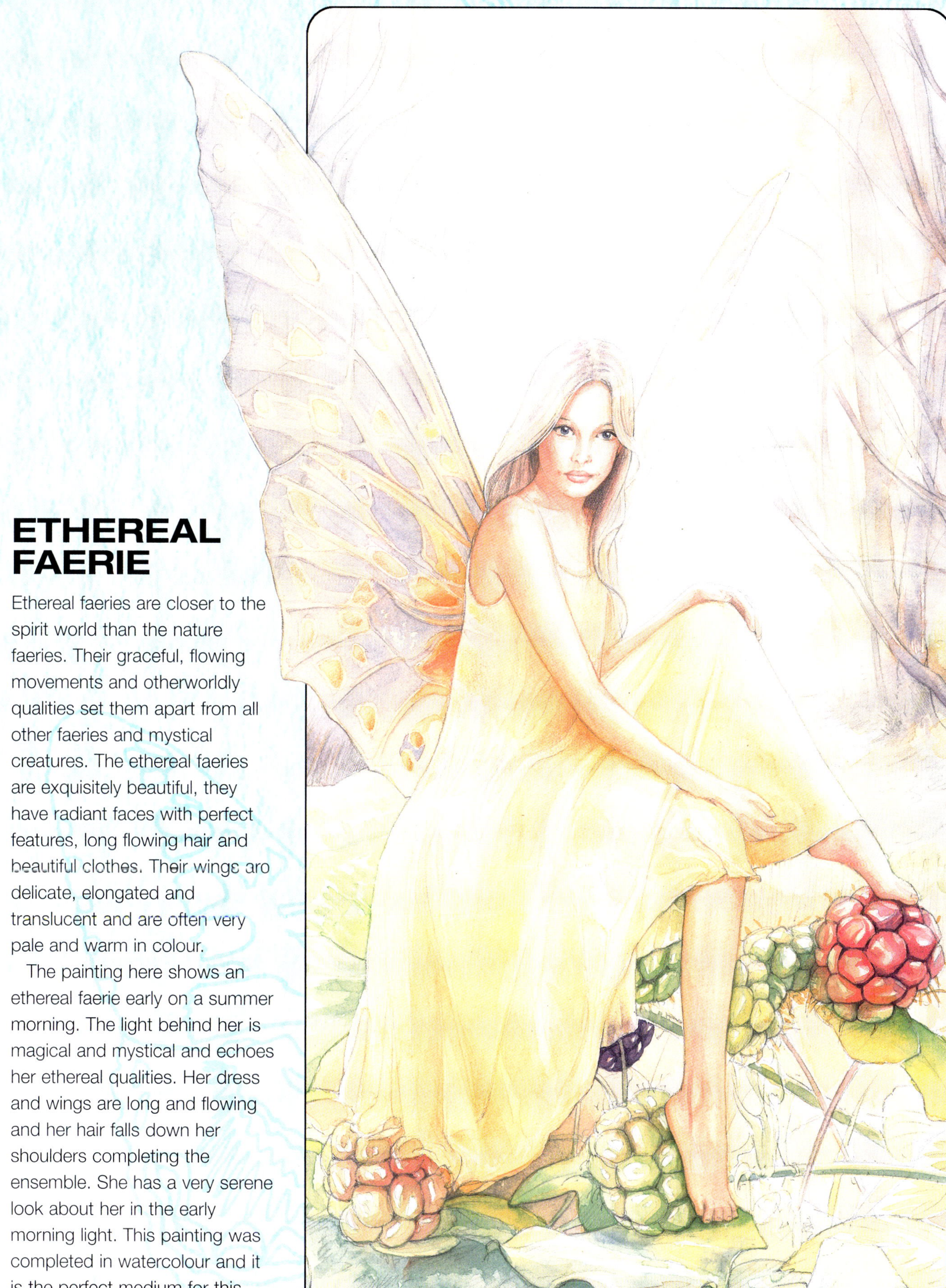

ETHEREAL FAERIE

Ethereal faeries are closer to the spirit world than the nature faeries. Their graceful, flowing movements and otherworldly qualities set them apart from all other faeries and mystical creatures. The ethereal faeries are exquisitely beautiful, they have radiant faces with perfect features, long flowing hair and beautiful clothes. Their wings are delicate, elongated and translucent and are often very pale and warm in colour.

The painting here shows an ethereal faerie early on a summer morning. The light behind her is magical and mystical and echoes her ethereal qualities. Her dress and wings are long and flowing and her hair falls down her shoulders completing the ensemble. She has a very serene look about her in the early morning light. This painting was completed in watercolour and it is the perfect medium for this type of faerie.

FLOWER FAERIES

Flower faeries are born in a flower whose characteristics they then take on, using the petals and leaves for clothes and flitting from flower to flower, nurturing them. They help plants and flowers to grow and each has their own special job in the garden. There are many different types of flower faeries and all of them love nothing more than to play and dance amongst the flowers and undergrowth.

Creating a flower faerie study

To make your flower faerie composition, start collecting photos, clippings and pictures and lay out those that you feel would work well together. I found and copied three photos that I think will work well as a faerie study.

▼ This butterfly is light and warm in colour and not only simple to draw because of its shape, but also easy to make into faerie wings.

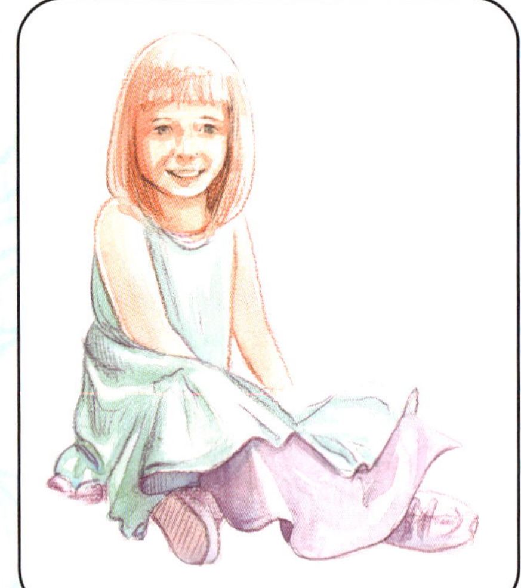

◀ I also found a picture of a small girl with a rounded appearance, sitting crossed legged. Her hair was petal shaped, her dress was long and flowing and I felt she would be the perfect candidate for a buttercup flower faerie.

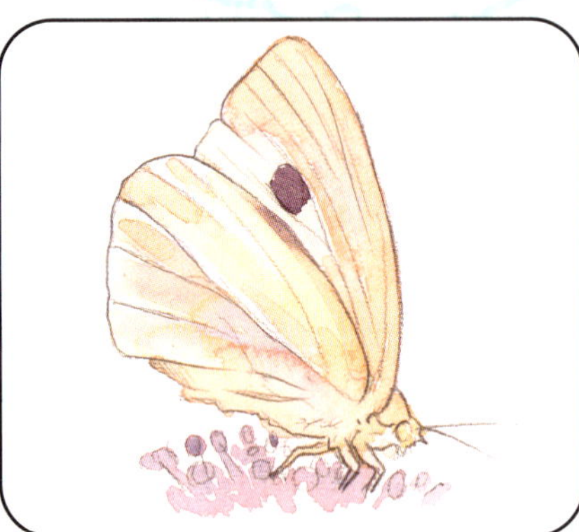

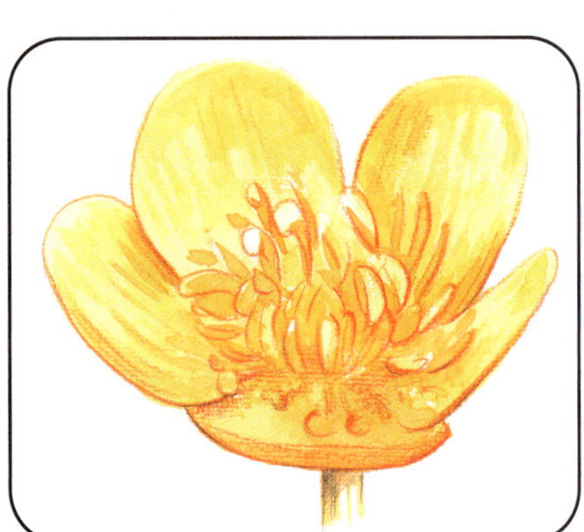

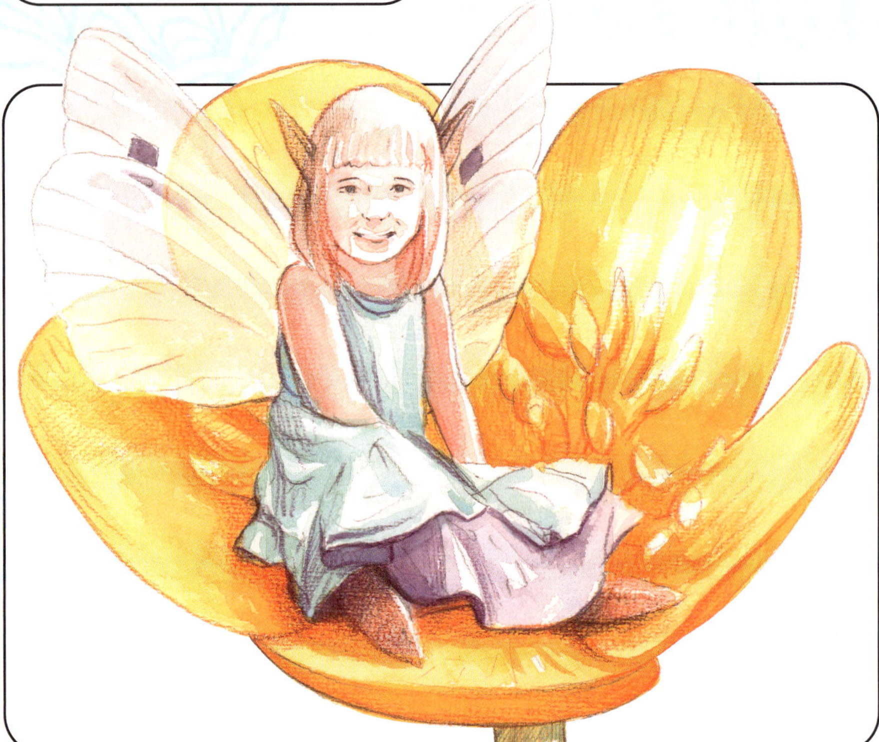

▲ The butterfly has a touch of yellow and is very round in shape so it reminded me of a buttercup. I felt the two would look great together so I have opted to create a buttercup flower faerie.

▲ Here the three images have been joined together. The flower is much larger to accommodate the faerie which gives scale to the image, and shows how small and delicate faeries are. I changed the little girl's shoes into pointed shoes and gave her pointed ears to match. Her wings join at her back between her shoulder blades, and I painted the flower behind a little lighter to show the wings' translucency.

Creating a full flower faerie composition

Now see if you can create a full painting of a flower faerie using the same process.

Collect photos and images that inspire you. You will need a background, a flower, a butterfly, a person and any clothing or accessories you wish to include. I chose to create a daisy faerie and found a close-up photo of a daisy. I felt that darker wings would add contrast and so chose a dark butterfly. I then found a photo of a child dancing, wearing a simple dress. Finally I found a smaller daisy and am going to work upon the idea that the daisy faerie is going to be holding a daisy in her hands as a parasol to shade her from the sunshine.

Next sketch ideas of how all these elements could fit together. Don't forget that the colours can be changed when you are working on your final painting; you could combine it all by integrating one colour theme throughout.

Using a soft pencil and some copy paper, sketch out a few ideas of how your composition could look. Place all your photos in front of you and try to fit them together. Don't forget to put the horizon line on one of the magic thirds, and think about where you will place the subject to be aesthetically pleasing. You can also try to emulate how a computer crops into a picture, so instead of having your faerie very small in the centre of the page, you can make her the main focus of the piece.

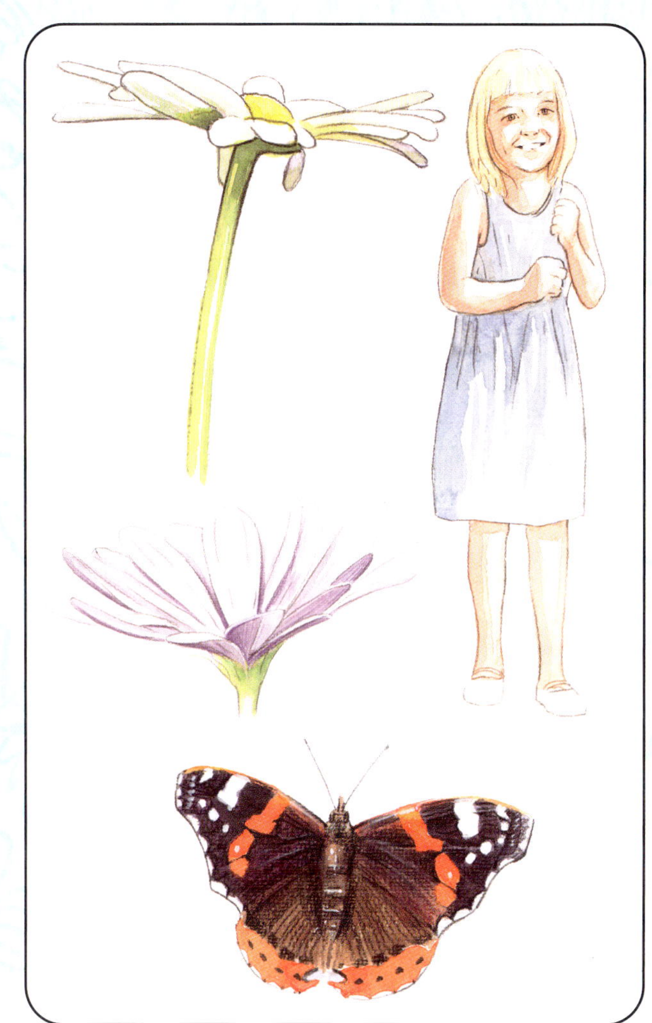

▶ To begin the process I sketched out the girl I wanted to turn into a flower faerie and fitted the butterfly wings on her back. I also worked out how she would hold the daisy so that she could hold it above her head as a parasol.

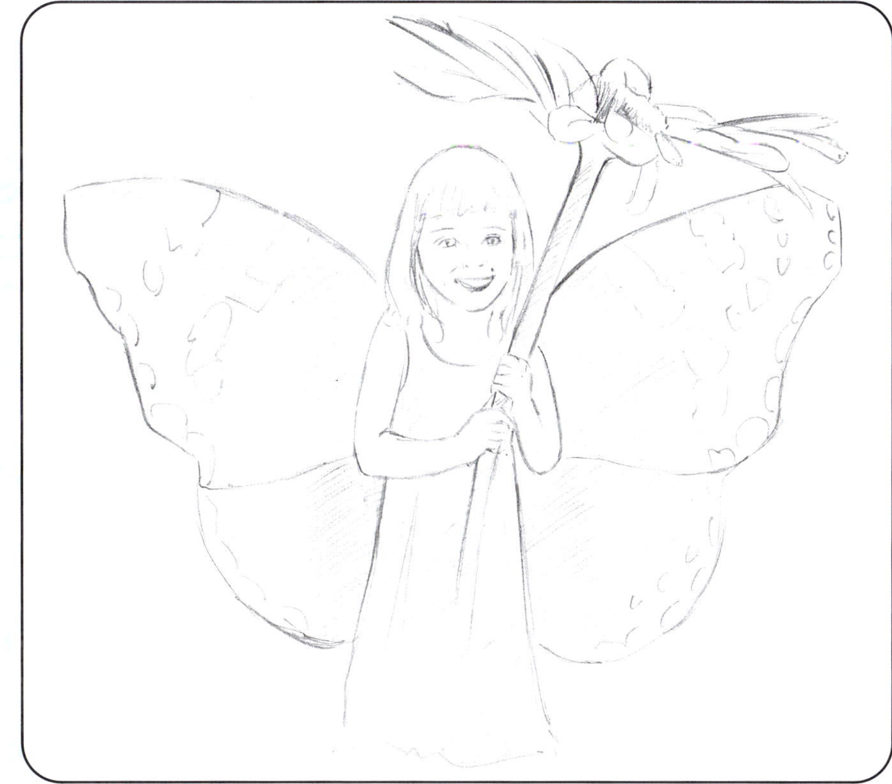

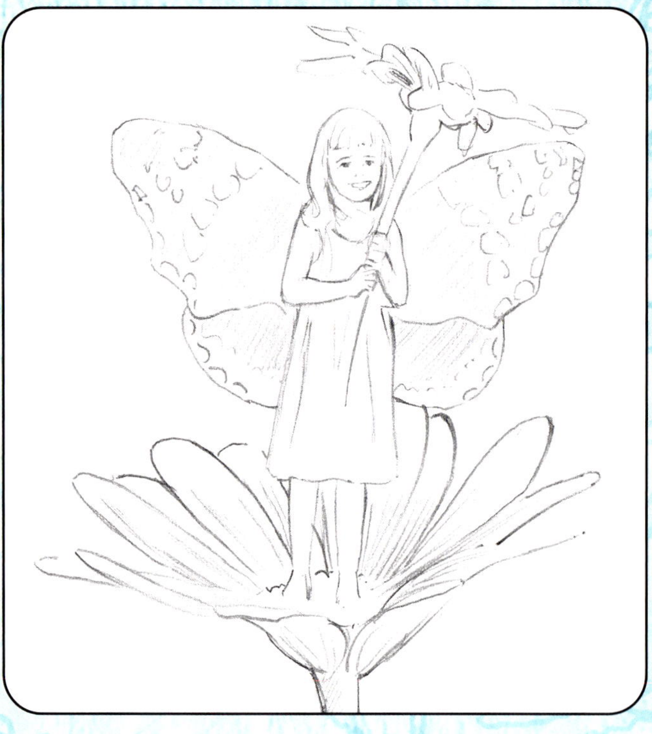

▲ I then needed to make sure the faerie could stand safely on the larger daisy. I sketched my idea again and felt that it could be a successful composition. I decided I wanted to paint it in watercolour as the beautiful translucent feel of the medium will enhance both the wings and the daisy.

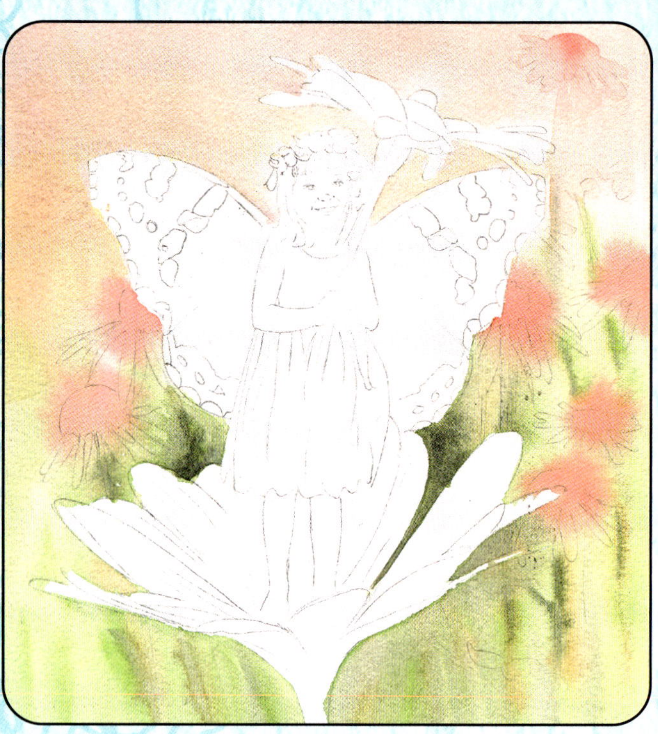

▲ I drew out my composition onto watercolour paper. The first stage was to paint a background using a wet-in-wet technique. I used a photo with red flowers in the distance which would pick up the red in the wings. The background is usually the first area to paint and, if you want, you can use masking fluid on the daisy and faerie shape. You must make sure it's thoroughly dry before starting on the next stage or removing the fluid.

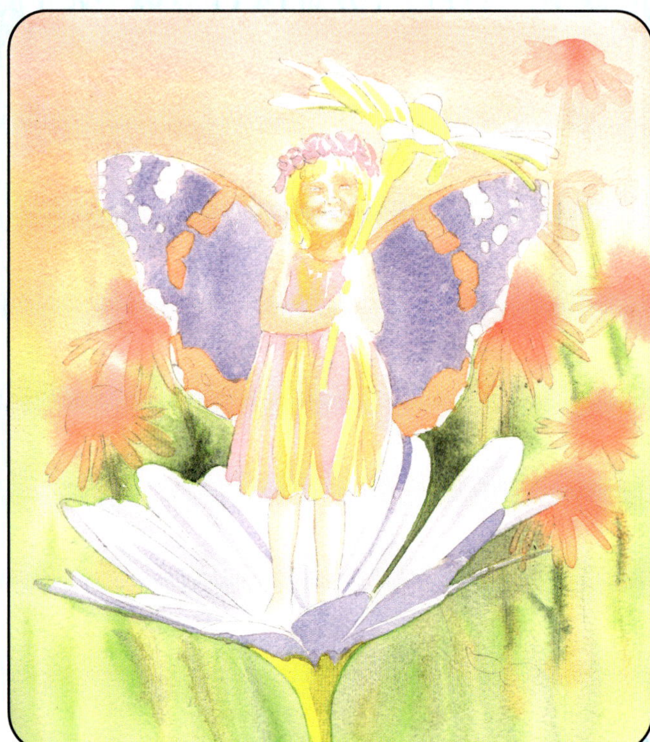

◀ The second stage is to paint in the faerie, the wings and the daisy but I have painted them as an undercoat. We only want to block in the basic colours. Remember to mix lots of water with your colours to keep them light, as the aim here is to keep the composition looking fairly translucent, so that you can still see the paper colour through the paint.

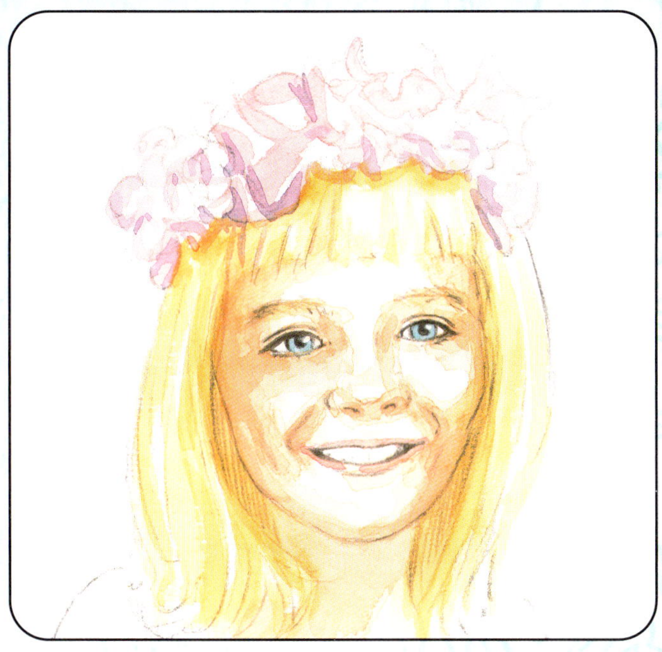

▲ I have drawn and painted a close-up of the faerie's face to show how much detail to add into the face itself. Try not to draw harsh outlines to the face, use a sharp pencil (preferably a 2B), and press lightly when drawing out the features. You can then use colour to lightly shade in the different tones.

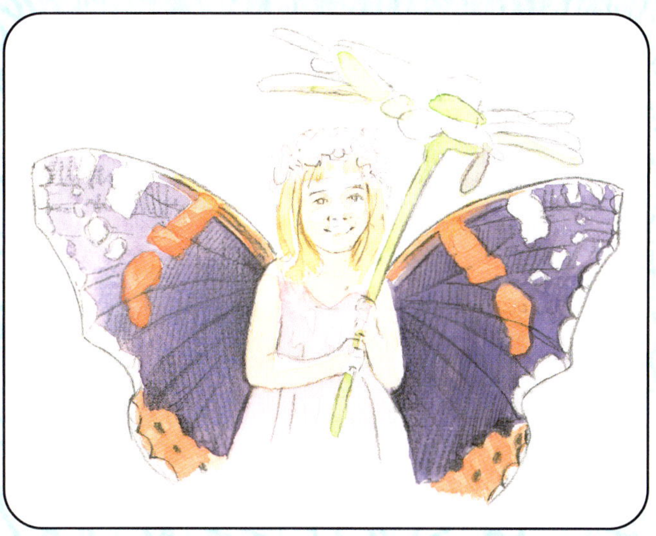

▲ This is a detail of the faerie and her butterfly wings. As you can see I have painted the wings a purple colour. The real Red Admiral's wings were brown, but this could have created a dull and muddy feel to the piece. Changing them to purple and blue instead keeps the wings looking fresh and pretty. A good tip for wings: lighten them as they get to the edges and tips, and keep them deeper in tone towards the body, because the faeries' body will cast a shadow on them.

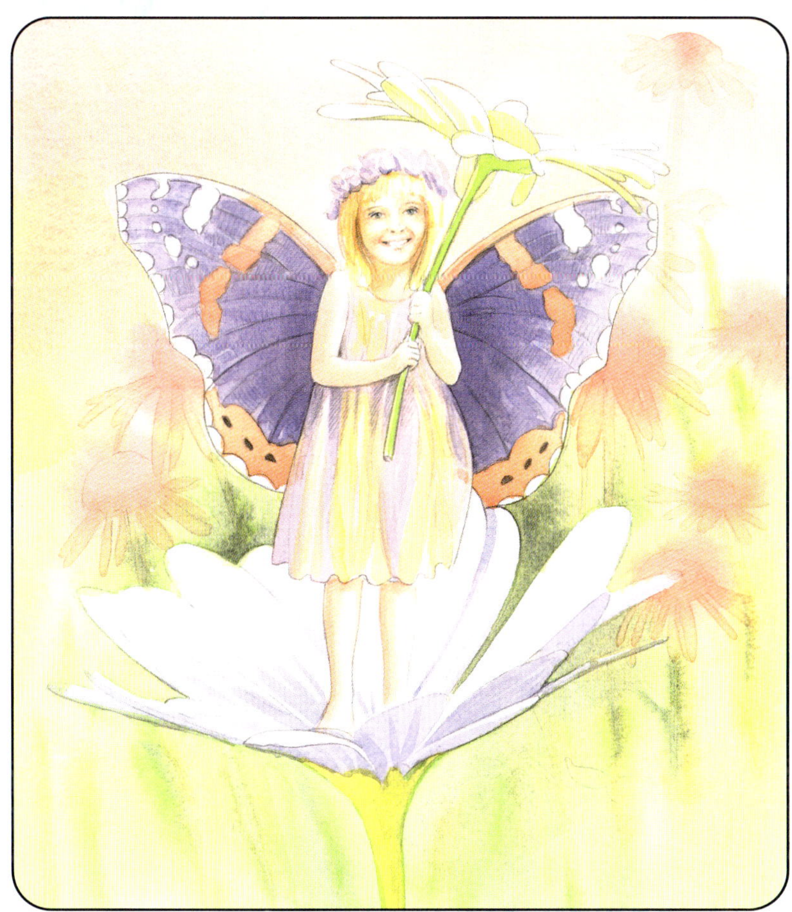

◀ Here is the final painting. Now that the last areas of detail have been added, you can see that the background had to be blurred to allow the foreground to come forward and be the focus of the scene. Using the wet-in-wet technique for the background is a good idea here, as it creates a beautifully soft and blurry effect. You can see that you don't need to use the watercolour too thickly: it's better to keep your colours light and fresh. If you feel you need to strengthen up some of the lines, you can add some coloured or graphite pencil in various places – particularly for the hands and face, as they may need a little definition. Don't forget to keep your pencils sharp at all times so that when you draw in these areas you will be using very fine lines.

DARK FAERIES

Not all faeries are charming, kind and concerned with protecting nature. There is another set of faeries that are the complete opposite: the dark faeries. These can be mysterious, dangerous and wicked. Unfortunately, the faerie kingdom is subject to evil just like the human realm and the dark faeries reveal themselves in many different forms.

The Snow Queen

This is a very beautiful faerie. She can be sweetness and light when she wants to be but she usually has a hidden agenda – in reality she is cold, icy and evil. This close-up of her face shows it is hidden by a magical mask so she cannot be recognised and can morph into the human world without being noticed.

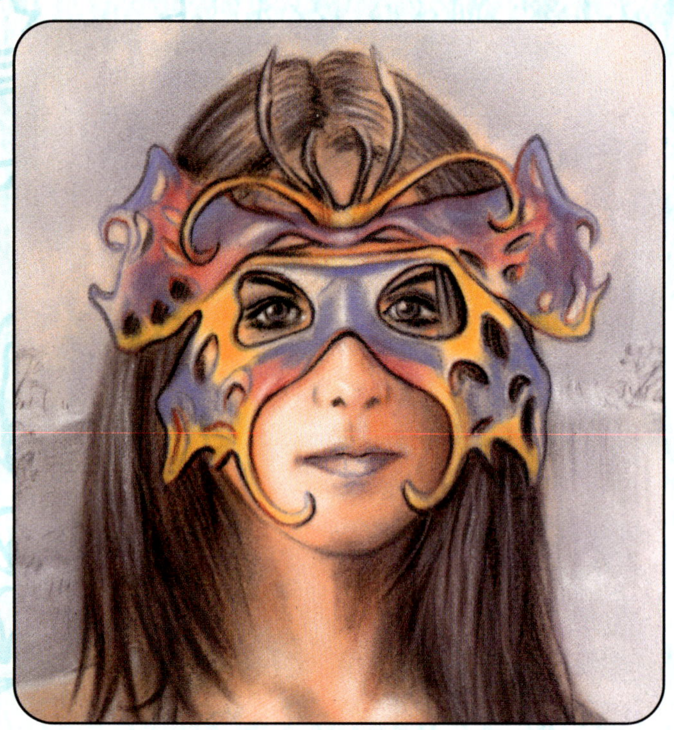

The illustration below shows the full image, which was drawn using pastel pencils and pastel sticks on velour paper. I found three photos to use for reference: a model for the Snow Queen, a mask to place on her face, and a photo of a snowy background. I also researched some dresses that I felt would be suitable to use and that a Snow Queen would possibly wear.

When you start, always sketch your ideas in your sketchpad so you know how the photos are going to fit together. Once you are happy, you can draw this out in an outline form on the paper you are using for your final drawing. I drew in the outline using a 2B pencil, then used the pastel sticks to add a base colour to the drawing. I used predominantly greys and blues to give a cold feeling across the entire piece. Some light oranges, yellows and cream colours came into play for the skin tones but always work with these delicately. It is important not to create too bright colours, especially for the Snow Queen as she needs to look icy and cold. If you find they are too bright, add a little white on the top to tone the colours down. I then chose to give her a brown/blue shade of hair and a blue/grey dress. As the entire piece was to have a cold feel I added yellows and blues into the mask, which helps it stand out and become the focal point of the piece. My final stage was to add the trees and hedgerows into the background to give the artwork a sense of depth and space.

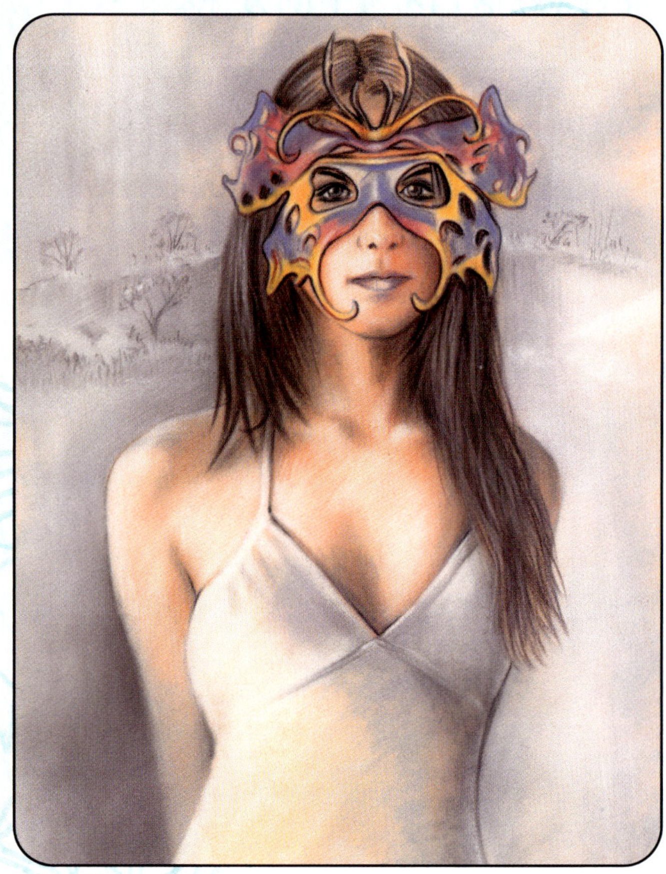

Gothic faerie

Gothic faeries are often dressed in black and dark clothes, they have very dark or sometimes white hair and often wear dark make-up. Not only can they be dark and menacing, they can also be seductive and feminine.

Gothic faerie wings Gothic faeries' wings can be painted and drawn in rich intense colours. The ideal colours for dark faeries' wings are blues, purples and reds. If you have metallic paints you could try using them to give the wings a shimmery feel. The three illustrations of these wings can be used for any dark faeries. Look at moths' wings for inspiration and then elongate the shape for a more dramatic look. You can also add jagged edges to them to give them a menacing feel.

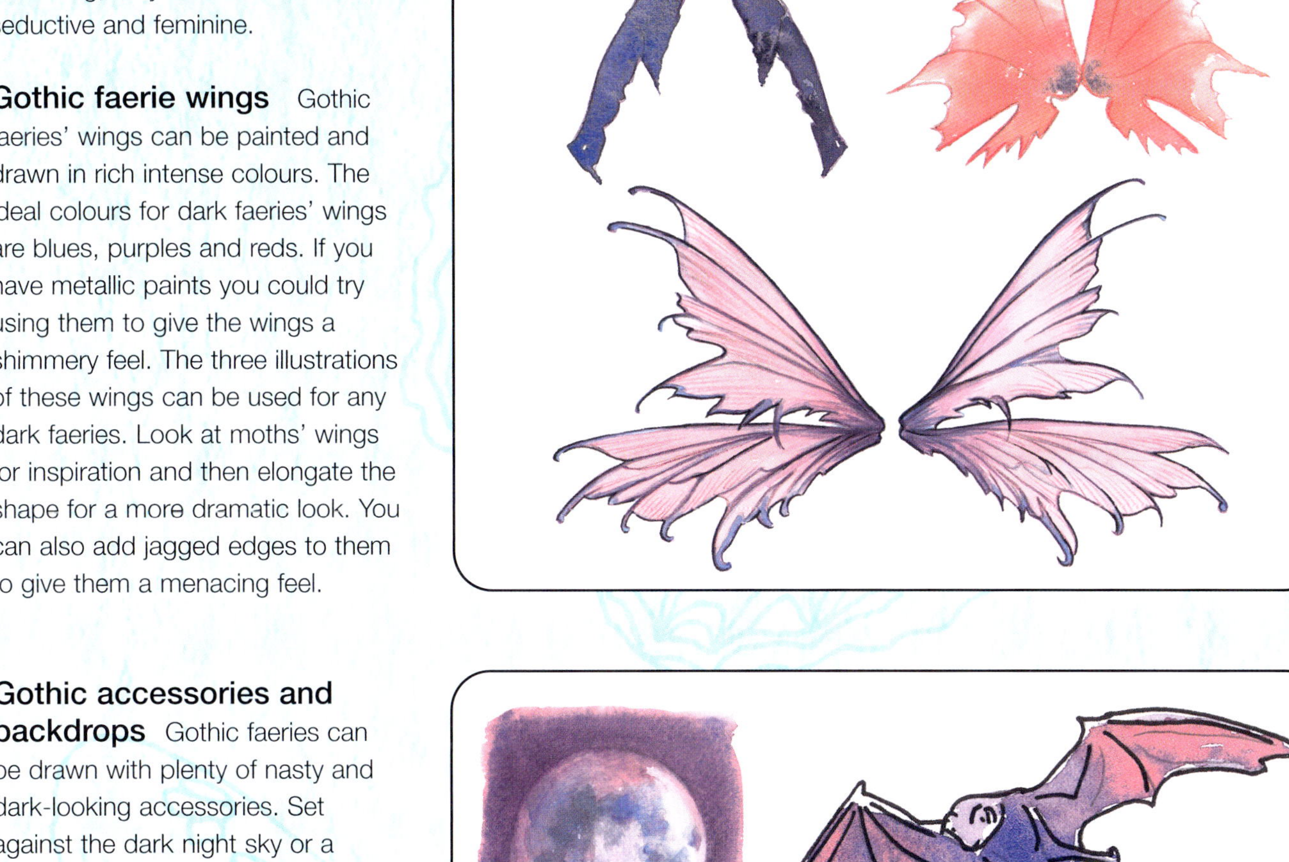

Gothic accessories and backdrops Gothic faeries can be drawn with plenty of nasty and dark-looking accessories. Set against the dark night sky or a gothic window, they could be surrounded by creatures of the night, either on them as decoration, or as live animals flying around or dangling from webs. The three illustrations here depict a bat, a spider and a moth, all painted in dark and cold colours. To give them an intense feel draw out your subject, then colour or shade the subject in and use a fine nibbed pen to outline the subject. It enhances them and adds detail where needed.

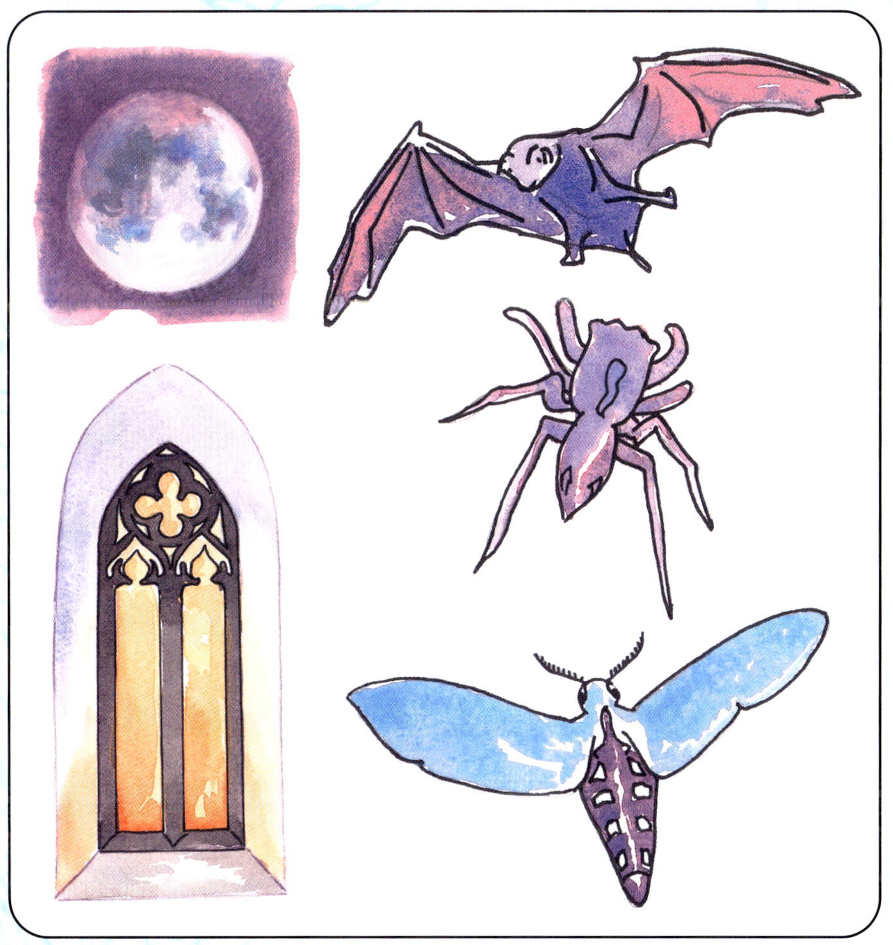

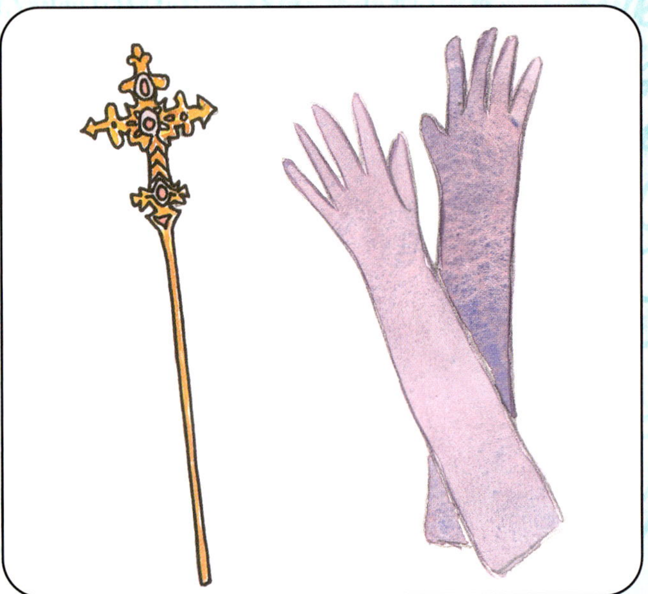

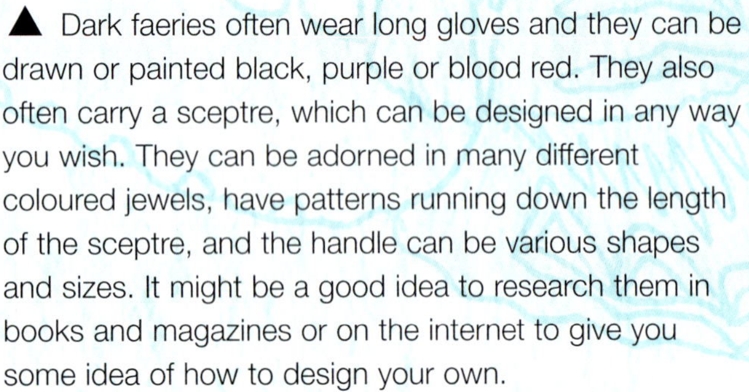

▲ Dark faeries often wear long gloves and they can be drawn or painted black, purple or blood red. They also often carry a sceptre, which can be designed in any way you wish. They can be adorned in many different coloured jewels, have patterns running down the length of the sceptre, and the handle can be various shapes and sizes. It might be a good idea to research them in books and magazines or on the internet to give you some idea of how to design your own.

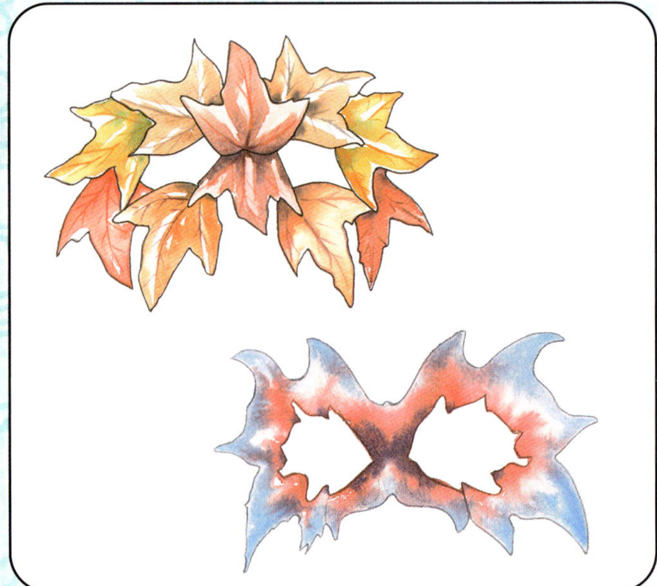

▲ Gothic faeries wear masks to hide their faces and these can vary greatly. The first mask here is made from autumn leaves. To make it look more terrifying you can create jagged edges to the leaves and outline them in fine nibbed black felt pen. The second is a glass ice mask, which is cold to the touch. Closer to the eyes, it is darker and redder: the wearer is so evil the glass begins to glow red hot, luring in innocent passers by and trapping them in the dark faeries' realm.

Step-by-step gothic faerie

For a gothic faerie drawing, choose reference photos of models posed with attitude. In this instance the model has her hand on her hip with a sneer on her face.

Research moths' wings and choose a few that you feel would look great elongated and stretched. Clothes are also important. Gothic faeries often wear seductive clothing, so corsets and bodices work well. If you would like to add any spiders, moths or bats flying around her, or you wish her to hold something then try to research your accessories at this early stage as it may be difficult to add one in later on.

Once you have collated your references, sketch out your ideas to make sure they fit together. Then draw a line drawing on the paper you wish to use. This particular drawing is going to be completed in pen, ink and wash. Once you have drawn the outline in pencil you can go over the lines in black pen and ink using a pen and nib. You can see I have not only elongated the wings, but also added curly lines to the ends of the jagged edges. This gives a very decorative feel to the wings and adds interest to the piece.

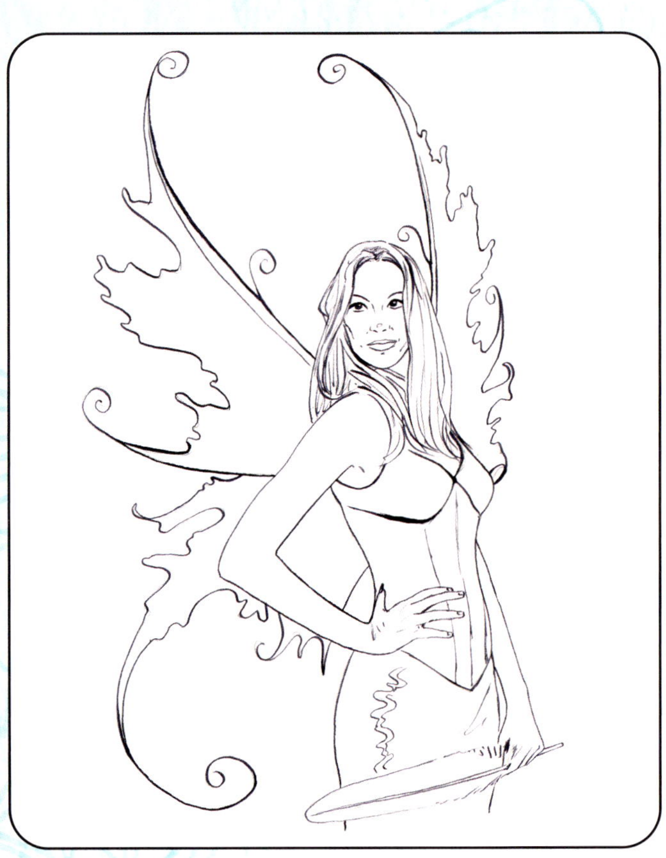

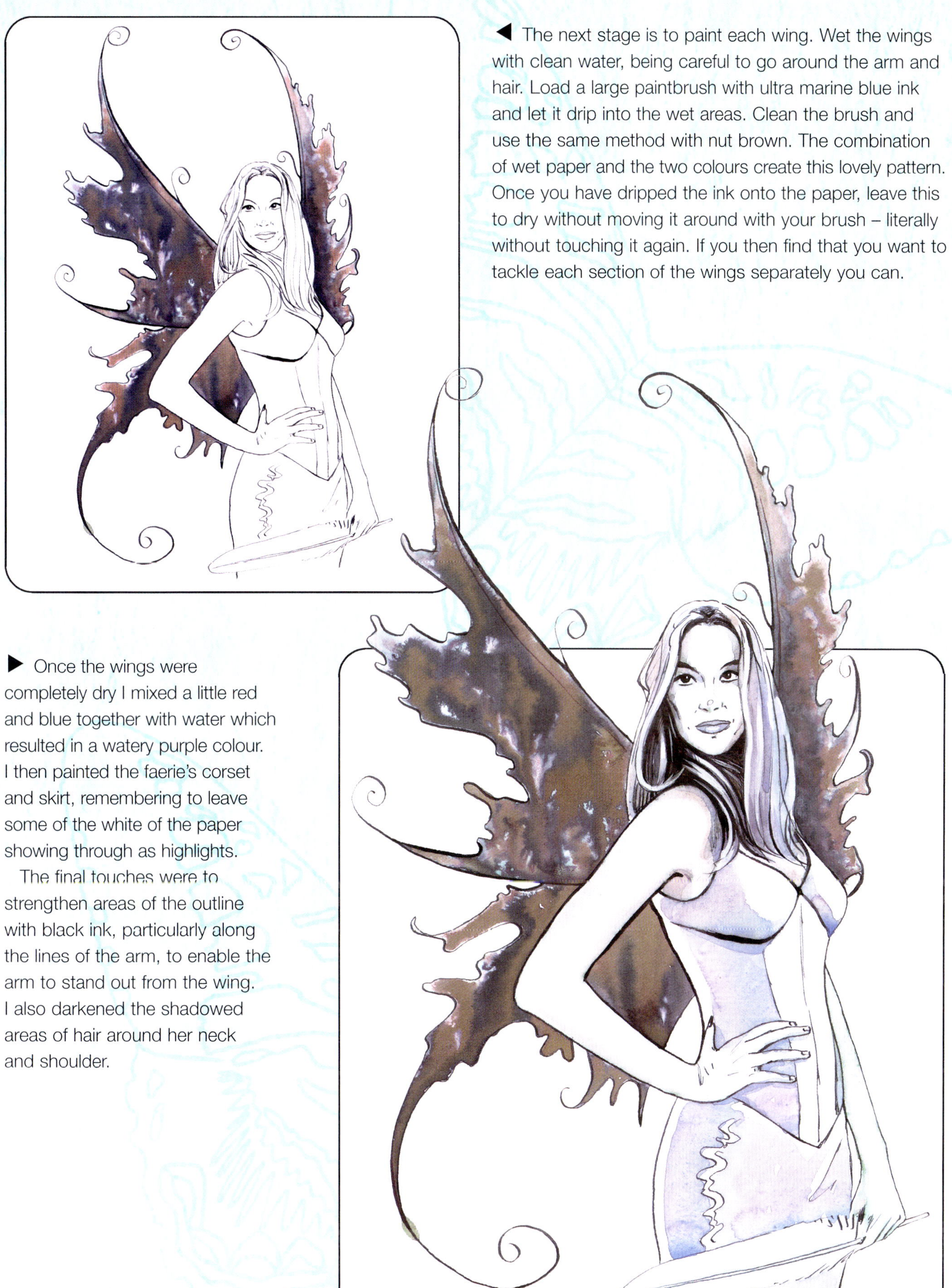

◀ The next stage is to paint each wing. Wet the wings with clean water, being careful to go around the arm and hair. Load a large paintbrush with ultra marine blue ink and let it drip into the wet areas. Clean the brush and use the same method with nut brown. The combination of wet paper and the two colours create this lovely pattern. Once you have dripped the ink onto the paper, leave this to dry without moving it around with your brush – literally without touching it again. If you then find that you want to tackle each section of the wings separately you can.

▶ Once the wings were completely dry I mixed a little red and blue together with water which resulted in a watery purple colour. I then painted the faerie's corset and skirt, remembering to leave some of the white of the paper showing through as highlights.

The final touches were to strengthen areas of the outline with black ink, particularly along the lines of the arm, to enable the arm to stand out from the wing. I also darkened the shadowed areas of hair around her neck and shoulder.

Backgrounds

Creating backgrounds to your faerie painting isn't as difficult as you may think. Also, the simpler the background, the more your subject will be the central focus of the piece. You can create moods with backgrounds to match with the character of your faerie: light and bright for good faeries and powerful and strong colours for the dark faeries. The following pages will give you a few ideas of how you can create simple backgrounds for your own faeries in a variety of media.

SIMPLE BACKGROUNDS IN WATERCOLOUR

The following two backgrounds are the easiest colour backgrounds you can create. They are rendered in watercolour and are created using just two colours and a wet-in-wet wash.

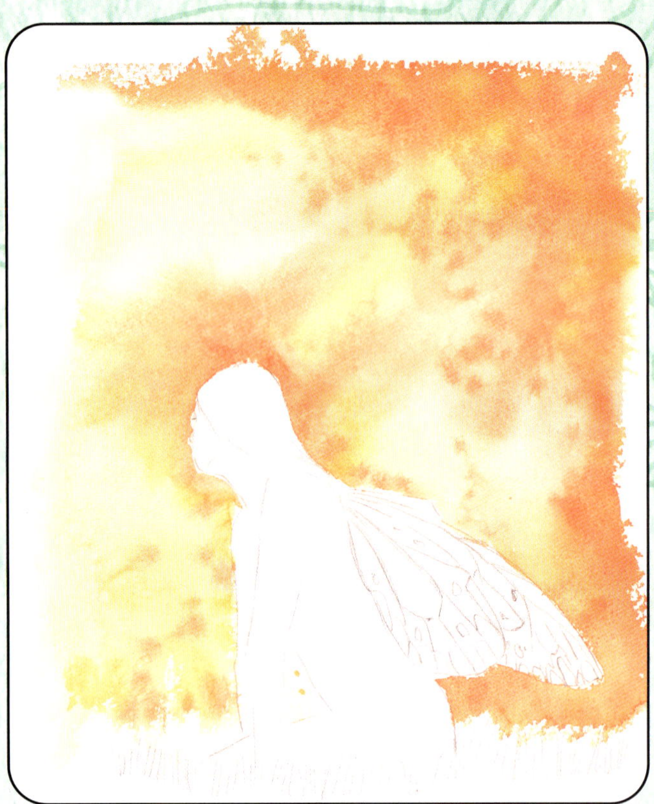

▲ Warm background

This scene shows a faerie looking into the distance in a warm, sunny and serene environment. Even though the faerie is not painted, we can tell from the warmth of the background that she is a good faerie enjoying the sunshine. To create this background, wet your watercolour paper, using a clean brush dipped in water and spreading it across the paper. Mix up two colours in your pallet; I have used yellow and orange. Load your brush with the orange and drop the colour in a few random places over the background. It will start to spread due to the water already on the paper. Rinse your brush well and load it with the yellow. Repeat the process, randomly dripping the yellow colour. Once you have covered the majority of the area, leave it to dry.

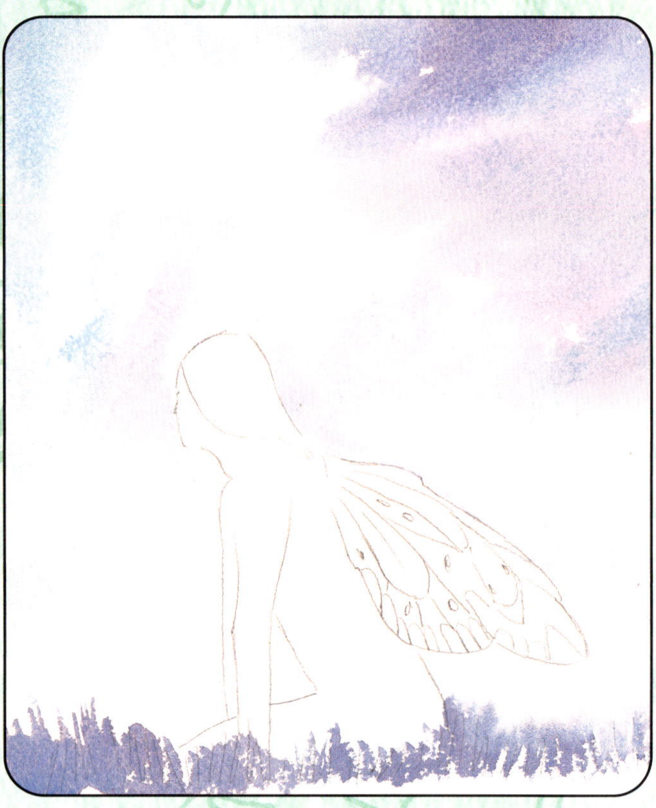

▲ Cold background

This background conveys a completely different mood. Even though the faerie is in exactly the same pose and still looks serene, the feeling is quite uneasy. She could either be in a cold moonlit night or just as the clouds are gathering for a storm. I wet the paper as before but this time I mixed two colours in the well of my pallet: blue and crimson. I then loaded a very large brush with crimson mixture and painted, starting at the top right hand corner of the page and allowing the colour to disperse. I purposely created a darker area at the top so that I could wash my brush and use a lighter version of the mixture nearer the faerie and the grass. Once you are happy with the placement of the paint and colour, leave it to dry thoroughly before continuing with the foreground.

▶ Flower background

If you want to add some detail within the wet-in-wet wash, you could add a flower behind the faerie in the middle ground of the painting. The background is a blurry wet-in-wet wash, the mid-ground is a flower which is only part in focus, and the foreground will be your in focus area. For this example I used clean water and a large brush to wet the background and the dandelion. Mixing some Sap Green I painted a light green wash, making sure to work around the dandelion. While the background was still wet I added some yellow into the main areas of the flower and this dispersed and merged into the green of the background. This allowed the dandelion to be partly blurred and to recede into the background. Once the green wash was dry I used some coloured pencil to add definition to the green under-petals and stem. This amount of detail ensures it stays in the middle ground and the blurry top of the dandelion helps it recede around the edges. The overall feeling of this background is sparkling springtime, with rich warmth coming through the grass.

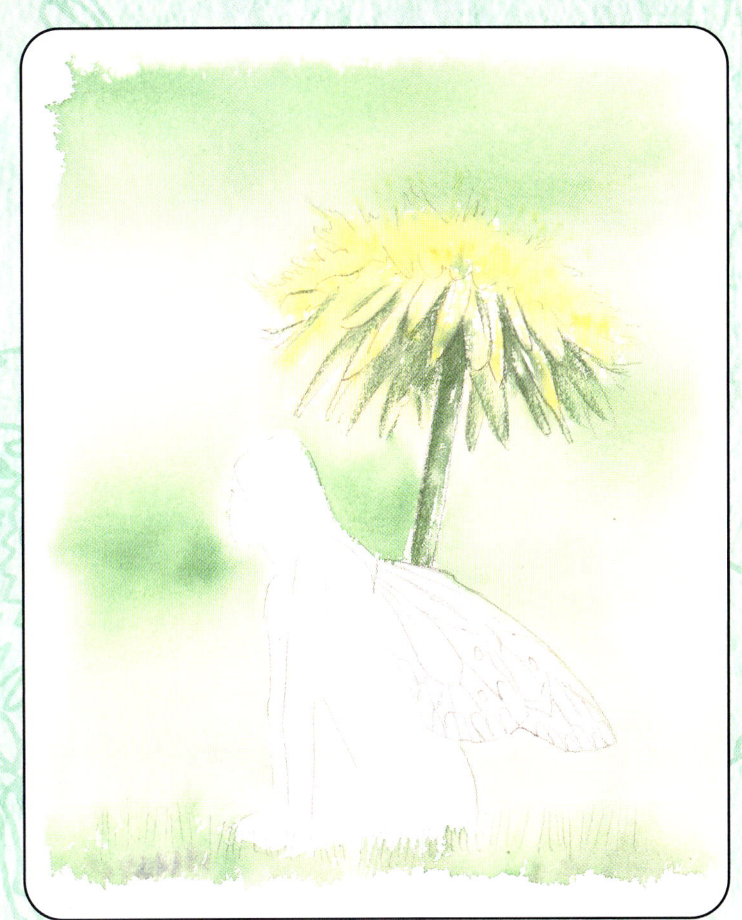

▶ Woodland background

This is a slightly more advanced background, using the same faerie. It is blurry enough that when you paint the subject in fully, she will come forward and the background will recede. The entire background was painted in one go. First, the background was wet using a clean brush and clean water. I then mixed up some Burnt Sienna, Yellow Ochre, Sap Green and French Ultra Marine in the different wells of my pallet and started with the Sienna at the top of the page. I loaded my brush and dropped in a little of the paint and then made sure to carefully wash my brush in clean water. After loading my brush with Sap Green, I painted the left hand side, the centre of the scene, the leaf and part of the acorn. The next step was to mix some of the Yellow Ochre and Burnt Sienna together to paint the acorn and then to leave the painting to dry. When you begin to paint the faerie in, the deeper tones in her clothing will stand out well against this very simple but striking background.

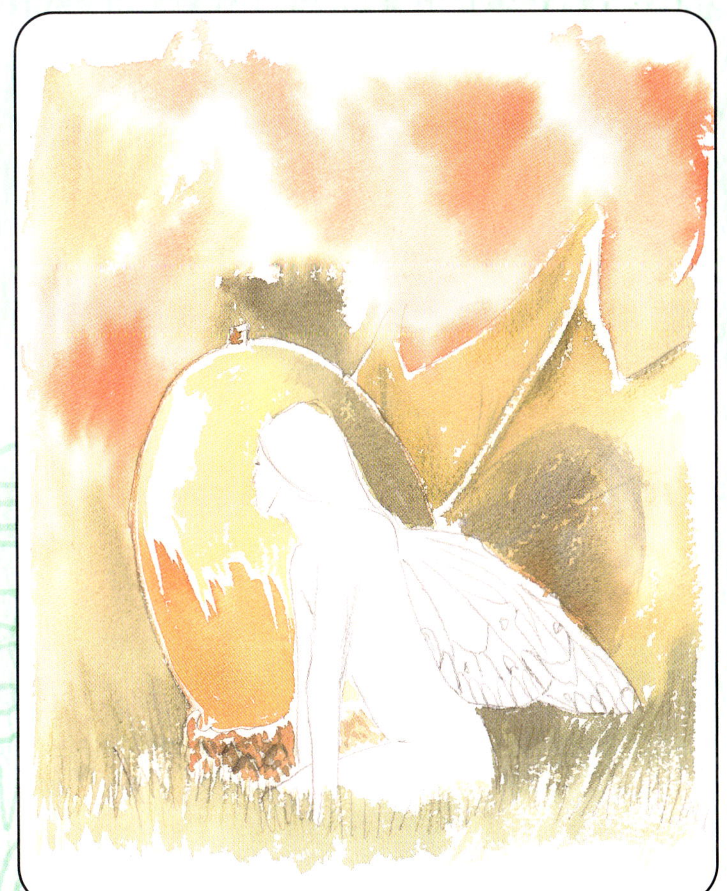

SIMPLE BACKGROUNDS IN PASTEL

Pastel drawings are a lovely way to create feeling in a faerie drawing, especially as you can use different coloured papers to work on. You can choose the paper colour to match the character of the faerie and the feeling you wish to create. It is also good to use a mixture of pastel pencils and pastel sticks to enable you to draw both fine detail and thicker blocks of colour.

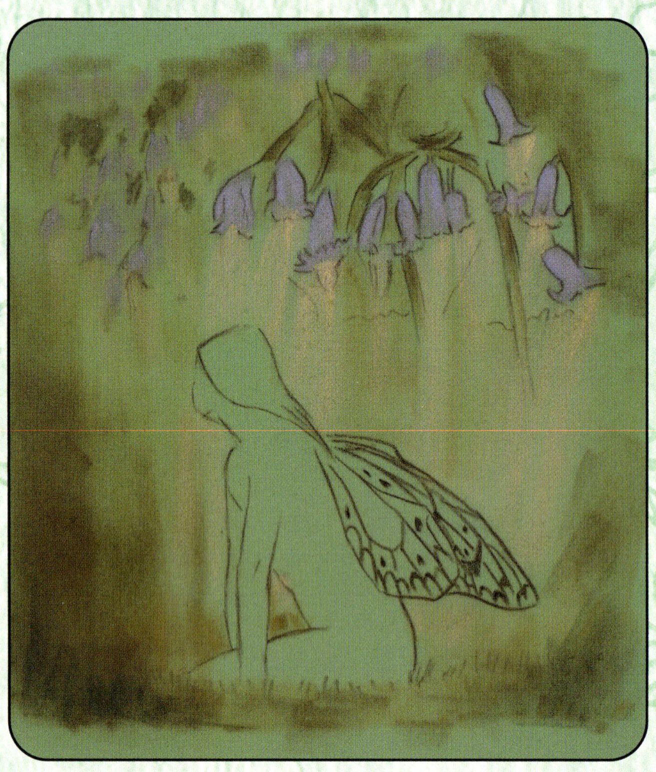

◀ Bluebell lights

This is a very simple background to create. It's a dynamic and interesting way of providing undergrowth for the faerie to sit in and lighting up the scene at the same time. The bluebell heads act as lights pouring down onto the faerie, lighting her way through the forest. The bluebells in the foreground are brighter and lighter than those in the background and this helps to give depth in the scene. To create a background like this, find some coloured pastel paper and use your pastel pencils to draw out your scene and faerie. Don't press too hard with your pastel pencils and try not to outline the bluebells too heavily; you can leave much of it up to the imagination. Once you are happy with the drawing, use your pastel sticks to shade in the background. When you are creating the light from the bluebells, use the blunt end of a creamy yellow pastel stick, and pull it down from the bluebell's head, lightening the pressure as you reach the base. This will create the impression of intensity of light from the top.

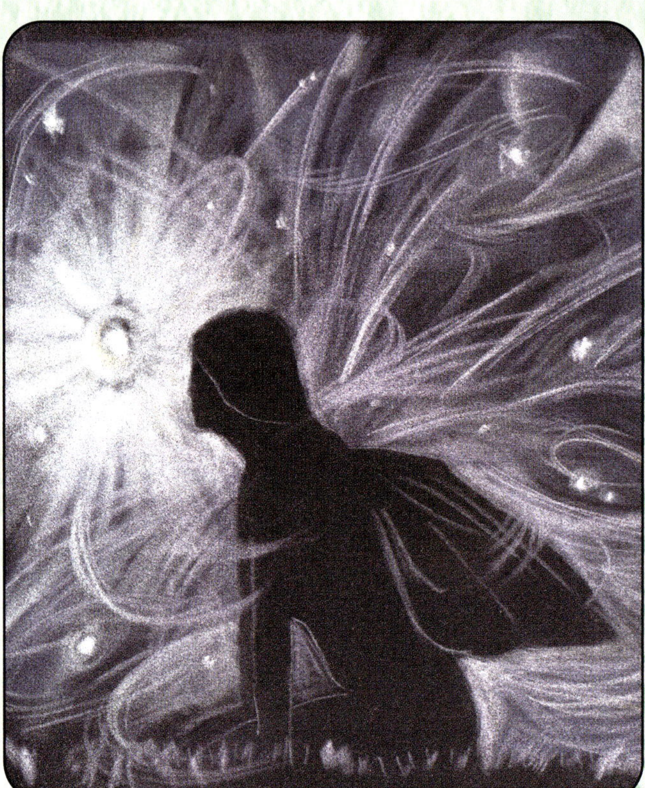

◀ Faerie dust

Another way to create a dynamic background is to use very dark pastel paper and draw only in white pastel pencils. Here I have used black velour paper and created a faerie dust effect. Start by drawing out your faerie using a white pastel pencil, then randomly place some white dots where you feel the faerie dust should be. Using a pastel stick, draw thick and thin lines using flowing movements around the faerie dust. Use your imagination with this and try to create a starry night sky effect. You can even use a little yellow for the centre of the faerie dust particles so that they really glow.

▶ Creating moods with pastel

Even though the following two illustrations were drawn on the same coloured paper, each has a different feel to it. One is serene and warm, the other cold and fresh.

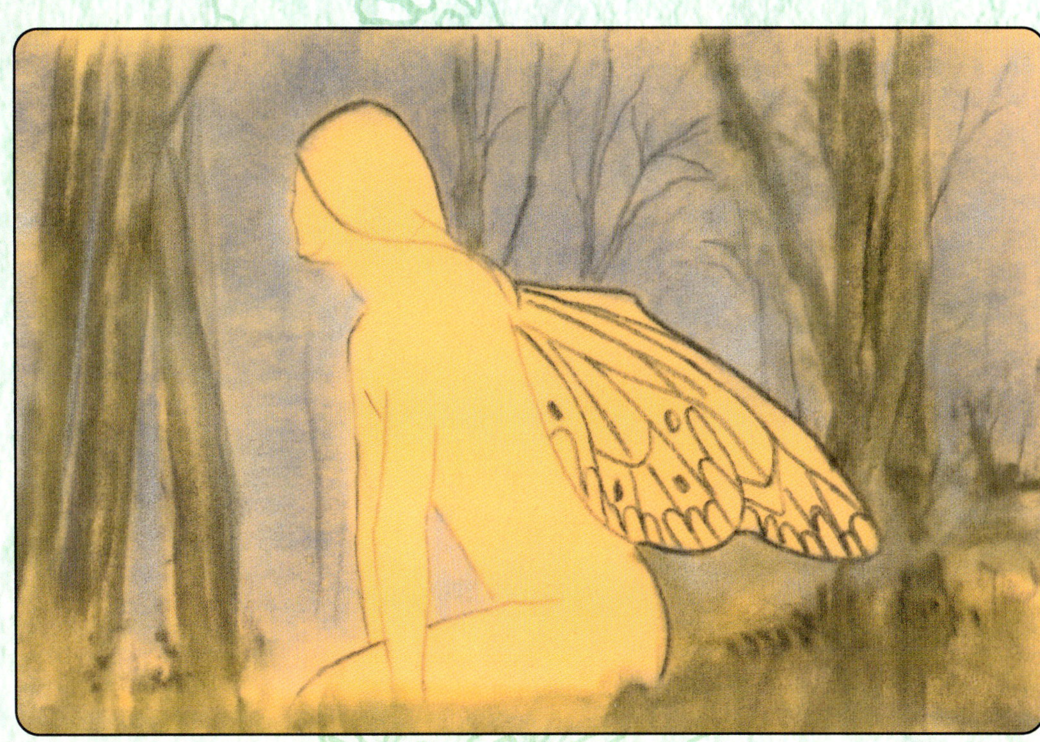

Creating a cold, fresh background in pastel is all about choosing the right colours. This woodland scene is an excellent background for a faerie, and the spaces between the trees can be coloured a cool blue colour to enhance the cool feel to the scene. Draw out your faerie and the background and then use olive green and brown colours for the trees. You can use pastel sticks to draw the thick areas and pastel pencils to draw in the twigs and thinner trees. Once these are placed in the scene, you can use a light blue pastel stick to fill in the background. The great thing is, if you use the stick on its side and sweep it across the trees near the tops, it pushes them back further into the distance and allows them to have a misty and eerie feel.

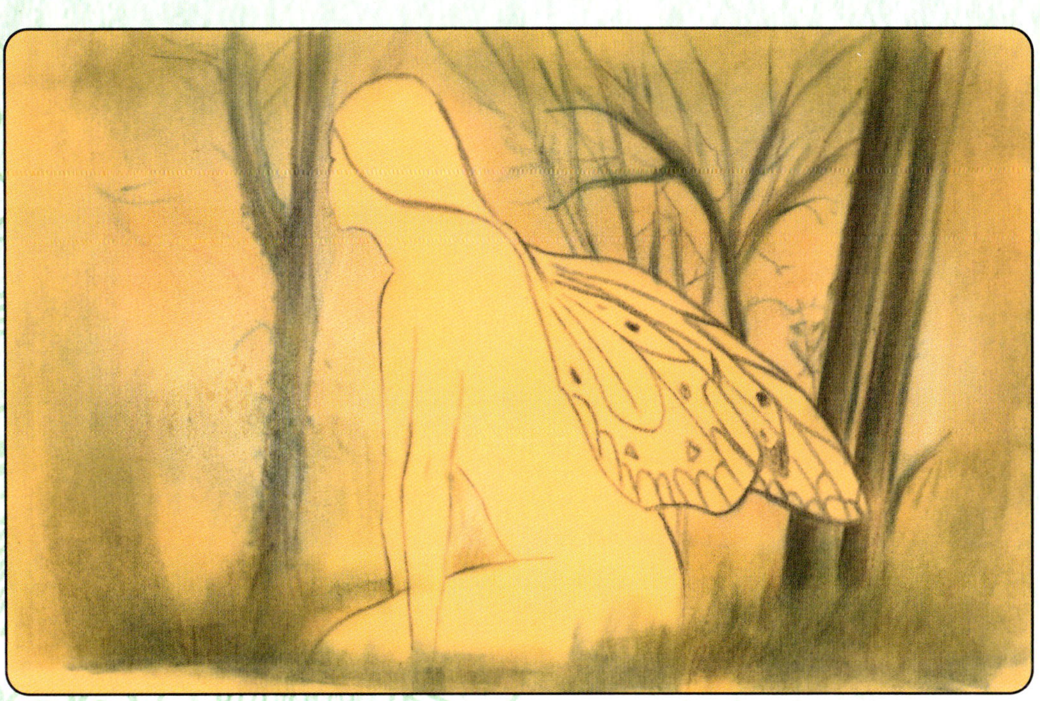

The method for creating a warm background is very similar to a cold one. Draw out your background trees and your faerie, and use a warmer Sap Green with the Olive Green to fill in the trees. You can use pastel pencils to draw in the thinner trees and the detail. Once you are happy with them, again use the side of a light yellow stick to sweep the colour across the trees. This will push them back into the distance and give the impression that warm light is flowing through the forest. You can make the trees as light at the top as you wish; the more light you place on top of the trees the more sunlight or mist you will create.

BACKGROUNDS IN GRAPHITE PENCIL

Graphite pencils are also a versatile medium for backgrounds; you can use a wide range of tones to bring depth and distance into your artwork.

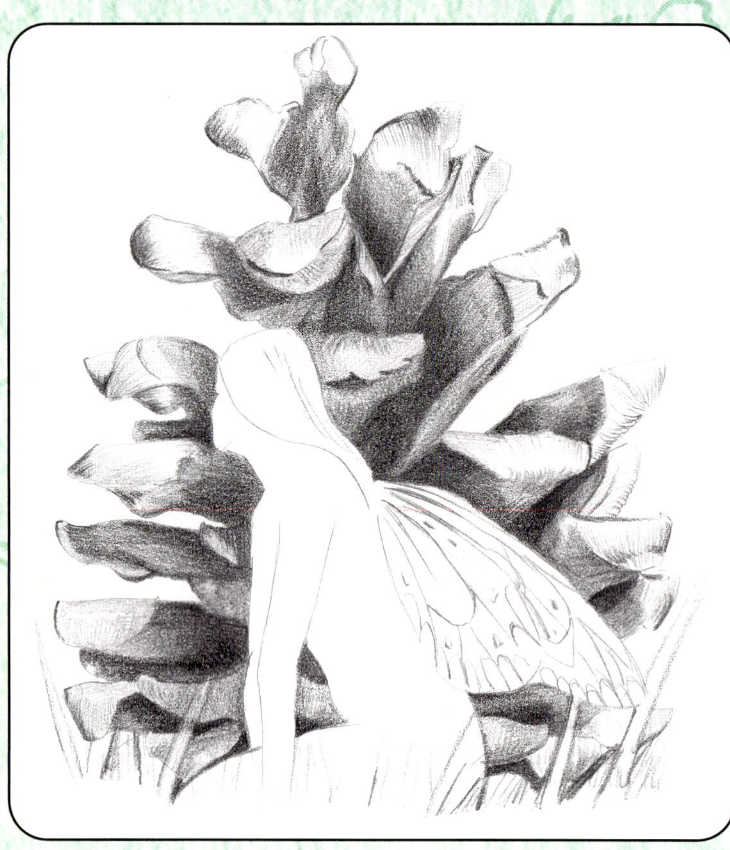

◀ The background of the faerie hiding behind the pine cone not only provides a great backdrop, but also gives the faerie scale. We can immediately see that the faerie must be very small and dainty. In this drawing the tones in the pine cone are very dark. If you were to draw in the faerie, it would be best to draw her lighter so that she stands out from the background. If you are drawing something similar to this, start off using a 2B and shade in the main tones lightly. You can then layer your graphite over the shadowed areas using softer pencils as you progress.

▶ The faerie sitting next to a large toadstool also gives a sense of picture scale. This background may look complicated to draw but actually it was relatively easy. If you draw out the toadstool with a 2B pencil and then build up your tones gradually, you will find the more tones you add the more depth you will create. We need to convey the feeling that the toadstool is in the undergrowth with long grass, so we can use the deeper tones to create more depth in the background. Don't forget to use different shading techniques to convey the various textures of the toadstool. The underside is going to be quite lined because of the gills, so make sure you draw your lines with the contours of the toadstool.

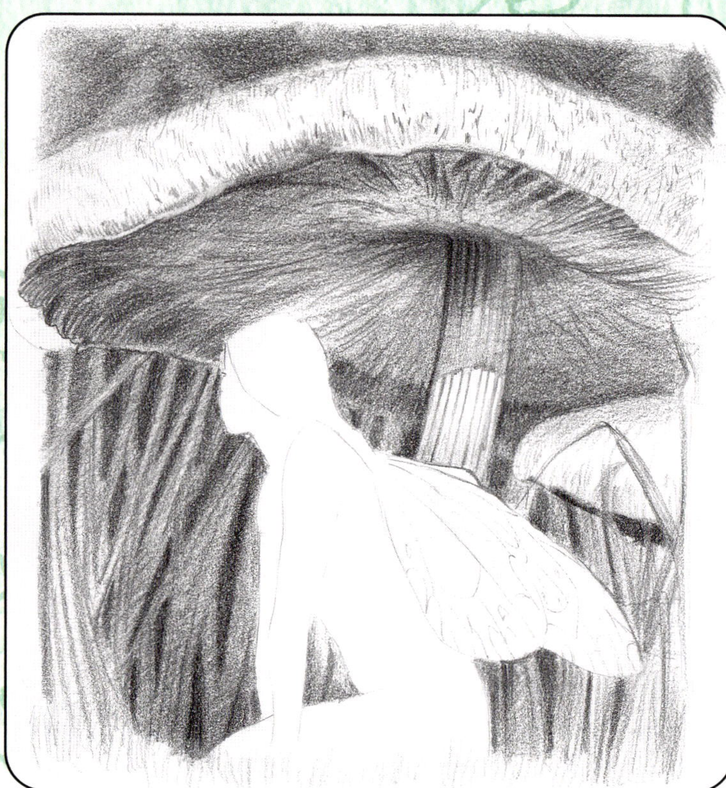

BACKGROUNDS IN PEN AND INK

Using pen and ink to create backgrounds also has its advantages, as you can use just line and wash or you can paint full colours with a brush and the ink. There are many colours and types of ink available to purchase and you can mix inks just like you can any other paint. So in fact, with only blue, yellow, red and brown, you can create a rainbow of colours.

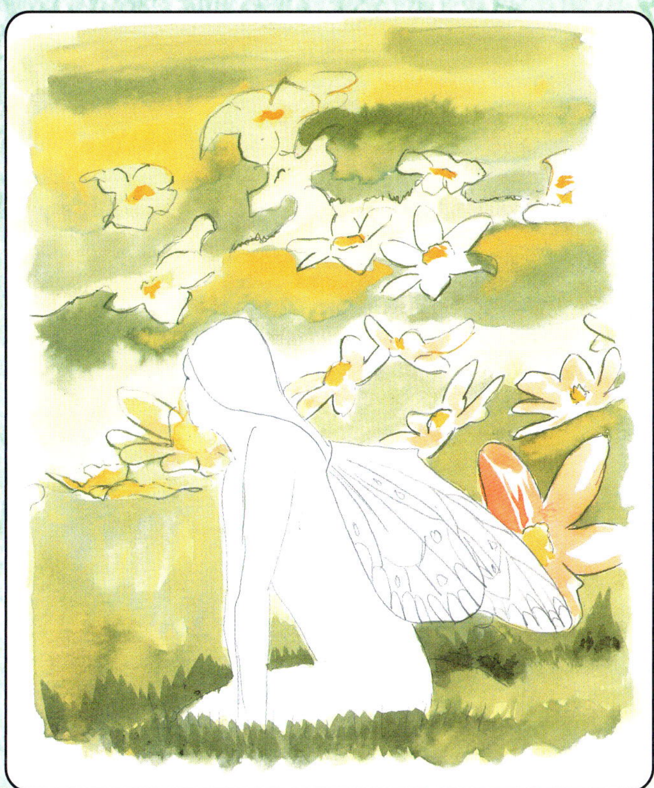

◀ The summery background I have created was very simple. I used a mixture of blue and yellow and, using a pen and nib, drew out a few flowers randomly across the page, and placed the faerie in the foreground. I then mixed a lighter mixture of blue and yellow and using a medium sized brush I created the yellow and green stripy effect running through the background. I left some lighter patches; you can create these by adding more water to your mix. Once the ink is dry you can use your pen to add detail to the flowers and draw the faerie.

▶ Ink is a very strong and vibrant medium, so here I have created a seasonal faerie sitting very carefully in amongst some holly and berries. I used a mixture of red and brown ink to draw the faerie, leaves and berries. With a brush, I then painted the berries a crimson colour, the leaves a lighter, more yellowy green, and the background a darker, more bluey, green. This is a very vivid drawing, so when you draw the faerie she will need to be light enough to stand out clearly enough from the background.

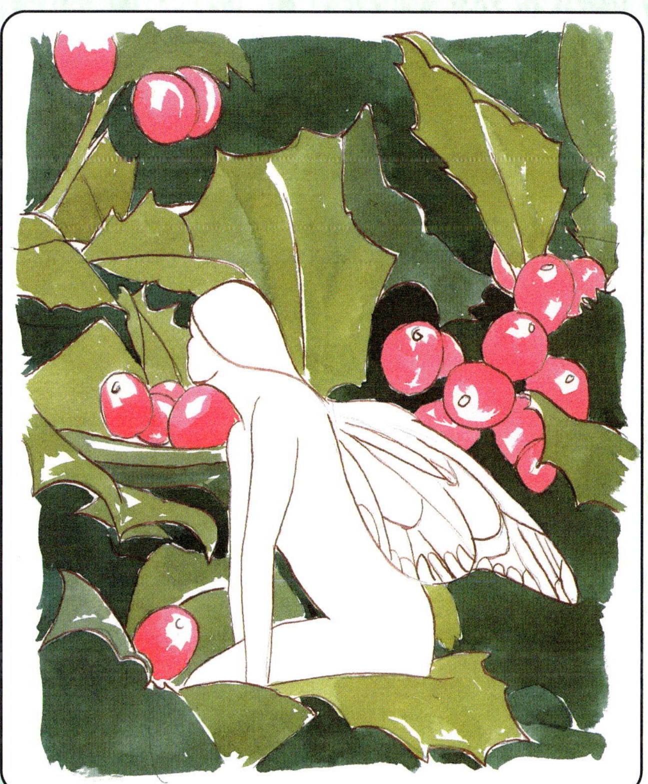

Faerie realm

The faerie realm is a magical world where faeries and faerie helpers reside. It is inhabited by unicorns, faeries, elves, pixies, gnomes and many other fabled and mystical creatures unseen by the human eye. When you draw your faerie realm you can allow your imagination to create magical places for the faeries to live. The easiest way to create these magical worlds is to think about where faeries might like to live in our human world. They could live in a cluster of toadstools, an old fallen tree, on lily pads on a pond, in a long-forgotten secret garden or simply next to your garden shed in some old clay plant pots – wherever, in fact, you wish them to be! Why not collect or take a few photos of where you think they might live and then turn them into your very own magical faerie realm? On these two pages we have two faerie realms in different toadstools, one shown at night and the other during the day.

DAY TIME TOADSTOOL FAERIE REALM

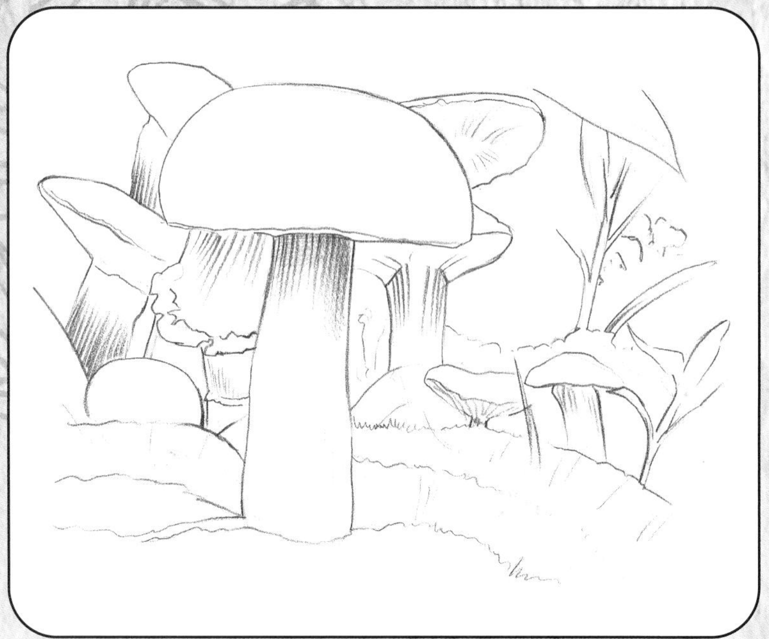

▶ I wanted to create a faerie realm in a woodland, centring on toadstools as the faeries' home. This sketch is based on a photo I took with toadstools growing randomly amongst some moss, grass and small plants. As you can see, by sketching out the photo you can pick out the most important areas and simplify the scene. Often, when you take photos of plant life there can be a lot of detail, so it's good to eliminate this. Sketching the photo beforehand therefore helps you to determine which areas you would like to use. The focus of this photo was the tall main toadstool in the foreground. The background toadstools lean into the picture which helps with the composition, and you can see that our horizon line is on the bottom third.

Once you have planned out your faerie realm, you can either continue working on top of the sketch or, if you find you've made too many unwanted lines, you can start afresh on a clean sheet of paper. You can even grid or trace your initial sketch. Using your imagination, add windows and doors where you think your faeries would like them. My front toadstool has a large door and a small window. I then imagned that once inside a faerie would travel up the centre of the stalk to the top of the toadstool. With this in mind, I added windows so she could look out as she walked up a spiral staircase inside. You could also add a staircase on the outside if you prefer. The moss gave me the opportunity to make smaller homes, and you can elongate the doorways to add variation and interest.

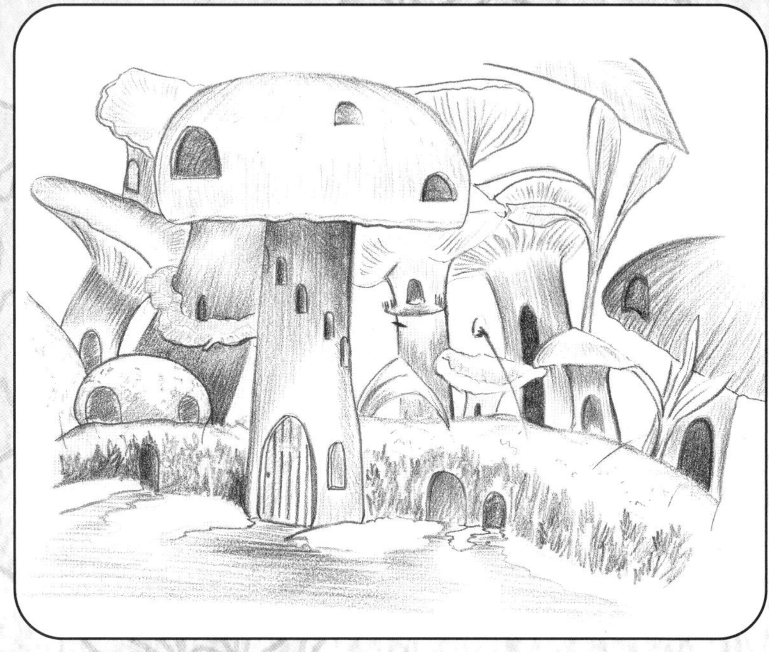

NIGHT TIME TOADSTOOL FAERIE REALM

▶ This time the photo I am using is much denser in comparison, and features a different variety of toadstool. As you can see, there is lots of scope for creating windows and doors. Using the same process as the daytime toadstool realm, I sketched out the main features of the toadstools, omitting anything that made the composition look muddled and cluttered. To create the night time effect you can add plenty of tone, so don't worry about drawing any objects in the background as these wont be seen in the dark.

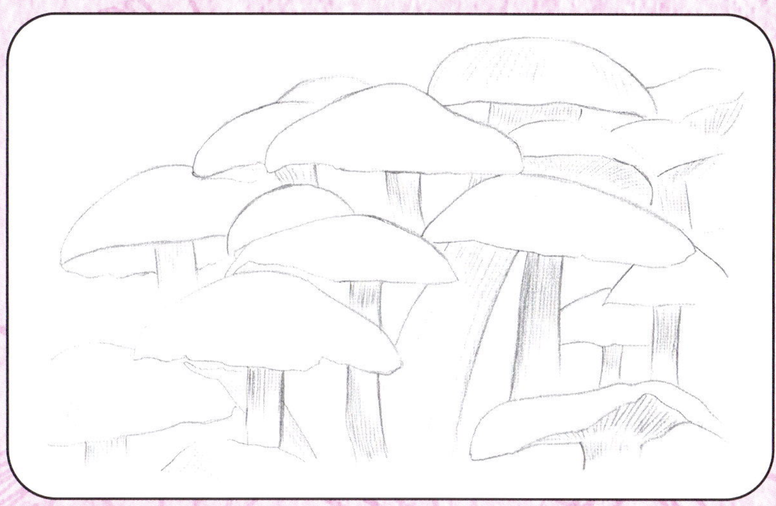

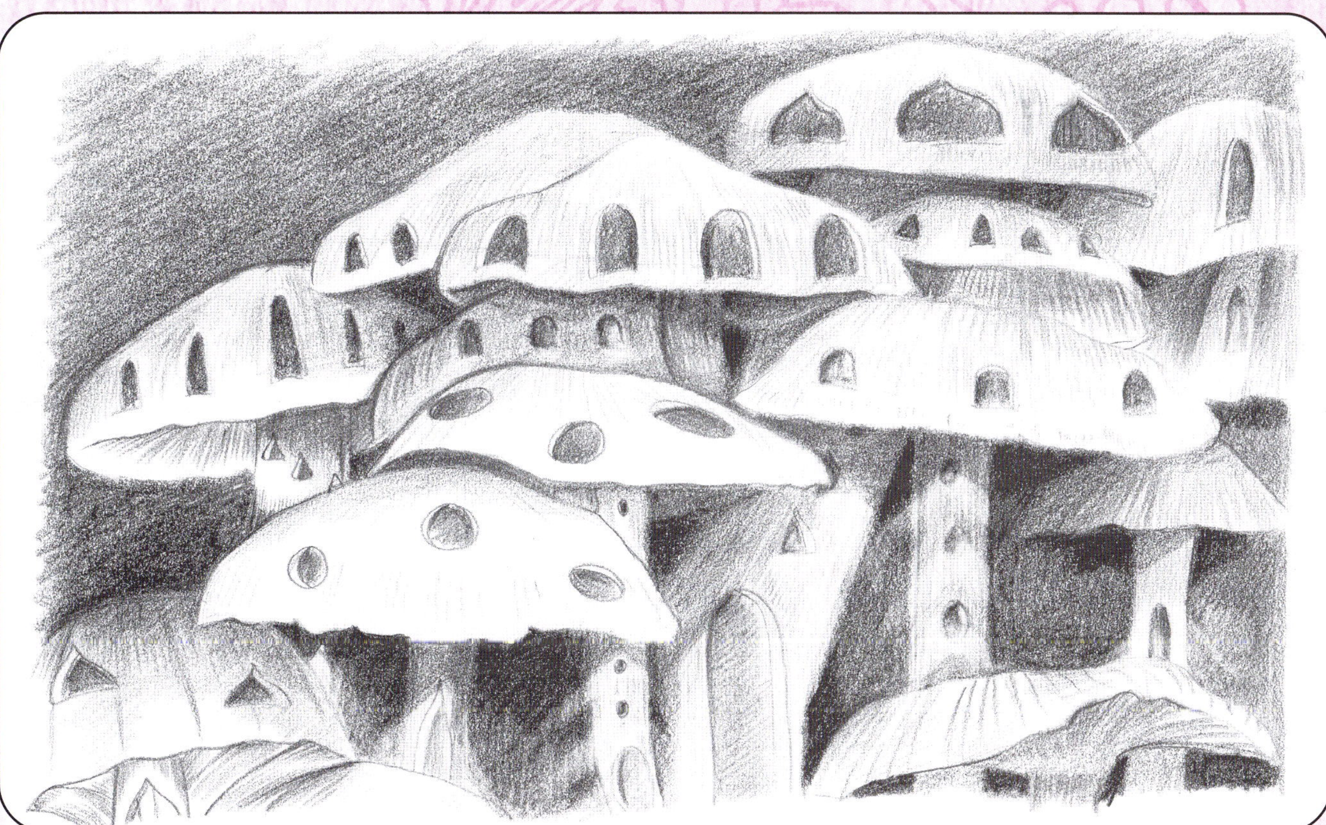

To create the finished drawing I drew out the main toadstools again on a separate sheet of paper. You can use a grid or trace yours if you need to. Start adding your windows and doors where you would like them to be placed. This time I used some round windows to mimic the spots and patters that can be found on the red Fly Agaric toadstool. Once you have created your windows start adding the tone into the background. I used a 6B to start with, building up the tones gradually. The more layers you shade over the deeper the tones will be. You can even use your 9B pencil to shade the very dark shadows underneath the toadstools. Remember, don't add pressure to your pencil to create the dark areas, just layer the graphite gradually over and over and this will give you a much more natural feel. You can use your putty eraser to create some light effects coming from the windows. This is a very simple technique; just place the putty eraser near the window and pull it downward, lessening the pressure as you go. If you erase on an angle, it will look like shafts of light flowing down from the rooms within the stalks of the toadstools.

FAERIE CASTLE

The most respected of all faeries will live in a faerie castle. Look at your photos and images to see where you could create your own castle. It could be in an old gnarled tree just like this step-by-step I have created. I gathered together two photos so that I could have a colony of faeries at the base of the tree and the castle in the tree above. Just as before, sketch out your photos in your sketch pad first to see if they will work well together.

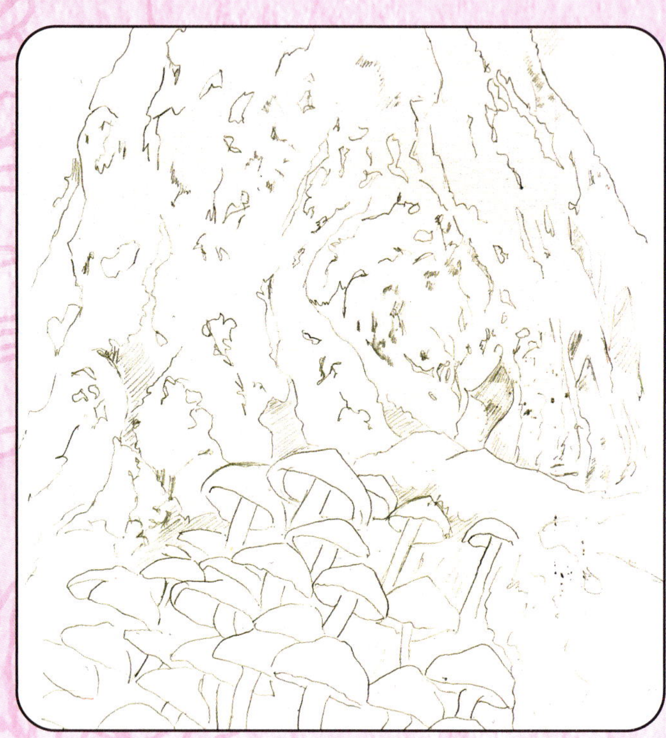

▶ The first stage is to make a simple line drawing, and with this one you can see quite easily that they are separate photos. We now need to integrate them so that they look as though they are really one image.

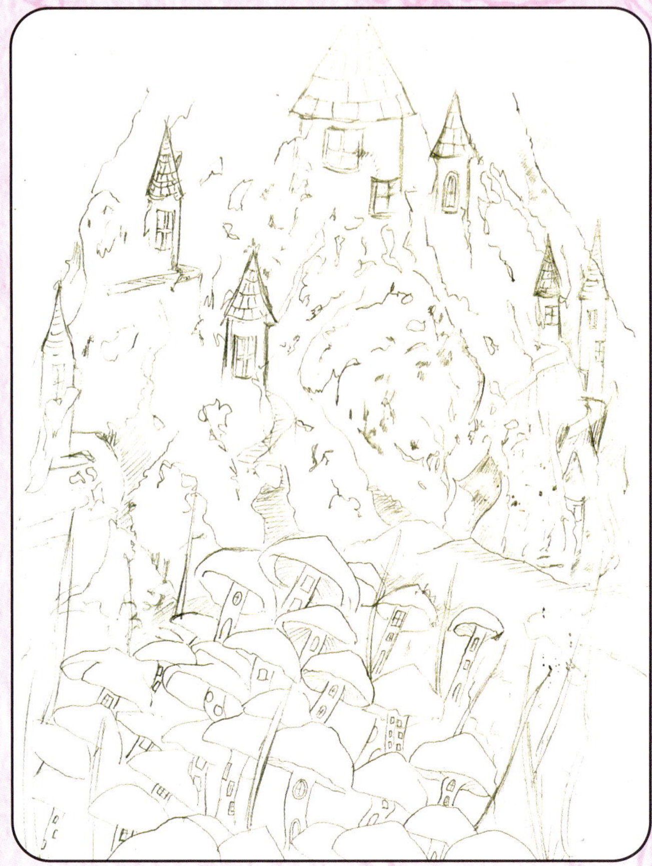

▲ The second stage is to start designing your castle turrets and windows in the toadstool village. You could place the turrets together or scatter them around the gnarled parts of the trunk. In this instance I have scattered them around the trunk and added steps to join each area of the castle from the outside.

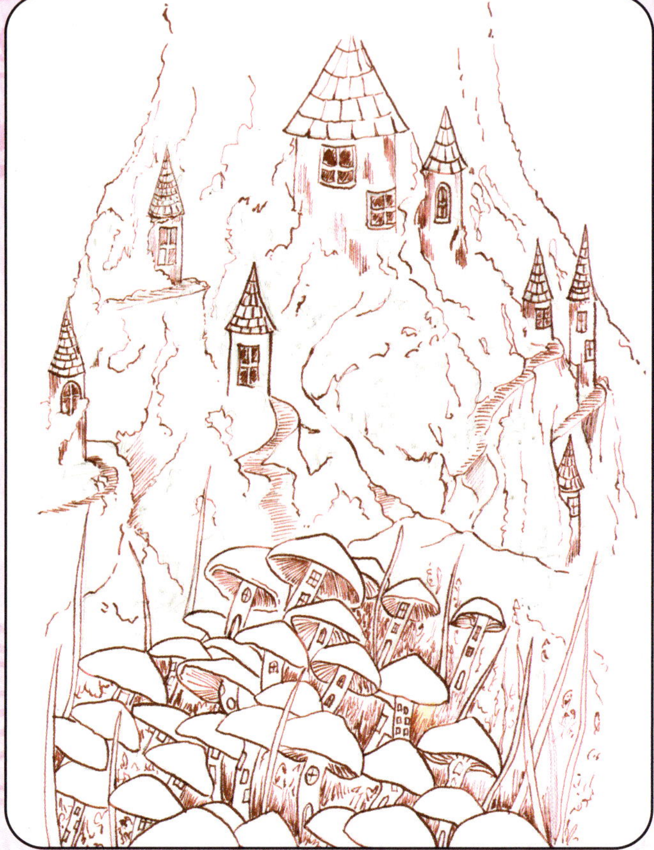

▲ Once you have drawn out and are happy with your castle, you can continue drawing in graphite pencil or use a sepia pen and ink as I have here. I have drawn over my lines, emphasizing the windows and the gnarled wood in the process.

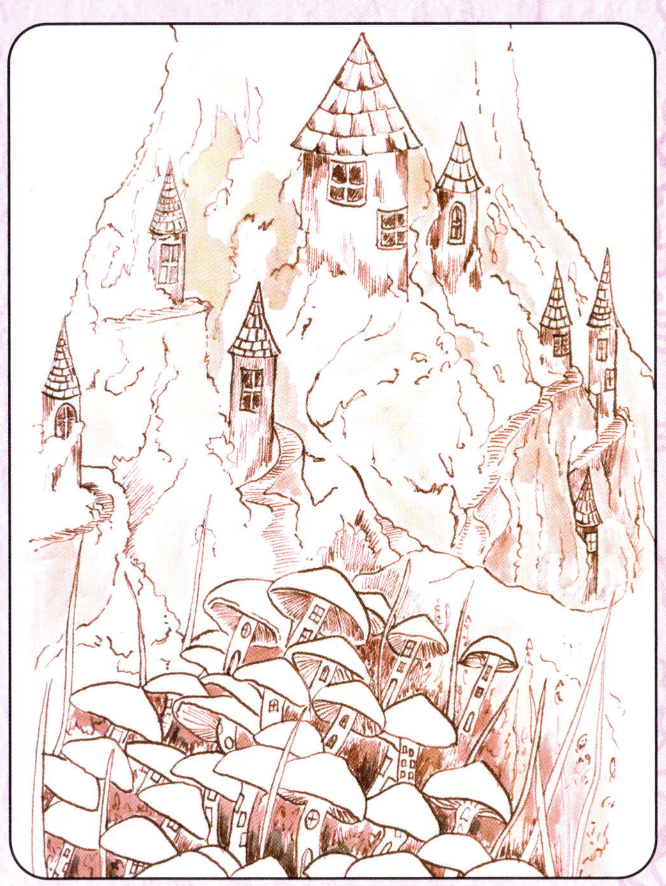

◀ Once you have finished drawing the outline you can use some ink and wash to add the shadows and dark areas within the tree and under the toadstool village.

▶ The final stage is to work back into the drawing with some detail and final lines. I have used a sharp 4B pencil to create the gnarled patterns on the tree bark and roots. Don't forget to draw within the contours of the roots and bark to give them a three dimensional appearance.

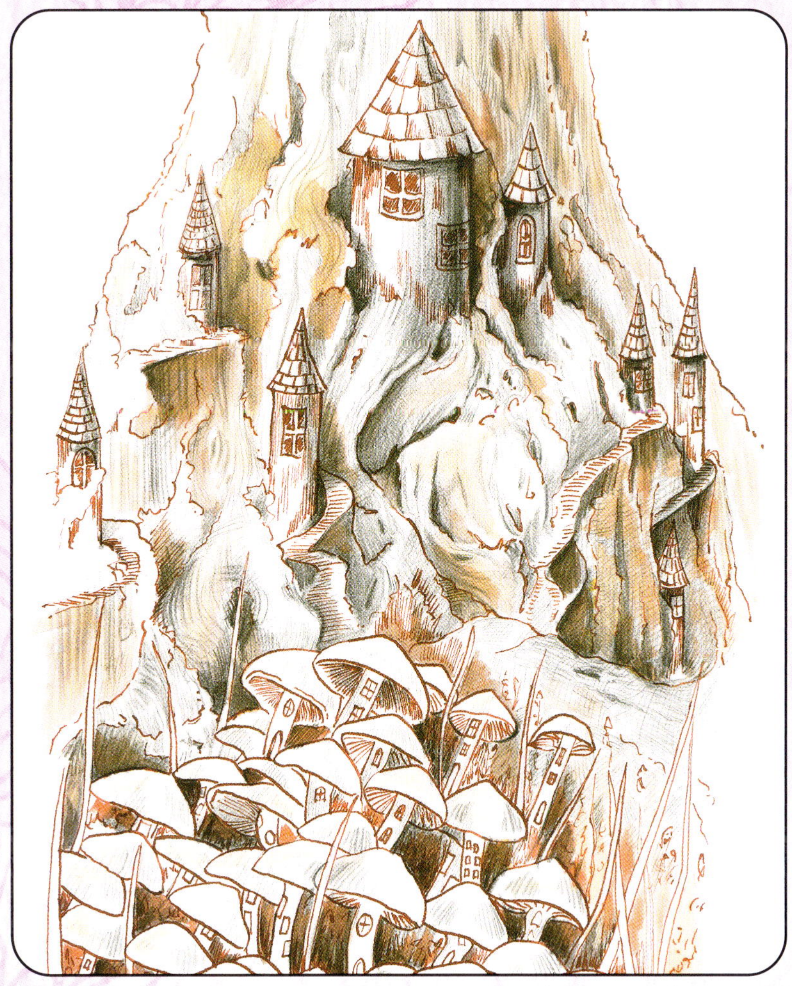

Faerie helpers

Faerie helpers are usually little faeries that help humans, like the tooth faerie or the faerie godmother. There are however, creatures in the human world who keep a watchful eye on the faeries too. They can help them if they are in trouble or warn them of danger. These helpers can take on many forms and I have illustrated a few here.

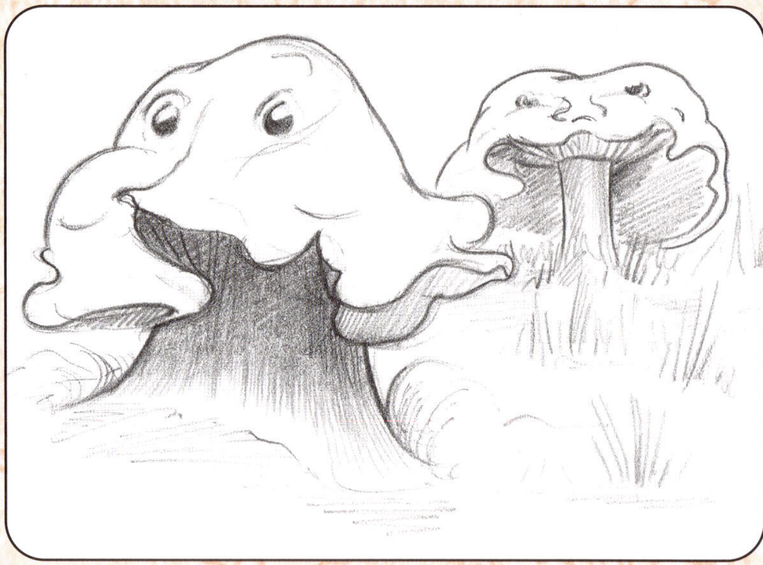

◀ Toadstool helpers

Toadstools are very happy creatures, have lots of character and don't mind faeries making their homes in them. As you can see from the sketch below it is quite easy to add a face to a toadstool, and you can use the stalk as their body and the cap as the head. The edge of the cap can be exaggerated to form a wide mouth, and eyes can be placed on the front for the toadstool creature to see. You can even create a nose and some rosy cheeks from the wrinkles. Try this for yourself. Be sure to choose a range of toadstools, from tall narrow ones to large fat round ones, and see if you can make a toadstool faerie helper.

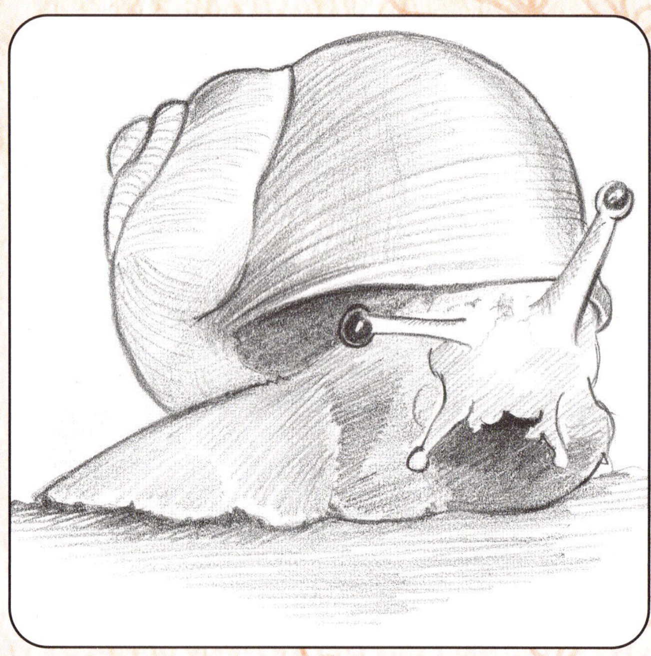

▲ Snail helpers

Snails are excellent helpers, as even though they are slow, they are able to move around, unlike toadstools and flowers. They have large eyes on stalks and can look in two directions at once, which is great when helping to keep the little faeries safe.

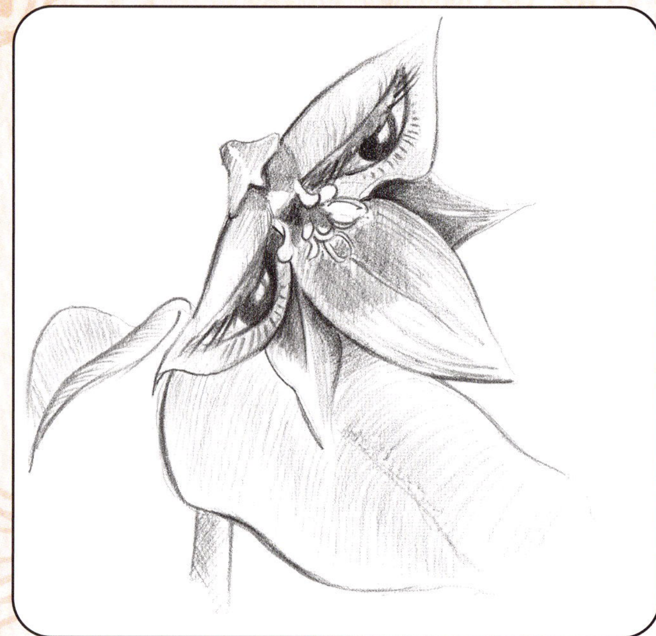

▲ Flower watchers

You can create many different faces in flowers. This drawing shows how simple it can be to add eyes into the petals and immediately create a living, seeing, faerie helper. You can use any flowers you wish, and you can imagine the flower being animated, with the leaves as arms and the head turning and looking all around, watching out for any danger.

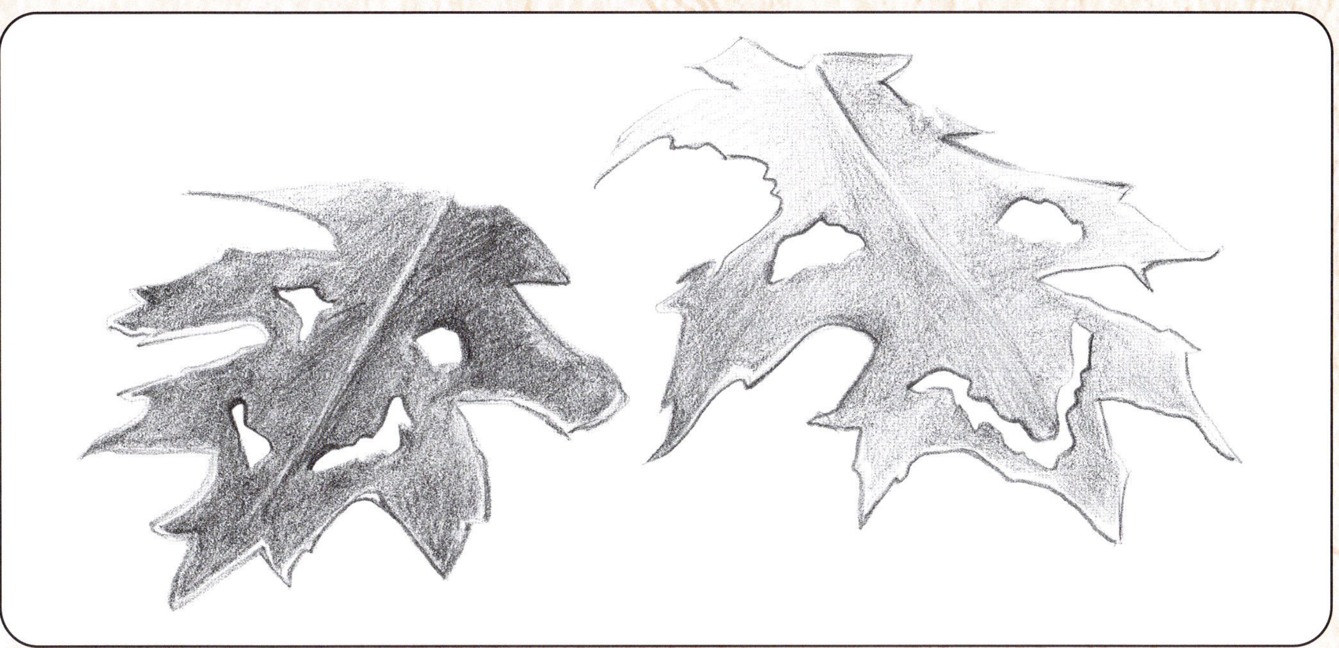

▶ Leaf overseers

Leaves are great friends with faeries. They not only protect the faeries when they are hiding in amongst the trees, but the leaves are always looking down on the faerie realm watching out for any danger on the horizon.

You can work with many different leaves and use your imagination to create the shapes within the leaves for the eyes and mouth – why not use the veins in the leaves to help you, for example? Always try to make the eyes an organic shape so that they feel natural within the leaf.

▶ Wood watcher

The wood watcher is a rare little creature; there aren't many found and to see one is wonderfully magical. The faeries really trust these creatures who live in the roots of very large trees. They are actually made from these roots and can only form when the tree is over a certain age. Try looking out for really gnarled old trees and see if you can create a similar drawing to this using your own reference photos. A fallen branch can often leave a round circle for the head and entwined roots can provide long fingers and arms.

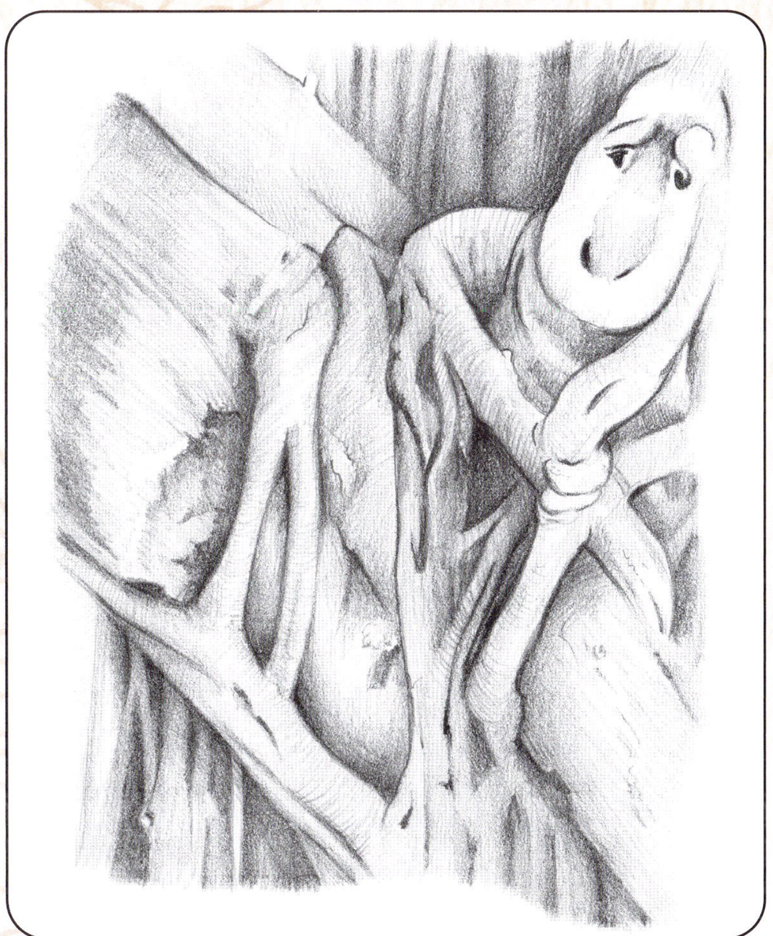

Putting it all together

STEP-BY-STEP FAERIE IN PEN, INK AND WASH

The following illustrations are a step-by-step final faerie drawing, using pen, ink and watercolour wash, and incorporating many of the techniques we have learnt so far.

Step one is to choose the photos or pictures that you would like to use for your faerie drawing. Collect plenty of references so you can be flexible with your choices and designs. The more sources of inspiration you can collect, the easier it will be to create a good composition. But remember, simplicity is the key.

▶ These are based on the three photos I am working from. I have sketched them out, removing the backgrounds. I like to sketch the area of the photo I am going to use so that I can work out the composition more easily. I have chosen a peacock butterfly, a young faerie model and a crown as an accessory. These are my main features for the painting, and I will add some grasses and a simple background in the composition and design stage.

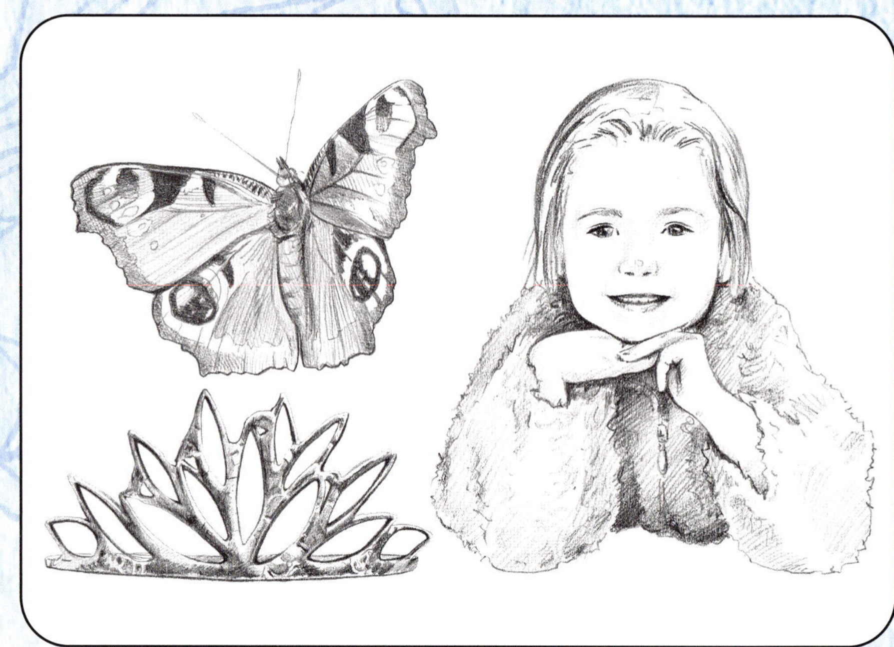

▶ Next you must design your composition. Remember to place your horizon line on one of the magic thirds, and create a light and blurry background so that the main feature of the painting stands out. As you can see I have decided to have the eye level on the bottom third, and have added some grass around the faerie to camouflage her. I want her to be a happy-go-lucky faerie basking in the sunshine, so I'm going to keep the mood of the drawing light and colourful.

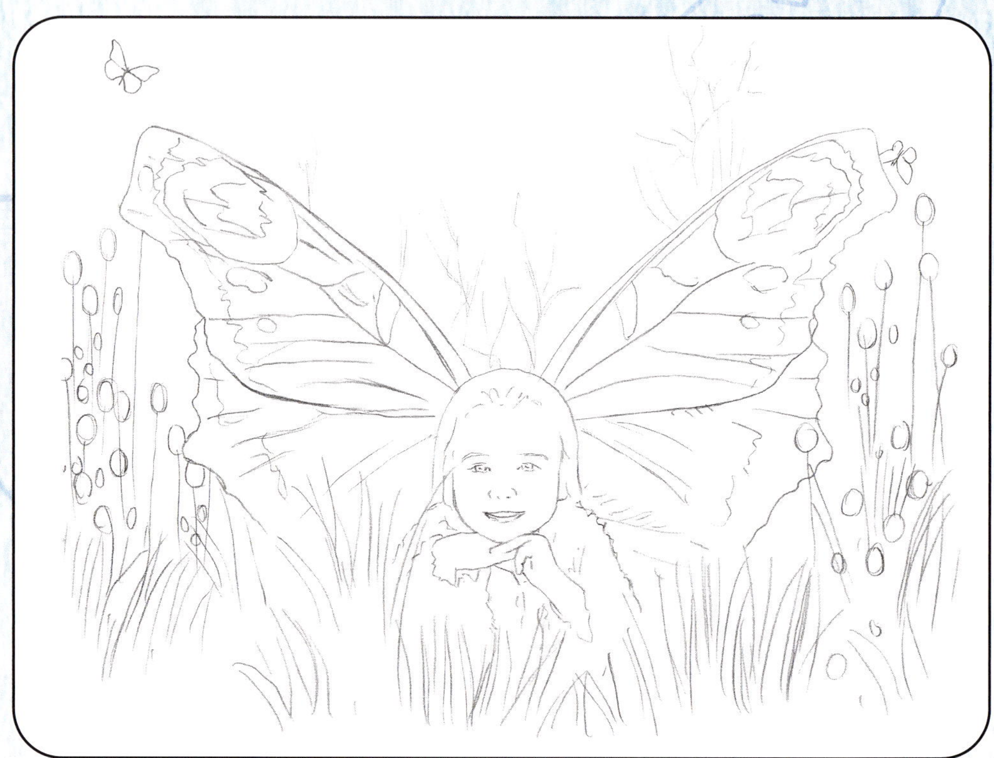

▶ Then draw around your main subject in sepia ink. I have also added a light wash in the background, to give a sense of warmth to the piece. It was a very simple wet-in-wet wash using a mixture of yellow and a little orange.

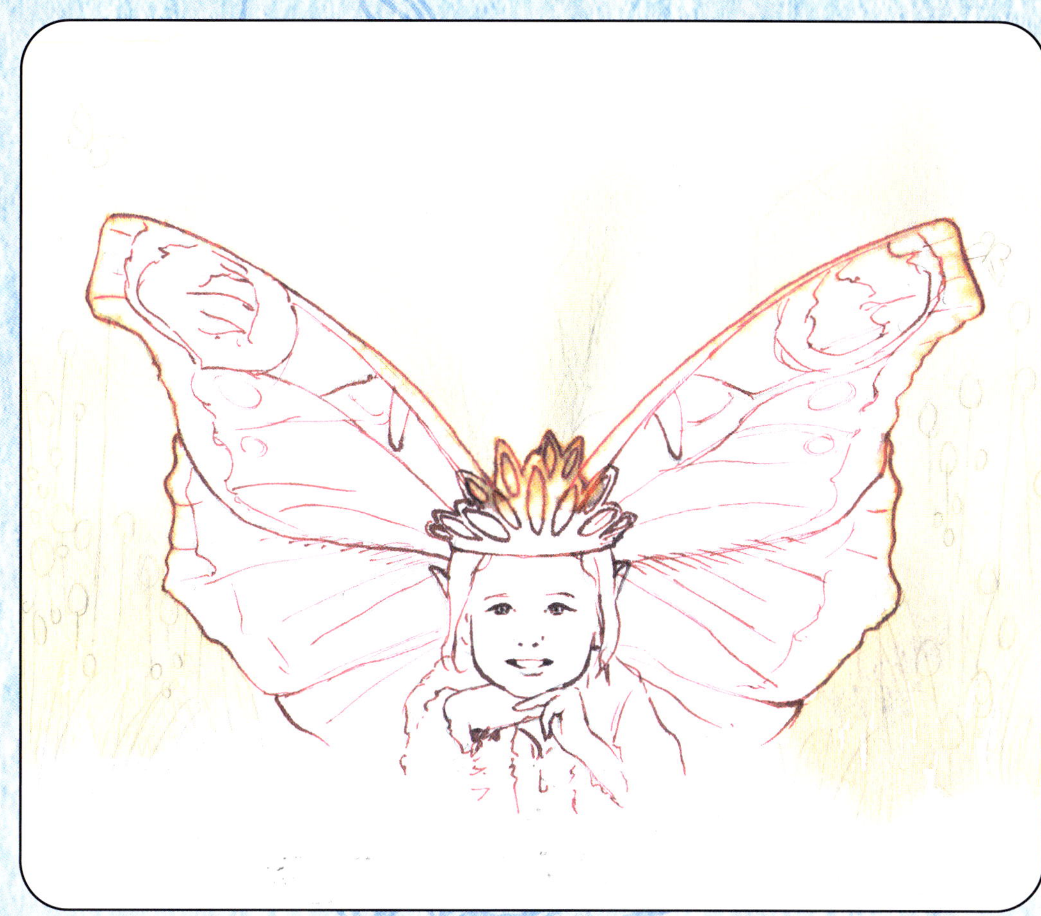

▶ Now we need to add some tones to the faerie and her wings. You can decide what colours your faerie's clothes will be and how you would like the wings to look. I have painted a simple purple colour in a fluffy texture for her clothing to echo the soft body of the butterfly. You could easily create these colours using pastel or coloured pencil if you preferred.

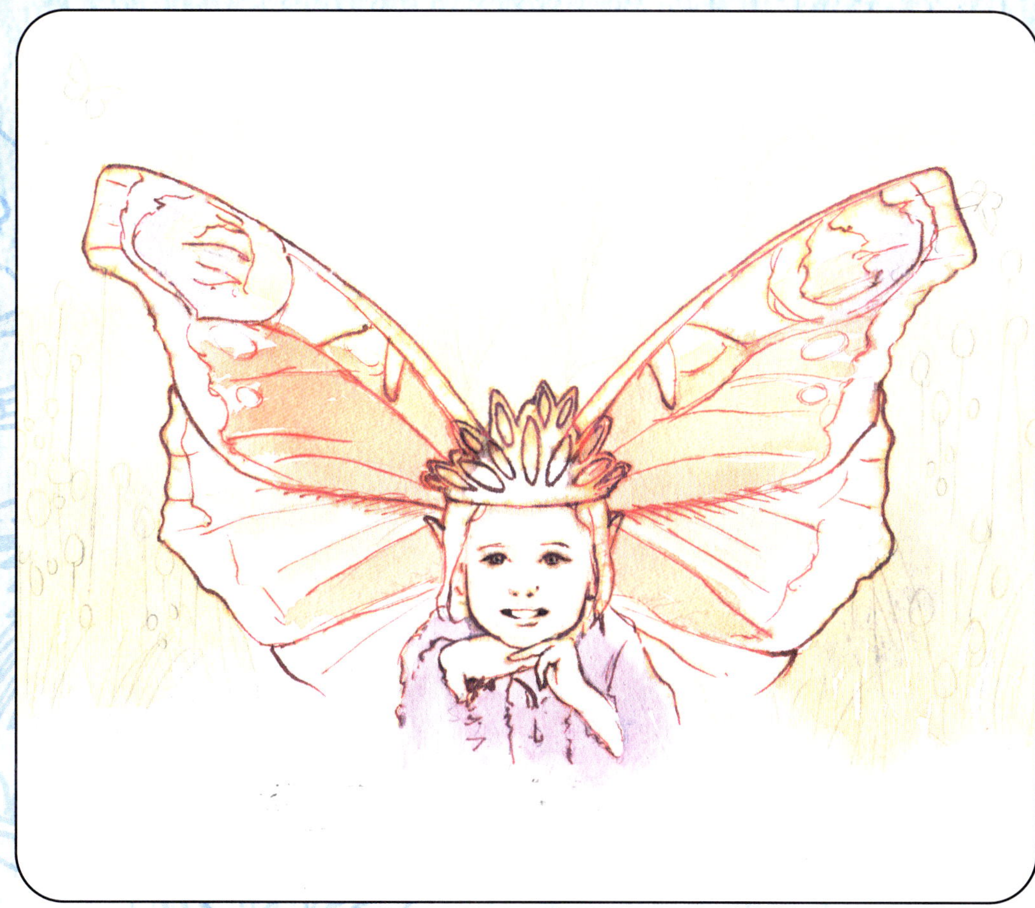

▶ We can now strengthen the colours in the wings to really make them stand out. Again, I have used watercolour but you could use pastel or coloured pencil, or a mixture of all three.

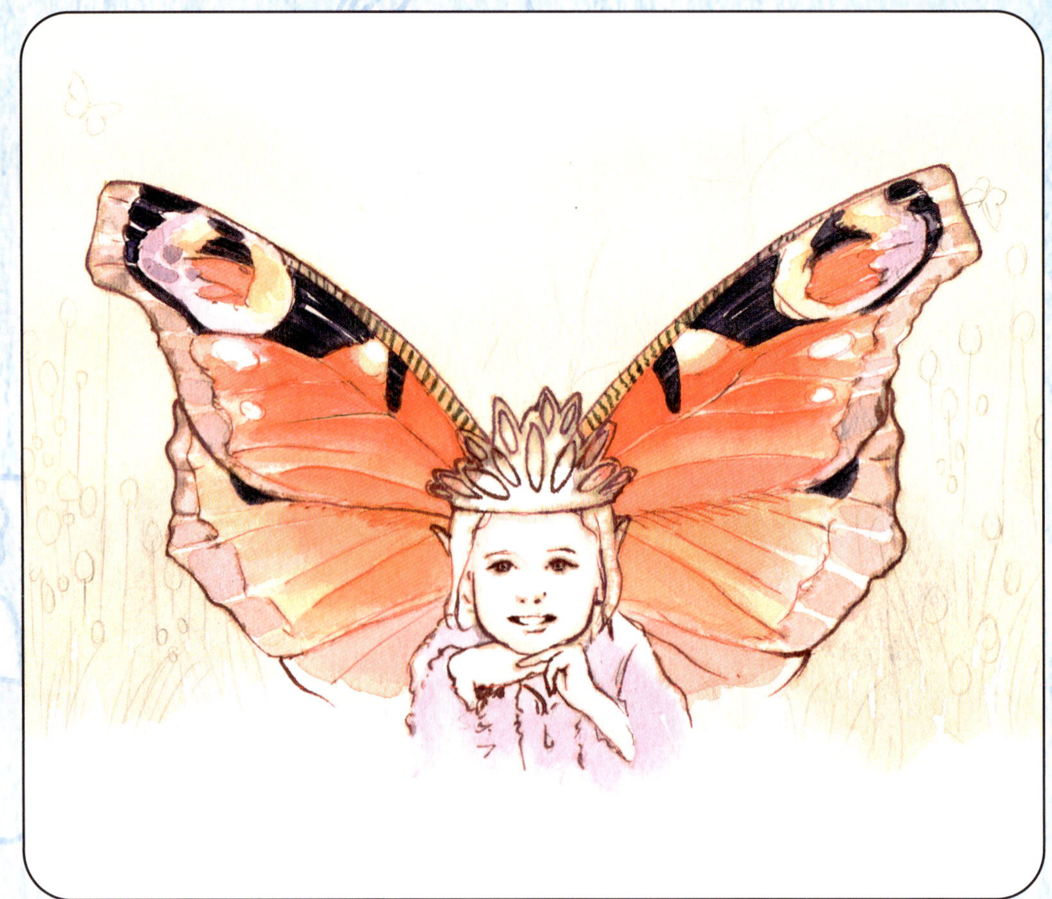

▶ Next you can add some colour to your faerie's face and start to paint in her crown. Here I used some white acrylic paint to make the crown bright and shiny.

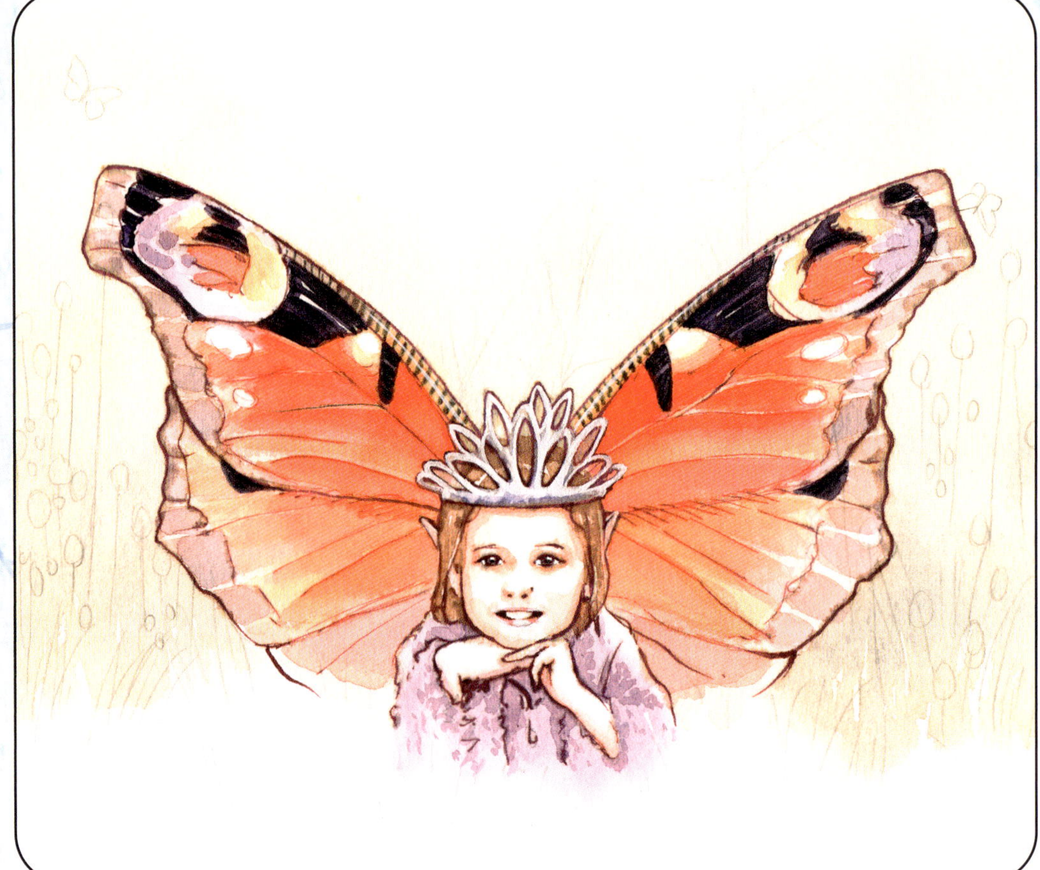

▶ Now, work back into the painting with your pen and ink nib, or with a fine pen if you have one. Create the grasses around the faerie very carefully, as once you place the pen line down you cannot erase it.

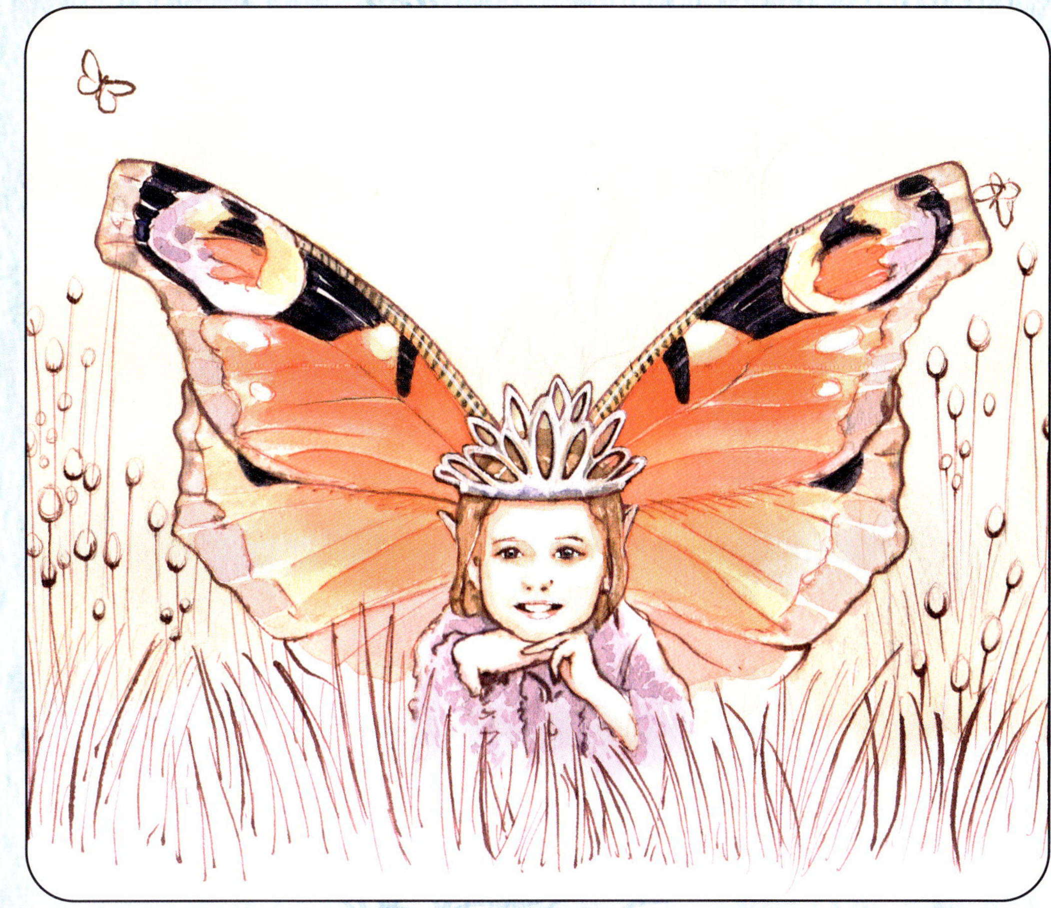

▶ The final stage: you can see I have added some trees faintly behind the faerie using watercolour. Don't forget to paint the background features much lighter then the foreground, as this gives the picture perspective and distance. Add lots of water into the mix. I also added a wash of green into the grass and a few extra details including the butterfly in the sky.

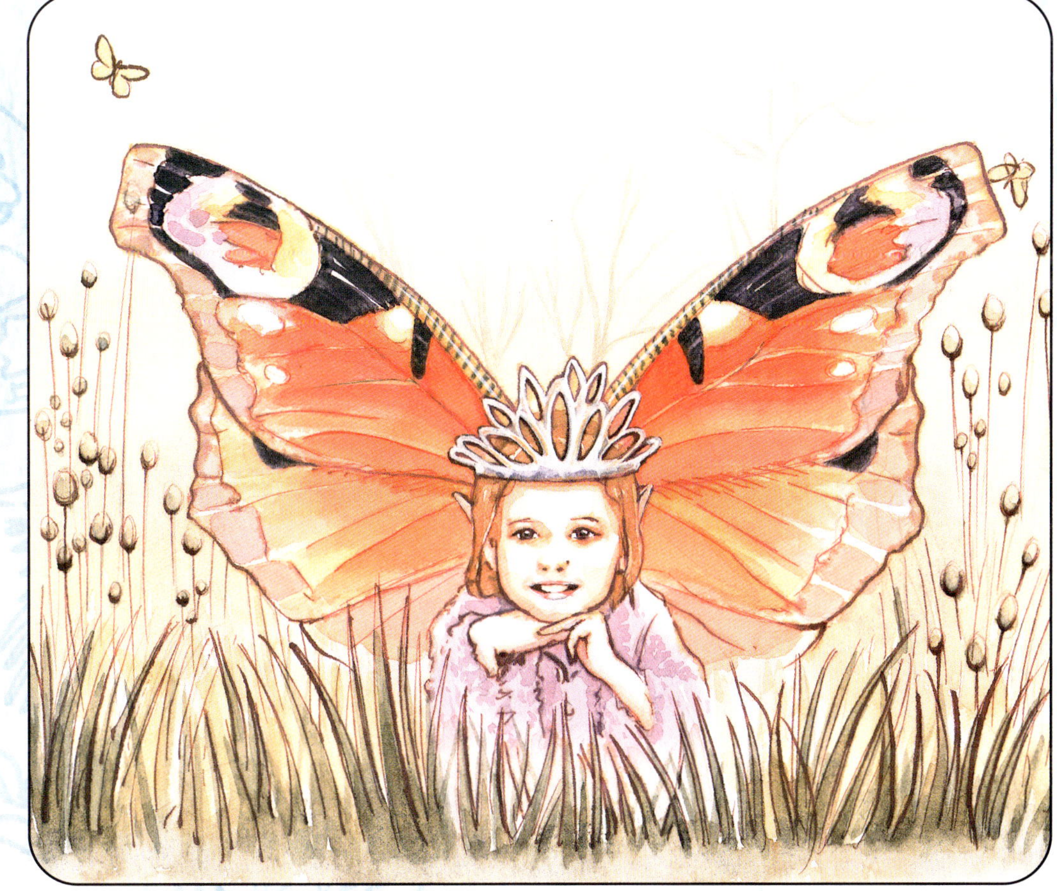

STEP-BY-STEP FAERIE USING A COMPUTER

Using a computer to create your faerie artwork produces a very different effect to traditional drawing and painting. All photo editing software is slightly different, but you should be able to follow this step-by-step guide to create a similar faerie composition using your own photographs.

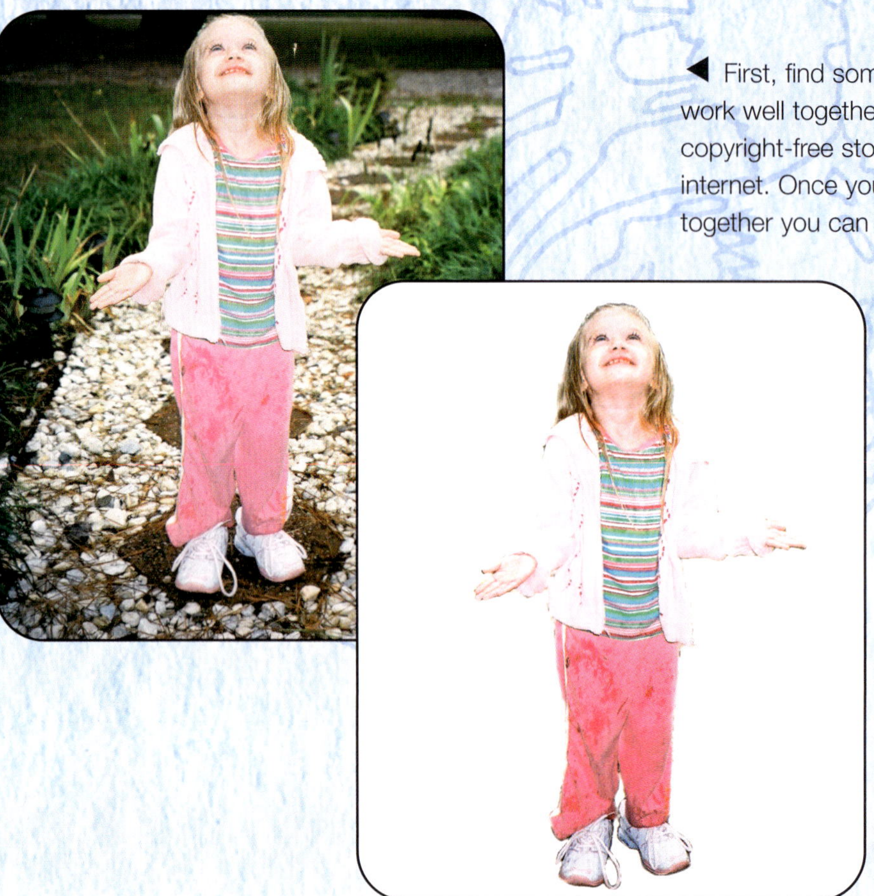

◀ First, find some reference photos that you feel would work well together. You could, for example, look at copyright-free stock photography websites on the internet. Once you have a few photos that work well together you can build on them and look for specific pictures to complement your images. I have a lovely photo of a child looking up into the air which I felt looked very faerie-like. The first step was to remove the background so I could see what would work well with her in the composition.

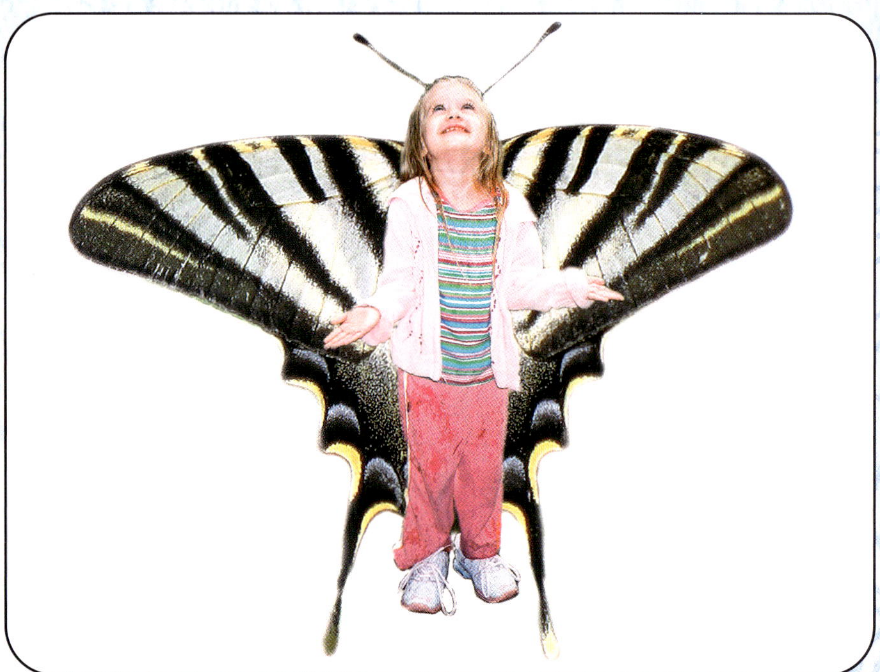

◀ Next I looked for a good photo of butterfly wings. Here I have used a swallowtail butterfly and placed the wings on the same page as the child, before removing the background from them.

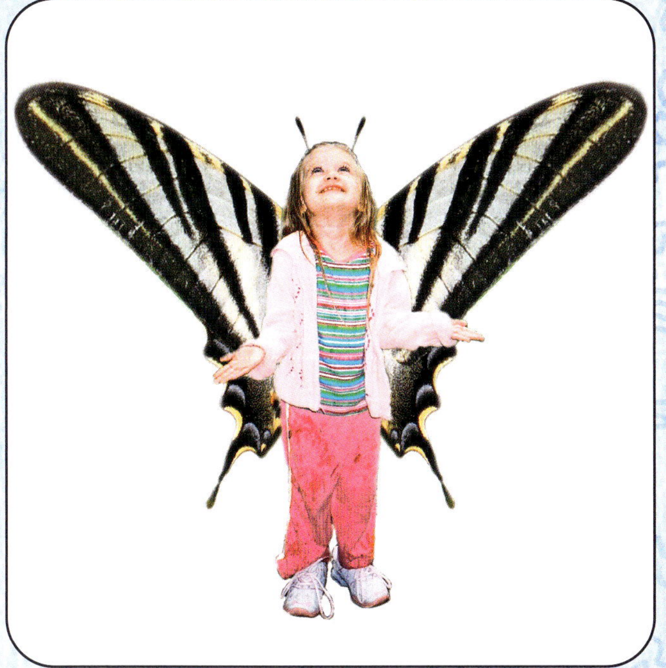

▲ As you can see, I have then manipulated each side of the wings using the distort feature in my software program. I separated the wings from each other so I could change the shape of each side separately.

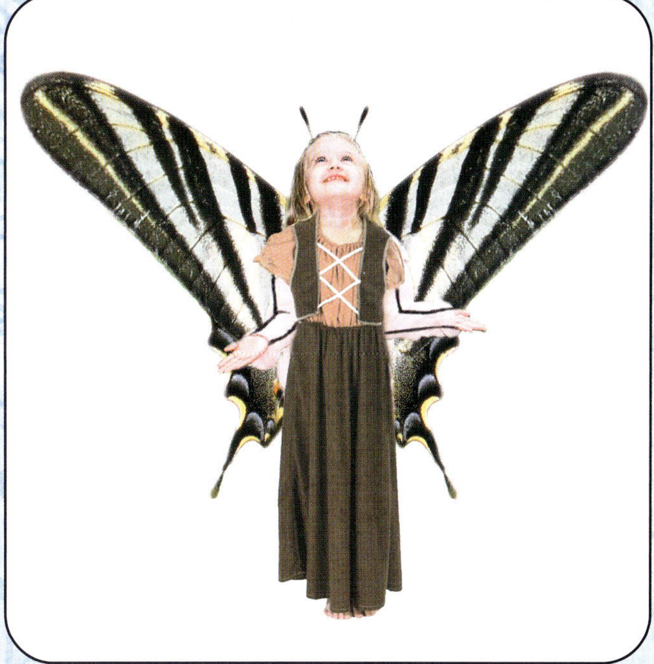

▲ Then I found some better clothing for my faerie to wear. This is a costume dress, but you could also use a tablet and pen to draw on top of the photo and create your own style of clothing.

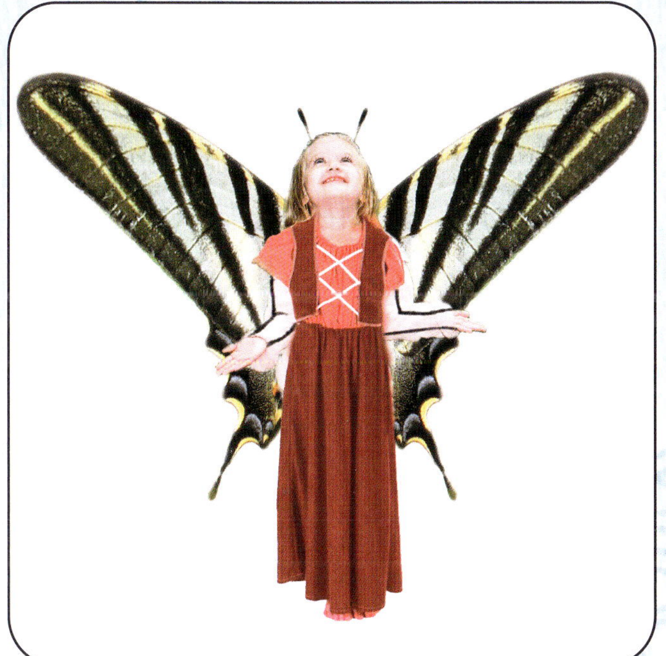

▲ I wanted a brighter colour for the dress, so I used the colour sliders to change the colours. If you have hand-drawn your clothes you could fill them using the paint brush tool.

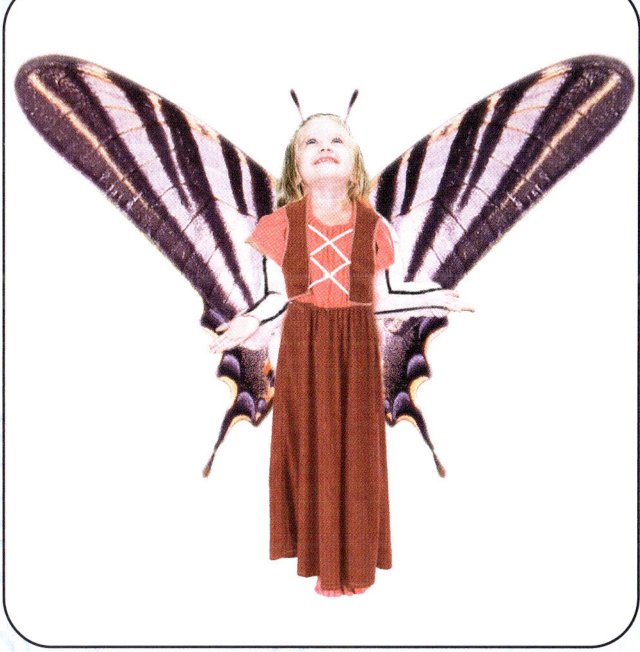

▲ I then changed the colour of the wings to match the dress and make them a little more magical.

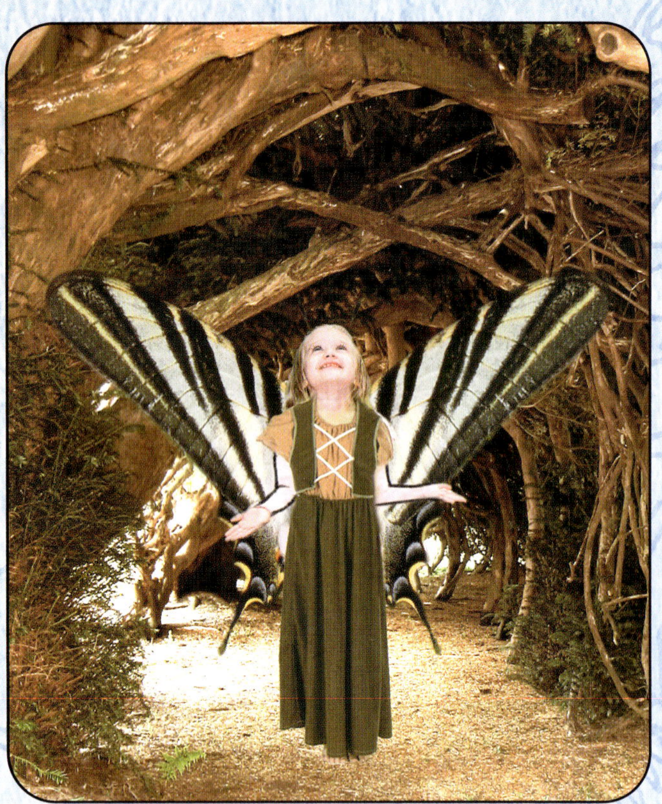

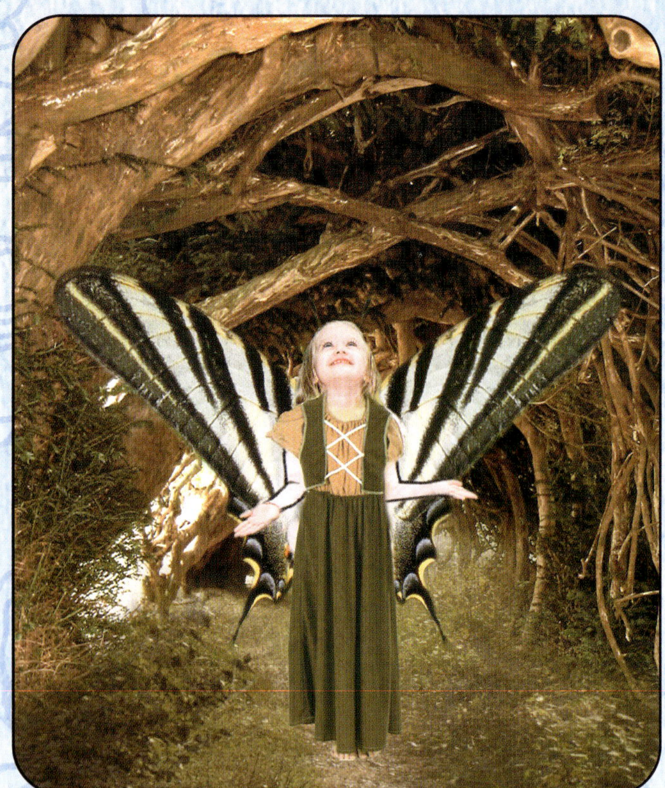

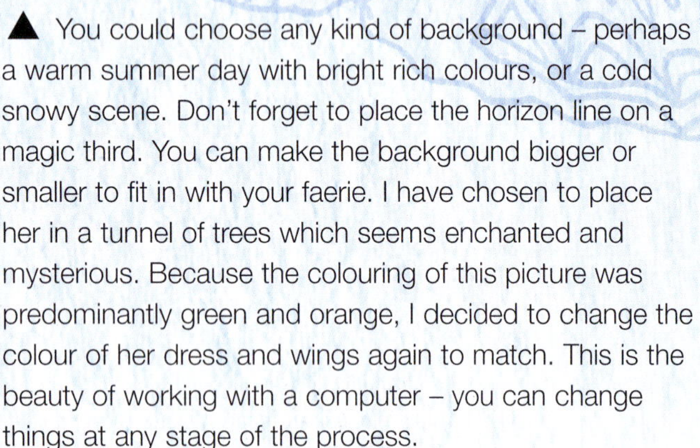

▲ You could choose any kind of background – perhaps a warm summer day with bright rich colours, or a cold snowy scene. Don't forget to place the horizon line on a magic third. You can make the background bigger or smaller to fit in with your faerie. I have chosen to place her in a tunnel of trees which seems enchanted and mysterious. Because the colouring of this picture was predominantly green and orange, I decided to change the colour of her dress and wings again to match. This is the beauty of working with a computer – you can change things at any stage of the process.

▲ Step eight is to add a separate photo for the ground. I wanted something a little more misty and grassy. I placed the new photo over top of the composition and erased the areas I didn't need with the eraser tool.

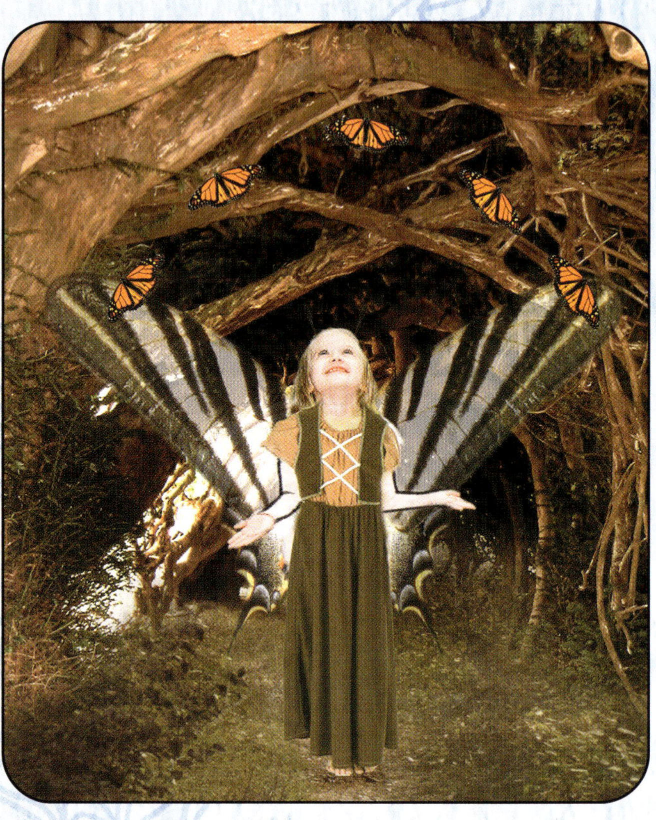

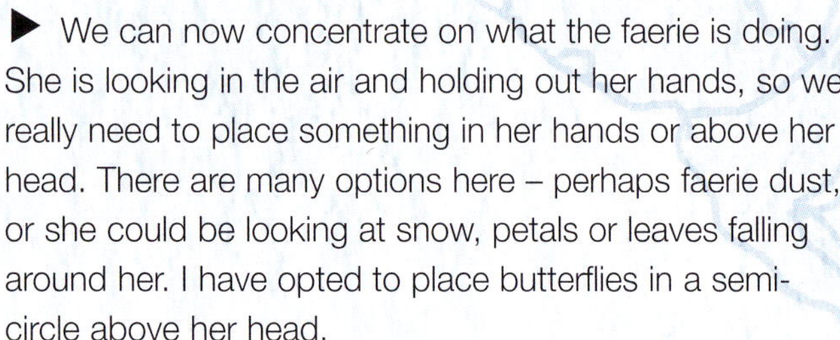

▶ We can now concentrate on what the faerie is doing. She is looking in the air and holding out her hands, so we really need to place something in her hands or above her head. There are many options here – perhaps faerie dust, or she could be looking at snow, petals or leaves falling around her. I have opted to place butterflies in a semi-circle above her head.

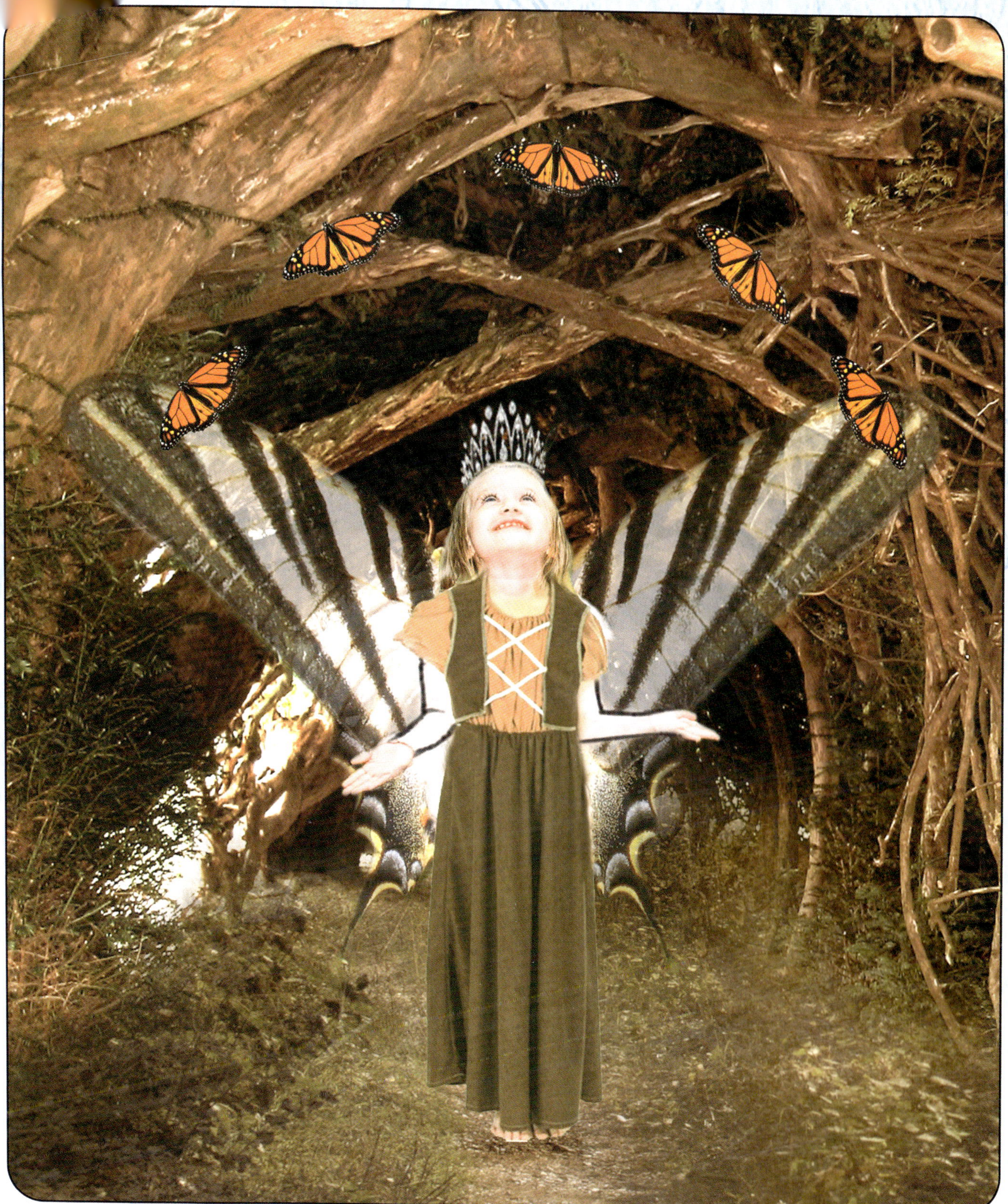

▲ The final stage is to add a small crown on her head, as I felt this area looked a little empty, and a shadow on the ground was needed to set her firmly on the path under the trees.

As long as you have some reference to work with and you use a little bit of imagination, you should be able to create your very own faeries, faerie helpers and faerie realms. Just follow the few simple rules and practise y drawing every day, and your faeries will be dancing i time. Most importantly: have fun!

Index